the NAZI
Officer's WIFE

the NAZI Officer's WIFE

■

HOW ONE JEWISH WOMAN
SURVIVED THE HOLOCAUST

■

EDITH HAHN BEER
with SUSAN DWORKIN

ROB WEISBACH BOOKS
WILLIAM MORROW AND COMPANY, INC. NEW YORK

In loving memory of my mother,
Klothilde Hahn

■

P R E F A C E

■

THE STORY THAT follows here was purposely buried for a long time. Like many people who survived a great calamity in which so many others lost their lives, I did not discuss my life as a "U-boat," a fugitive from the Gestapo living under a false identity beneath the surface of society in Nazi Germany, but preferred to forget as much as possible and not to burden younger generations with sad memories. It was my daughter, Angela, who urged me to tell the story, to leave a written record, to let the world know.

In 1997, I decided to sell at auction my archive of wartime letters, pictures, and documents. The archive was bought at Sotheby's in London by two longtime friends and dedicated philanthropists of history—Drew Lewis and Dalk Feith. Their intention was to donate it to the United States Holocaust Memorial Museum in Washington, D.C., and there it resides today. I am enormously grateful to them for their generosity and concern. The papers in that archive have helped to trigger many memories. I am grateful to my collaborator, Susan Dworkin, for her sympathy and understanding in helping me to express them.

Many thanks to Nina Sasportas of Cologne, whose detailed research has enabled us to augment my recollections, and to Elizabeth LeVangia Uppenbrink of New York, who translated all the documents and letters into accessible and idiomatic English. Many thanks as well to Nicholas Kolarz; to Robert Levine; to Suzanne Braun Levine; to our editor, Colin Dickerman, and his associate, Karen Murphy; and to our publisher, Rob Weisbach—all treasured critics and comrades who have contributed gifts of spirit, energy, and wisdom.

Finally, this book owes everything to Angela Schlüter, my daughter, for it was the loving spirit of her inquiry, her need to know, her search for the strange, miraculous past, that inspired me to tell the story at last.

—EDITH HAHN BEER
NETANYA, ISRAEL

ONE

■

The Small Voice from Then

𝔄FTER A WHILE, there were no more onions. My coworkers among the Red Cross nurses at the Städtische Krankenhaus in Brandenburg said it was because the Führer needed the onions to make poison gas with which to conquer our enemies. But I think by then—it was May 1943—many citizens of the Third Reich would have gladly forgone the pleasure of gassing the enemy if they could only taste an onion.

At that time, I was working in the ward for the foreign workers and prisoners of war. I would make tea for all the patients and wheel it around on a little trolley, trying to smile and give them a cheery *"Guten Tag."*

One day when I brought the teacups back to the kitchen to wash, I interrupted one of the senior nurses slicing an onion. She was the wife of an officer and came from Hamburg. I believe her name was Hilde. She told me the onion was for her own lunch. Her eyes searched my face to see if I knew that she was lying.

I made my gaze vacant and smiled my silly little fool's smile and went about washing up the teacups as though I had absolutely no idea that this nurse had bought her onion on the black market especially to serve to a critically injured Russian prisoner, to give him a taste he longed for in his last days. Either thing—buying the onion or befriending the Russian—could have sent her to prison.

Like most Germans who defied Hitler's laws, the nurse from Hamburg was a rare exception. More typically, the staff of our hospital stole the food meant for the foreign patients and took it home to their families or ate it themselves. You must understand, these nurses were not well-educated women from progressive homes for whom caring for the sick was a sacred calling. They were very often young farm girls from East Prussia, fated for life-long backbreaking labor in the fields and barns, and nursing was one of the few acceptable ways by which they could escape. They had been raised in the Nazi era on Nazi propaganda. They truly believed that, as Nordic "Aryans," they were members of a su-perior race. They felt that these Russians, Frenchmen, Dutchmen, Belgians, and Poles who came into our clinic had been placed on earth to labor for them. To steal a plate of soup from such low creatures seemed not a sin but a perfectly legitimate activity.

I think we must have had more than ten thousand foreign pris-oners in Brandenburg, working in the Opel automobile factory, the Arado airplane factory, and other factories. Most of those whom we saw in the hospital had been injured in industrial acci-dents. While building the economy of the Reich, they would mangle their hands in metal presses, burn themselves in flaming forges, splash themselves with corrosive chemicals. They were a slave population, conquered and helpless; transported away from their parents, wives, and children; longing for home. I did not dare to look into their faces for fear of seeing myself—my own terror, my own loneliness.

In our cottage hospital, each service was housed in a separate building. We on the nursing staff ate in one building, did laundry in another, attended to orthopedic cases in another and infectious diseases in yet another. The foreign prisoners were rigorously separated from German patients, no matter what was wrong with them. We heard that one time, a whole building was allocated to foreigners suffering from typhus, a disease that comes from contaminated water. How they had contracted such a disease in our beautiful historic city—which had inspired immortal concertos, where the water was clean and the food was carefully rationed and inspected by our government—was impossible for simple girls like us to comprehend. Many of my coworkers assumed that the foreigners had brought it on themselves, because of their filthy personal habits. These nurses managed not to admit to themselves that the disease came from the unspeakable conditions under which the slave laborers were forced to live.

You must understand that I was not really a nurse but rather a nurse's aide, trained only for menial tasks. I fed the patients who could not feed themselves and dusted the night tables. I washed the bedpans. My first day on the job, I washed twenty-seven bedpans—in the sink, as though they were dinner dishes. I washed the rubber gloves. These were not to be discarded like the thin white gloves you see today. Ours were heavy, durable, reusable. I had to powder their insides. Sometimes I prepared a black salve and applied it to a bandage and made compresses to relieve the pain of rheumatism. And that was about it. I could not do anything more medical than that.

Once I was asked to assist at a blood transfusion. They were siphoning blood from one patient into a bowl, then suctioning the blood from the bowl and into the veins of another patient. I was supposed to stir the blood, to keep it from coagulating. I became nauseated and ran from the room. They said to themselves: "Well, Grete is just a silly little Viennese youngster with almost no education, the next thing to a cleaning woman—how much can be expected from her? Let her feed the foreigners who have chopped off their fingers in the machines."

I prayed that no one would die on my watch. Heaven must have heard me, because the prisoners waited for my shift to be over, and *then* they died.

I tried to be nice to them; I tried to speak French to the Frenchman to assuage their homesickness. Perhaps I smiled too brightly, because one August morning my head nurse told me that I had been observed to be too friendly with the foreigners, so I was being transferred to the maternity service.

You see, there were informers everywhere. That was why the nurse who was preparing the forbidden onion for her Russian patient had been so frightened of me, even me, Margarethe, called "Grete" for short. An uneducated twenty-year-old nurse's aide from Austria. Even *I* could conceivably be working for the Gestapo or the SS.

IN THE EARLY fall of 1943, shortly after my transfer to the maternity service, an important industrialist arrived in an ambulance, which had brought him all the way from Berlin. This man had suffered a stroke. He needed peace and quiet and uninterrupted therapy. The Allies had been bombing Berlin since January, so it seemed to his family and friends that he would recover more speedily in Brandenburg, where no bombs were falling and the hospital staff was not beset with emergencies and he could count on more personal attention. Perhaps because I was the youngest and least skilled, and not badly needed elsewhere, I was taken away from the babies and assigned to care for him.

It was not very pleasant work. He had become partly paralyzed, and he had to be led to the bathroom, hand-fed every morsel, bathed and turned constantly; and his flaccid, powerless body had to be massaged.

I did not say much about my new patient to Werner, my fiancé, because I believed it might trigger his ambition, and that he would begin to press for the advantages we could gain from my close association with such an important personage. Werner was always on the lookout for advantages. Experience had taught him that advancement in the Reich occurred not because of talent and ability but because of connections: friends in high places, powerful relatives. Werner himself was a painter, imaginative and quite talented. Before the Nazi regime, his gifts had brought him nothing but joblessness and homelessness; he had slept in the forest under the rain. But then better times came. He joined the Nazi Party and become a supervisor of the paint department at the Arado Aircraft factory, in charge of many foreign workers. Soon he would be an officer in the Wehrmacht and my devoted husband. But he didn't relax—not yet, not Werner. He was always looking for something extra, an angle, a way to climb upward to a spot where he would finally receive the rewards he felt he deserved. A restless and impulsive man, he dreamed of success. If I told him everything about my important patient, he might dream too much. So I told him just enough, no more.

When my patient received flowers from Albert Speer, the Minister for Armaments and War Production, himself, I understood why the other nurses had been so eager to give me this job. It was risky to take care of high-ranking party members. A dropped bed-pan, a spilled glass of water, could get you into serious trouble. What if I turned this patient too quickly, washed him too roughly, fed him soup that was too hot, too cold, too salty? And—oh, my God—what if he had another stroke? What if he *died* while I was the one taking care of him?

Quaking at the thought of so many possibilities for doing something wrong, I tried with all my strength to get every single thing just right. So of course the industrialist thought I was wonderful.

"You are an excellent worker, Nurse Margarethe," he said as I was bathing him. "You must have considerable experience for one so young."

"Oh, no, sir," I said in my smallest voice. "I have only just come from school. I do only what they taught me."

"And you have never taken care of a stroke patient before . . ."

"No, sir."

"Amazing."

Every day he recovered a little more motion and his voice became less slurred. He must have been encouraged by his own recovery, for his spirits were high.

"Tell me, Nurse Margarethe," he said as I was massaging his feet, "what do people here in Brandenburg think about the war?"

"Oh, I don't know, sir."

"But you must have heard something. . . . I am interested in public opinion. What do people think about the meat ration?"

"It is quite satisfactory."

"What do they think about the news from Italy?"

Should I admit that I knew about the Allied landings? Did I dare? Did I dare *not*? "We all believe that the British will be defeated in the end, sir."

"Do you know anyone whose boyfriend is fighting on the Eastern front? What do the men write in their letters home?"

"Oh, the men don't write about the fighting, sir, because they don't like to worry us, and also they fear that they might give away some important detail and the enemy might capture the mail and read it and their comrades might be endangered."

"Have you heard that the Russians are cannibals? Have you heard that they eat their young?"

"Yes, sir."

"And do you believe that?"

I took a chance. "Some people do, sir. But I think that if the Russians ate their babies, there would not be so many Russians as there apparently are."

He laughed. He had warm, humorous eyes and a gentle manner. He even reminded me a little of my grandfather, whom I had cared for years before when he suffered a stroke . . . so long ago, in another life. I began to relax with the important industrialist and let down my guard a little.

"What could the Führer do to make his people happy, Nurse? What do you think?"

"My fiancé says that the Führer loves Germany like a wife, and that is why he has no wife himself, and that he would do anything he could to make us happy. So if you could speak to him, sir, perhaps you could tell the Führer that we would be very very happy if he would send us some onions."

This amused him very much. "You are good medicine for me, Margarethe. You are plainspoken and kindhearted, the true soul of German womanhood. Tell me, is your fiancé fighting at the front?"

"Not yet, sir. He has special skills, so he is working to prepare aircraft for the Luftwaffe."

"Ah, very good, very good," he said. "My sons are also fine young men; they are doing very well these days." He showed me a picture of his tall handsome sons in their uniforms. They had risen high in the Nazi Party and become important men. He was very proud of them.

"It's easy to be a cardinal," I said, "when your cousin is the pope."

He stopped bragging and took a long, hard look at me. "I see you are not such a simple girl," he said. "I see you are a very clever woman. Where were you educated?"

My stomach tightened. My throat went dry.

"That is something my grandma always said," I said, turning him over to wash his back. "An old saying in our family."

"When I return to Berlin, I would like you to come with me as my private nurse. I shall speak to your superiors."

"Oh, I would love that, sir, but my fiancé and I are planning to be married soon, and so you see, I could not leave Brandenburg—it would not be possible! But thank you, sir! Thank you! I am honored! Most honored!"

My shift ended. I bade him good night and walked, trembling and unsteady, out of his room. I was wet with perspiration. I told the coworker who arrived to replace me that this was because exercising my patient's heavy limbs was such hard work. But in truth it was because I had almost revealed my disguise. The smallest indication of sophisticated wit—a literary reference or historical knowledge no ordinary Austrian girl could hope to have—was, for me, like a circumcision, a complete giveaway.

As I walked home to the Arado apartment complex on the east end of town where Werner and I lived, I admonished myself for the millionth time to be more careful and hide every sign of intellect, to keep my gaze vacant, my mouth shut.

IN OCTOBER 1943, the other members of the Red Cross nursing contingent gave me a great honor. The municipality of Brandenburg was planning a rally, and each group of workers had to
send a representative. For one reason or another, none of the senior
nurses could attend; I suspect that they didn't feel like celebrating
because they had heard how badly Germany's forces were faring
in Russia, North Africa, and Italy (although how they would have
heard that I cannot imagine, since German radio did not fully
report it and everybody knew that to listen to Radio Moscow, the
BBC, the Voice of America, or Beromünster of Switzerland was
a criminal act akin to treason). I was selected to represent our
workers' group at the rally.

Werner was very proud of me. I can imagine him bragging to
his colleagues at Arado, "No wonder they chose my Grete! She's
a true patriot of the Fatherland!" He had a good sense of humor,
my Werner, a real flair for life's little ironies.

I dressed carefully for the big day. I wore my Red Cross nurse's
uniform. My plain brown hair I combed in a simple natural style,
no barrettes, curls, or pomade. I wore no makeup and no jewelry
except a thin little gold ring with the tiniest diamond chip, a gift
from my father on my sixteenth birthday. I was a small girl, not
much more than five feet, and I had a lovely figure in those days.
However, I kept it covered with baggy white stockings and a
shapeless pinafore. It was not a time when a person like me wanted
to look especially attractive in public. Nice, yes; neat, yes. But
most important, plain. Nothing to draw attention.

The rally turned out to be quite different from those to which
we had grown accustomed. There were no stirring drums or stri-
dent marches, no beautiful young people in uniforms waving

flags. This rally had a purpose, and that was to overcome the defeatist mood which had begun to fall over Germany since the debacle at Stalingrad the past winter. Heinrich Himmler had been appointed Minister of the Interior in August with this mandate: "Renew German faith in the Victory!" Speaker after speaker exhorted us to work harder and harder to support our valiant fighting men, because if we lost the war, the terrible poverty which most Germans recalled from the days before the Nazi era would return and we would all lose our jobs. If we had grown tired of our evening *Eintopf*, the one-dish meal that Joseph Goebbels had proclaimed the proper self-sacrificing fare for a nation engaged in "total war," we should remind ourselves that after the Victory, we would feast like kings on real coffee and golden bread made with white flour and whole eggs. We were told that we should do everything in our power to keep up productivity in the workplace, and turn in anybody we suspected of being disloyal, especially people who were listening to enemy radio and the "grossly exaggerated" news of German defeats in North Africa and Italy.

"My God," I thought. "They are worried."

The Nazi "masters of the world" were beginning to quake and waver. I felt giddy, a little breathless. An old song began to sing itself inside my heard.

Shhh, I thought. *It's too soon to sing. Shhh.*

That night, when Werner and I tuned in to the BBC, I prayed that the news about German military misfortune would mean an early end to the war and, for me, release from the prison of my pretense.

But I did not dare share my hopes, even with Werner. I kept my elation secret, my voice soft, my persona unobtrusive. Invisibility. Silence. These were the habits that I wore when I lived as what survivors of the Holocaust now call a U-boat, a Jewish fugitive from the Nazi death machine, hiding right in the heart of the Third Reich.

For a while, in later years, when I was married to Fred Beer and living safely in England, I cast off those wartime habits. But now that Fred is gone and I am old and cannot control the impact of my memories, I put them on again. I sit here as I sit with you today in my favorite café on the square in the city of Netanya by the sea in the land of Israel, and an acquaintance stops to chat and says, "So tell us, *Giveret* Beer, what was it like then, during the war, living with a Nazi Party member inside Germany, pretending to be an Aryan, concealing your true identity, always fearing exposure?" I answer in a little voice that is dazed by its own ignorance, "Oh, but I do not know. I think I do not remember this anymore." My gaze wanders and loses focus; my voice turns dreamy, halting, soft. It is my voice from those days in Brandenburg, when I was a twenty-nine-year-old Jewish law student on the Gestapo's "Wanted" list, pretending to be an ignorant twenty-one-year-old nurse's aide.

You must forgive me when you hear this small voice from then fading and faltering. You must remind me: "Edith! Speak up! Tell the story."

It has been more than half a century.

I suppose it is time.

TWO

•

The Hahns of Vienna

WHEN I WAS a schoolgirl in Vienna, it seemed to me the whole world had come to my city to sit in the sunny cafés and enjoy coffee and cake and matchless conversation. I walked from school past the opera house, the beautiful Josefsplatz, and the Michaelerplatz. I played in the Volksgarten and the Burggarten. I saw dignified ladies with rakish hats and silk stockings; gentlemen with walking sticks and golden watch chains; rustic workmen from all the provinces of the bygone Hapsburg empire, plastering and painting our fancy facades with their thick blunt skilled hands. The stores burst with exotic fruits and crystal and silk. Inventions sprang up in my path.

One day, I squirmed into a crowd and found myself looking into a store window where a uniformed parlor maid was demonstrating something called a "Hoover." She scattered dirt on the floor, turned on her machine, and like magic whisked the dirt away. I squeaked with delight and raced off to tell my schoolmates.

When I was ten years old, I joined a long line before the offices of a magazine called *Die Bühne*, "The Stage." Soon I was sitting at a table before a large brown box. A nice lady put earphones on my head. The box came to life. A voice. A song. Radio.

I raced to my father's restaurant to tell my family. My sister Mimi, only a year younger than I, could not have cared less. The baby—little Johanna, called Hansi—was too young to understand. And Mama and Papa were too busy to listen. But I knew I had heard something special, the force of the future, a god-to-be. Remember that radio was brand-new in 1924. Imagine what a power it represented, and how helpless people were to resist its messages.

I bubbled to Professor Spitzer of the Technical University, my favorite customer among the regulars: "The person who speaks can be very far away, Professor! But his voice flies through the air like a bird ! Soon we will be able to hear the voices of people from everywhere!"

Eagerly I read the newspapers and magazines that Papa kept for his customers. What most interested me were the law columns, with cases, arguments, and problems to make your head spin. I raced around our "waltz city," forever searching for someone to talk to about what I had read and seen.

School was my delight. There were only girls in my class; Papa did not believe in coeducation. Unlike my sisters, I loved to study and never found it difficult.

We were taught that the French were our archenemies, that the Italians were traitors, that Austria had lost the First World War only because of a "stab in the back"—but I must tell you, we were never sure who had done the stabbing. Often, the teachers would ask me what language we spoke at home. This was a not-so-subtle way of discovering if we spoke Yiddish (which we didn't) and were therefore Jewish (which we were).

They wanted to know, you see. They were afraid that with our typical Austrian faces, we might be able to pass. They didn't want to be fooled. Even then, in the 1920s, they wanted to be able to tell who was a Jew.

One day Professor Spitzer asked my father what he intended for my future education. Papa said I would finish grammar school and then be apprenticed as a dressmaker, as my mother had been.

"But you have here a very bright girl, my dear Herr Hahn," the professor said. "You must send her to high school, perhaps even to university."

Father laughed. If I had been a boy, he would have beggared himself to educate me. As I was a girl, he had never even considered it. However, since the distinguished professor had raised the question, Papa decided to discuss it with my mother.

MY FATHER, LEOPOLD Hahn, had a beautiful black mustache, curly black hair, and a humorous, outgoing personality well suited for a restaurateur. He was the youngest of six brothers, so by the time he was ready for his education, the family's money had run out. Therefore, he studied to be a waiter. I know it is hard to believe, but in that time and place, a waiter's training took several years. People liked Papa. They trusted him, told him their stories. He was an inspired listener. That was his gift.

He was much more worldly and sophisticated than he ever expected us to be. He had worked on the Riviera and in the Czechoslovakian spas of Carlsbad and Marienbad, and had experienced some wild nights. He fought with the Austro-Hungarian Army in the First World War. He was wounded, then captured; but he escaped and returned to us. The wound to his shoulder caused a loss of motion in his arm. He could not shave himself.

The restaurant, at Kohlmarkt in Vienna's busy center, was my father's life. It had a long, burnished bar and a dining room in back. His customers came every day for years. Papa knew what they wanted to eat before they ordered. He stocked their favorite newspapers. He provided them with service and comfort, a little world of dependabilities.

We lived in a two-bedroom apartment in what was actually an old converted palace at Number 29 Argentinierstrasse in Vienna's Fourth District. Our landlord, from the Hapsburg-Lothringen Company, came from royal stock. Since Mama worked side by side with Papa in the restaurant, seven days a week, we girls took our meals there. The household help did the cleaning and took care of us when we were little.

My mother, Klothilde, was pretty, short, buxom, attractive but not coquettish. She kept her long hair completely black. She had a patient, bemused air; forgave people their stupidities; sighed often; knew when to hold her peace.

I lavished all my affection on Hansi, my baby sister, seven years younger than I. To me, she looked like a cherub from one of our baroque cathedrals, with chubby pink cheeks, delicious flesh, and bouncing curls. My sister Mimi I disliked. The feeling was mutual. She had weak eyes, thick glasses, a sour personality—mean-spirited, jealous of everybody. Mama, intimidated by Mimi's unhappiness, gave her whatever she wanted, assuming that I, the "carefree one," could fend for myself. Since Mimi could make no friends, and I was popular, like my father, I had to share my friends with her and take her everywhere with me.

Papa took care of us all and shielded us from knowledge of the world's seamy side. He made our decisions, saved for our dowries.

In good times, if he was feeling a bit flush, he would stop at an auction house on his way home from work and buy my mother some jewelry as a surprise—a gold chain, amber earrings. He would lean on one of our leather chairs waiting for her to open the package, cherishing her excitement, anticipating her embrace. He adored my mother. They never fought. I mean it: they *never* fought. In the evening, she did her sewing and he read his paper and we did our homework and we had what the Israelis call *shalom bait*, peace in the home.

I THINK MY father knew how to be Jewish, but he did not teach us. He must have thought we would absorb it with our mother's milk.

We were sent to the *Judengottesdienst*, the children's service at the synagogue on Saturday afternoons. The maid was supposed to take us. But she was a Catholic, like most Austrians, and she feared the synagogue; and my mother—a working woman, dependent on her help—feared the maid. So we went infrequently and learned almost nothing. However, one song from that time stayed in my head.

> One day the Temple will be rebuilt
> And the Jews will return to Jerusalem.
> So it is written in the Holy Book.
> So it is written. Hallelujah!

In addition to the theme of faith—*Shema. Yisrael. Adonai eloheynu. Adonai echod*—this baby song about the Temple was all I knew of Jewish prayer and practice.

Too bad I didn't know more.

Thank God I knew that much.

Father's restaurant closed on Rosh Hashanah and Yom Kippur. (Like our home, it did not serve pork or shellfish, but otherwise it was not kosher at all.) On these high holidays, we went to synagogue mostly to meet our relatives. Mama and Papa were distantly related; each came from a family named Hahn. Between Mama's two sisters, and her brother, and Father's six brothers and three sisters, there were more than thirty Hahn cousins in Vienna. You could always find some Hahn or other at the third café in the Prater. Each branch of the family observed the Jewish religion differently. For example, Aunt Gisela Kirschenbaum—one of Papa's sisters, who also ran a restaurant—opened her place to the poor for a free seder on Passover. Mama's brother Richard, an outright nonbeliever, married a stylish furniture heiress from Topolčany, near Bratislava. Her name was Roszi. She had been raised Orthodox, and she couldn't stand the Hahns' assimilated ways, so she always went home to Czechoslovakia for the holidays.

Sometimes my parents startled me with an outburst of Jewish consciousness. For example, I once ate a blood sausage sandwich at a friend's house. "Absolutely delicious!" I reported to Mama. She literally gagged. Her sincere horror astounded me. On another occasion—just for the sake of conversation—I asked my father if I could marry a Christian. With black eyes blazing, he answered: "No, Edith. I could not bear that. It would kill me. The answer is no."

Papa felt that Jews had to be better than everybody else. He expected our report cards to be better, our social consciousness to be more highly developed. He expected us to have finer manners, cleaner clothes, immaculate moral standards.

I didn't think about it at the time, but of course now I realize that my father's insistence that we Jews must be better was based on our country's firm belief that we were not as good.

MY MOTHER'S PARENTS owned a gray stucco bungalow in Stockerau, a pretty little town north of Vienna. We went there on weekends and for holidays and birthdays. That was where my closest cousin Jultschi lived.

When Jultschi was nine years old, her mother (Mama's sister Elvira) dropped her off at Grandmother's house, went home, and killed herself.

Jultschi's father stayed on in Vienna. But Jultschi—traumatized by her past, always needful, easily intimidated—remained with our grandparents, who raised her as though she were their own child.

A soft, large, brown-haired, brown-eyed girl with full, deeply sculpted lips, Jultschi had a big heart and—unlike my sister Mimi— a great sense of humor. She played the piano, badly but well enough for our tone-deaf clan, and we made up operas to her good-natured banging. While I, the "intellectual," was discovering a passion for gothic novels full of mystery and desire, Jultschi was becoming addicted to movies and swing music.

Grandmother Hahn—a short, fat, strong woman and a strict disciplinarian—would assign us housework and then go off to the market, and of course we would not do what she asked but would instead spend the entire afternoon playing. As soon as we caught a glimpse of her coming back down the road, we would dive into the house through the open windows and get to work, so that she would find us dusting and sweeping like proper children. I am sure we never fooled her for one minute.

Grandmother seemed always to be busy adding to the richness

of the world, knitting delicate lace doilies or teaching Jultschi how to bake *Stollen* or tending to her hens and geese, her dog (named Mohrli), and her hundreds of potted plants. She had every sort of cactus. She would notify Mama in advance: "Klothilde! The cactus will bloom on Sunday. Bring the children to see." And we would stand in the yard at Stockerau, admiring the hardy desert flowers as they struggled to survive in our cold country.

Grandfather Hahn, a shopkeeper, sold sewing machines and bicycles and served as the agent for Puch motorbikes. Grandmother worked alongside him in the store on Sunday, the big shopping day for the local farmers, who would come from church, meet at the pub, have an early drink, and do their marketing for the week. They all knew my grandparents. Stockerau officials would always invite the Hahns to sit with them at carnival time, to watch as each guild gave its program.

On Grandfather's birthday, our task was to copy a poem out of Mama's *Wunschbuch* and then recite it in Grandfather's honor. I remember him sitting like a rotund little king listening to our pretty recitations, his eyes glistening with pride. I remember his hug.

Near my grandparents' house was a tributary of the Danube, where Jultschi and I loved to go swimming. To reach the water, you had to cross a high wooden bridge. One day, when I was seven, I got up before anyone else, ran down to the bridge, slipped, and went flying down and down and down into the water. I bobbed to the surface, howling and hysterical. A young man leaped in and saved me.

After that, I was terrified of heights. I did not ski in the Alps. I did not climb to the top of towering buildings and hang socialist banners from the dome. I tried to stay close to the ground.

■ ■ ■

IN 1928, WHEN inflation was so high in Austria that a customer's lunch would double in price while he ate it, Papa decided to sell the restaurant.

Luckily, he soon found work with the Kokisch family, who had employed him on the Riviera. They had now opened a new hotel in Badgastein, an Alpine resort famous for its medicinal hot springs. Papa managed the hotel's restaurant.

The Hotel Bristol nestled among green meadows, beneath snowy mountains, where springs of healing waters percolated up into marble spas. Wealthy families would walk along the garden pathways, feeding the fat squirrels, murmuring their conversations in a mannerly hush. Some rich girl whose parents thought she had a little talent was always playing the piano or singing at an afternoon concert in the gazebo. We visited Papa there every summer—a heavenly life.

As the only kosher hotel in that area, the Bristol attracted Jewish guests from everywhere. The Ochs family, who owned the *New York Times*, came there; and so did Sigmund Freud and the writer Sholem Asch. One day a tall blond man, wearing lederhosen and a Tirolean hat with a chamois-hair brush, came in for lunch. Papa thought surely he had come to the wrong place. But then the man took off his hat, put on a *yarmulke*, and stood up to make a *brucha*.

"I guess even the Jews can't always tell who the Jews are," Papa remarked with a laugh.

For the first time in Badgastein, we met rabbis from Poland, religious men with beautiful long beards who walked slowly through the halls of the hotel, their hands clasped behind their backs. They filled me with a sense of mystery and peace. I believe that one of them saved my life.

I was sixteen, unwise and self-indulgent. I stayed too long in one of the baths and developed a chill and a fever. My mother put me to bed, made me tea with honey, and put compresses on my brow and wrists. As night fell, one of the Polish rabbis knocked on our door. He could not reach the *shul* in time for the evening prayers, he said, and asked if he could say them in our house. Of course Mama welcomed him. When he had finished his prayers, she asked if he would say a blessing for her sick daughter.

He came to my bedside, leaned over me, and patted my hand. His face radiated warmth and good nature. He said something in Hebrew, a language I never expected to know. Then he left. And I got well.

In later years, at moments when I thought I was going to die, I remembered that man and comforted myself with the thought that his blessing would protect me.

Of course there were some things about working in this paradise that weren't so wonderful, but they were part of life then, and to be truthful, we accepted them. For example, kosher slaughtering was not allowed in the province where the hotel was situated. So the *schoichet* had to slaughter the meat in the next province and then transport it to the Bristol. To take another example, our grandparents' generation usually lived in Vienna's outlying towns—Floritzdorf, Stockerau. It was not until our parents reached maturity that Jews were permitted to reside in Vienna proper.

So you see, we had all the burdens of being Jewish in an anti-Semitic country, but none of the strengths—the Torah learning, the prayers, the welded community. We spoke no Yiddish or Hebrew. We had no deep faith in God. We were not Polish Chasidim or Lithuanian yeshiva scholars. We were not bold free Americans—remember that. And there were no Israelis then, no soldiers in the desert, no "nation like other nations." Hold that in your mind as I tell you this story.

What we mostly had was intellect and style. Our city was the sophisticated "Queen of the Danube," "Red Vienna," with social welfare and workers' housing, where geniuses like Freud and Herzl and Mahler whirled in the ferment of their ideas: psychoanalysis, Zionism, socialism, reform, renewal—throwing off lights for the whole world to see by.

In that respect, at least—that "light unto the nations" part—my assimilated Vienna Jews were as Jewish as anybody.

THREE

■

Pepi Rosenfeld's
Good Little Girl

MY FATHER'S DECISION to let me go to high school had a monumental effect on my life, because for the first time I had friends who were boys. It had nothing to do with sex, I assure you. Girls from my social group felt obligated to remain virginal until they were married. No, it was about intellectual development.

You see, in those days, boys were simply better educated than girls. They read more, traveled more, *thought* more. So now, for the first time, I began to have friends with whom I could really talk about the things I cared about—history, literature, society's many ills and how to cure them completely so that everybody would be happy.

I loved mathematics, French, philosophy. I took class notes in shorthand and knew them completely thereafter; I never had to study them again. One girlfriend, a terrible math student—Mama dubbed her "Fräulein Einstein"—arrived at my doorstep every morning before school seeking help with her math homework. I tried to explain without making her feel worse than she already did. The reward I received for my delicacy was a bitter complaint: "How come you Jews are always so smart?"

I was a teenage bluestocking, passionate about ideas, dreaming of adventure. I would travel to Russia and live among the peasants and write best-selling novels about my romantic liaisons with commissars. I would be a lawyer, maybe even a judge, and dispense justice to the common man. This notion first occurred to me in September 1928, during the trial of young Philippe Halsmann, sometimes called the Austrian "Dreyfus case."

Halsmann had gone hiking with his father in the Alps near Innsbruck. He pulled ahead, lost sight of his father, and returned to find him fallen from the trail and dead in a brook below. The son was accused of murdering his father. The prosecution—lacking any motive or proof—based its case on anti-Semitic slander, for Halsmann was Jewish and many Austrians were prepared to believe that the Jews were murderers by inclination. A preacher declared from the pulpit that by insisting on his innocence and not repenting, young Halsmann deserved worse hellfire than Judas. A policeman said that the father's ghost had appeared to him like King Hamlet to accuse his son.

Philippe was wrongly convicted and sentenced to ten years' hard labor. He served two years. Then, through the intervention of people like the Nobel Prize–winning author Thomas Mann, his sentence was commuted to time served and he was allowed to leave the country. He ended up in America, where he became a famous photographer.

His trial inspired me. I fantasized about sitting on the bench, dispensing justice to all. In the court of my dreams, the innocent would never be convicted.

I did not break any rules, never, except that I cut gym all the time. Nobody cared because nobody could imagine a situation in which a girl like me would have to be physically strong. I was a little *zaftig*—that was considered lovely then—and the boys liked me.

I see them before me. Anton Rieder, handsome, tall, impoverished, a strict Catholic. We eyed each other from a distance. Rudolf Gischa, smart, ambitious; he called me his "witch" and made me promise to marry him right after he finished his studies. I said of course I would marry him, but right now we should just keep it our secret. Actually I knew that if I told my father I was going to marry a non-Jew, he would lock me in the house and never let me go to university, a privilege for which I lobbied ceaselessly and which had become much more important to me than any boy.

Out of thirty-six students in my class, three were Jews—Steffi Kanagur, Erna Marcus, and I. One day somebody wrote on their desks: "Jews, get out, go to Palestine!" Nobody wrote on my desk, because those girls came from Poland and I came from Austria and they seemed (actually they were) more overtly Jewish than I was.

It was 1930.

Erna Marcus was a Zionist. My father had once allowed a Zionist meeting in his restaurant, and he had concluded that the whole idea of rebuilding a Jewish state on its original soil in Palestine was a pipe dream. But with so much anti-Semitic propaganda in the air, many young Viennese Jews were drawn to the Zionist plan, among them my little sister Hansi. While I was reading Kant and Nietzsche and Schopenhauer, while I was lost in a dream of Goethe and Schiller, Hansi was joining Hashomer Hatzair, the left-wing Zionist youth group, and planning to take the *hachshara* course to prepare her for life as a pioneer in Israel.

Steffi Kanagur was a Red. So was her brother Siegfried. On a certain Saturday, I told my parents that I was going to attend one of his communist demonstrations against the Christian Democratic government. In truth, I was going to meet Rudolf Gischa in the park.

"How was the demonstration?" Papa asked when I arrived home.

"Marvelous!" I exclaimed. "There were bunches of red balloons. Everybody was carrying a red flag! The Communist Youth League chorus sang beautifully, and there was a band with many horns and a big drum . . . and . . . what's the matter?"

Papa was scowling. Mama had buried her face in her apron, to stifle an explosion of giggles.

"There was no demonstration," Papa said. "It was canceled by the government."

Banished to my room, disgraced, I played chess with Hansi and wondered why in the world the government would cancel Siegfried Kanagur's demonstration.

You see, I had no head for politics. For me, political activity was fun, an ideological romp with smart kids. When Mimi and I joined the high school socialist club, it was not for the sake of ideology but to get ourselves a new social center, where we could listen to lectures on the plight of the workers and learn socialist songs and meet some new boys from other schools—like "Lugubrious" Kohn, who was studying to be a doctor; and "Jolly" Zich, who was planning to go skiing for the rest of his life; and Wolfgang Roemer, short, dark, charming; and Josef Rosenfeld, whom everyone called Pepi.

Pepi was only about six months older than I was, but a full year ahead of me in school and much more mature. A lithe, slender young man, he had—at age eighteen—already begun to lose his hair. But he had bright blue eyes and a sly pussycat smile, and he smoked cigarettes. And of course Pepi was brilliant, absolutely brilliant; there was that too.

While we danced at the high school ball, I talked his ear off about the plays of Arthur Schnitzler.

"Meet me in the park at the Belvedere next Saturday at eight," he said.

"Very well," I answered. "See you then." And off I waltzed with Zich or Kohn or Anton or Wolfgang or Rudolf.

Well, along came Saturday. I decided to go shopping and asked Wolfgang to come along. He agreed. It began to rain, and I got all wet. So Wolfgang took me home to his mother, Frau Roemer, one of the sweetest women I have ever known. She dried my hair and fed me strawberries in cream. Her husband and his happy-go-lucky brother Uncle Felix arrived. Then Wolfgang's younger sister Ilse came in, shaking out her umbrella. They pulled back the carpet, rolled out the gramophone, and put on some new swing records, and we all started to dance. And in walked Pepi Rosenfeld, soaked to the skin.

"That girl from the socialist club—she agreed to meet me at the Belvedere and I waited for her for an hour and finally I gave up. I am so annoyed! Mother was right! Girls are impossible!"

He stood there looking at me, dripping. The music was playing.

"I'm sorry," I said sweetly. "I forgot."

"Dance with me," he said, "and I will tell you how angry I am with you."

The next day a boy named Suri Fellner came to our house with a letter, signed by both Wolfgang and Pepi. Apparently they had discussed the situation and had decided that I must choose between them. The one I selected would be my boyfriend. The other would withdraw, brokenhearted.

On the bottom of the letter, I wrote "Wolfgang," and I sent my answer back with the dutiful emissary. A few weeks later I went on a holiday with our family in the mountains and completely forgot that I had "chosen" Wolfgang Roemer. Luckily, so did he.

In my last year of high school—it was 1933—I wrote a final essay on *Thus Spake Zarathustra* by Nietzsche. For my research, I decided to go to the National Library. (I also agreed to pick up my sister Mimi in front of the twin columns at the Karlskirche on my way home.) Pepi Rosenfeld appeared suddenly, out of nowhere. He had a way of doing that, coming upon you like a cat or a sprite, on silent feet, with his subtle smile. Without a word, he seized my heavy books and fell into step with me.

"Have you ever been to the National Library before?" he asked.

"No."

"Well, I go there very often now that I'm enrolled in the law program at the university, and I can tell you, it's extremely gigantic. As you are unfamiliar with the layout of the place, you may not know which entrance to use. Why, you could become lost even before you get inside! Better let me lead you."

So I did. We walked and walked, past the palaces, through the parks, scattering the pigeons, not even hearing the tolling clocks of the city.

"My paper has to be very long and complex," I said. "I shall cite all the great thinkers—Karl Marx, Sigmund Freud."

"What about Adolf Hitler?"

"Oh, him. He's not a thinker. He's just a ranter and raver."

"There may come a time," said Pepi, "when people cannot tell the difference."

"Impossible," I solemnly predicted. "I have read Hitler's book *Mein Kampf* and also some works by his colleague Herr Alfred Rosenberg because I am a fair-minded, objective person and I believe one should always hear out all sides before making a decision, and so I can tell you from firsthand knowledge that these men are idiots. Their ideas about how the Jews have poisoned their so-called superior Aryan race and caused all of Germany's troubles are utter nonsense. No intelligent person could possibly believe them. Hitler is laughable. He will soon disappear."

"Just like all your old boyfriends," Pepi said with his sly smile.

We stopped for cake and coffee, as people of our type habitually did in the midafternoon. He told me about his studies, his professors, his great future as a doctor of jurisprudence. The sun sparkled on the spires of the churches. In the park at the Belvedere, he interrupted my chatter with a little kiss. I completely lost my train of thought. He set down my books and took me in his arms and kissed me properly. We never did get to the National Library. I never did pick up my sister Mimi (who complained about my lack of consideration for years afterward). But by the end of that afternoon, what Pepi Rosenfeld had said came true: all my old boyfriends had just disappeared. Poof. Like that. Gone.

Pepi could always get my attention. I'd be in class, in a bookstore, in a café, and suddenly I would feel a tingling on my scalp or at the nape of my neck. I'd turn around and there he would be, staring at me. He never talked nonsense. He always had a point to make. I felt that my long search for someone to share my passion for ideas and books and art had finally ended. Soon I was madly in love with him and could think of no one else. When my old amour Rudolf Gischa wrote to me from his university in the Sudetanland, Czechoslovakia, declaring that he had decided to join

the Nazi Party, that Adolf Hitler was obviously right about everything, including the Jews, and that I should please return to him
his promise of love and marriage, I did so with pleasure.

BY THE TIME I met Pepi, his father had died—in Steinhof, the
famous insane asylum that the Kaiser built. Pepi's uncles, important
men in the city of Eisenstadt, provided a monthly pension for
Pepi's mother, Anna. She had converted to Judaism in order to
marry but had really always remained a candle-lighting, mass-going
Catholic. After Herr Rosenfeld's death, Anna pretended to continue to be Jewish so his family would continue to support her.
She also kept it a secret when, in 1934, she married Herr Hofer,
an insurance man from Ybbs—so that the money would keep
coming in.

Pepi had a sort of bar mitzvah; really it was just a party which
his mother gave in order to elicit some presents. She was disappointed because, instead of cash, his uncles gave him a set of beautifully bound books by Schiller and Goethe. Strange—but I think
that if Pepi felt any connection to things Jewish, it may have been
because of those wonderful German books. He knew he would
never have received them from his mother's family. He knew that,
intellectually, he was connected to the Jewish side. And Pepi's
whole personality was his intellect—remember that.

Anna wasn't a stupid woman, but she was uneducated, full of
superstitions and unveiled fears and desires. Hefty, always short of
breath, florid, she dressed with unsuitable flash for a woman of her
age and size. She wore a big false smile full of big teeth. Set her
reddish hair in little pin curls and used beer as a lotion. She spent
her days gossiping and read nothing.

She slept in the same room with her son, even when he was

fully grown. She waited on him as though he were a king, serving him lunch on the good china every day and hushing the neighbors' children when he took his daily afternoon nap.

She always knew which child in the district had been born with a deformity, and she always had a theory as to why: a harelip because of the mother's vanity, a gimpy leg because of the father's philandering. She told Pepi that his father had suffered from dementia at the end—a sure sign of syphilis, she said. I don't know to this day whether it was true. Maybe she got the idea from the same wellspring of Austrian poison that caused Hitler to believe that syphilis was a "Jewish disease."

Anna bought "new wine," which she said "had not yet aged" so it "contained no alcohol and could not make you tipsy." At the end of the day, Pepi and I would find her in the living room of their flat at Number 1 Dampfgasse, drinking the "new wine" and listening to the Nazi radio station with a worried look on her face.

"For heaven's sake, Mother!" Pepi protested. "Why do you distress yourself by listening to that irrational propaganda?"

Anna turned to us with wide, frightened eyes. "We have to pay attention to them," she said.

"Oh please . . ."

"They are very very dangerous, my dear son!" she insisted. "They hate the Jews. They blame the Jews for everything."

"No one listens," Pepi said.

"*Everybody* listens!" she cried. "In church, in the marketplace, I hear people talking and I know, everybody listens and *everybody agrees!*"

She seemed intensely emotional, close to tears. I assumed it was because of the wine.

■　■　■

MY FATHER GAVE IN. He sent me to the university. I decided to study law.

In those days, those who hoped to be judges and those who hoped to be lawyers took the same course of study, and specialized only after they had taken their final examinations. We studied Roman law, German law, and church law; civil, criminal, and commercial procedures; the Law of Nations; political science; economic theory; and also certain new subjects, like psychiatry and forensic photography, pertaining to criminal behavior.

I bought a little box camera and took snapshots of people.

Pepi's mother bought him a Leica. He set up a darkroom at home and took soulful pictures of objects: dominos spilled on a table, arranged in a slanting beam of sunlight; books and fruit.

While Hitler was coming to power in Germany, I was hiking in the mountains with the girls from the socialist youth group. I remember Heddy Deutsch, the daughter of a Jewish member of parliament; and Elfi Westermayer, a medical student. We slept in the hay in farmers' barns near the lakes at Saint Gilden and Gmunden. We wore blue shirts, hammered studs into the soles of our boots for better traction on the pebbly trails, and went out singing in the brittle mountain air. I remember all the songs. The "International," "Das Wandern Ist des Müllers Lust," "La Bandiera Rossa" ("The Red Flag").

During the school year, my friends and I gathered at the socialist hall and concentrated on saving the world. In those tumultuous days, other young people lived politics; they were ready to die for their beliefs. But our group mostly talked.

There were two boys, Fritz and Franck, who played Ping-Pong incessantly but never too strenuously. The steady, indolent beat of their game captured nothing of the outside world's mad rhythm.

A couple of the girls brought cake that their mothers had baked. Another boy brought records for dancing. Pepi contributed his chess set. He and Wolfgang and I played all the time. Occasionally, I even beat them.

"Oswald Spengler says that our great cultural achievements are over," Pepi mused, moving his rook. "He says we're all just sinking into materialism and becoming philosophers instead of men of action."

"Ah, the Nazis must love him," Wolfgang said, looking over my shoulder, silently planning my next move, "since they consider themselves men of action."

"The Nazis have banned Spengler," Pepi commented. "They don't like anyone who says the worst is yet to come."

"For them the future is beautiful," I chimed in, deftly cornering Pepi's king. "They anticipate a thousand-year Reich in which they will be the *Übermenchen* and everybody else will be the *Untermenschen* and do all the world's work for them."

"And what do you anticipate, Edith?" Fritz called from the Ping-Pong table.

"I anticipate having six children, all sitting around the table for lunch with big white napkins tucked in their collars, saying, 'Mama, this strudel is yummy!' "

"Who's going to bake the strudel?" Pepi joked. "What if Grandmother Hahn is busy that day?"

I poked him. He squeezed my hand.

"Did you hear that Hitler is taking children away from their mothers?" Wolfgang said. "If they don't teach National Socialist doctrine, they lose their kids."

"But surely the courts will not agree to that!" I exclaimed.

"The courts have been packed with Nazis," Pepi answered.

"How can a gang of pompous little men so quickly destroy the democratic institutions of a great country?!" cried Wolfgang, pounding on the table in frustration, making the chess pieces topple.

"Freud would tell you it is a triumph of the ego," Pepi said. "They think they are big men and their belief in themselves creates a light so blinding that all around are dazzled. The trouble with these Nazis is that they have no self-critical faculty, so in their efforts to achieve greatness, they achieve nothing but a parody of greatness. Caesar conquered nations, took their leaders captive, picked their brains, and so enriched his empire. Hitler will burn down nations, torture their leaders to death, and destroy the world."

We sat stunned and silent at Pepi's prediction. Our friends stopped dancing and chattering. The Ping-Pong game came to a halt.

"So what should we do, Pepi?"

"We have to fight for the rule of law, and have faith in the inevitability of the socialist paradise," Pepi answered, throwing his arm around my shoulders. "One class. No masters. No slaves. No black. No white. No Jew. No Christian. One race—the human race."

How can I describe my pride at that moment? To be Pepi's girl, to be the chosen consort of our undisputed intellectual leader— this was exactly the place I wanted in society, and his vision was exactly the future I wanted for humankind.

WHILE I WAS attending the University of Vienna from 1933 to 1937, we had endless political turmoil in Austria. Chancellor Dollfuss, determined to preserve us as a religious Catholic country, outlawed the Socialist Party. The socialists responded in ways that I, a socialist myself, often found downright foolish.

I went to an illegal socialist meeting. I seem to remember that Bruno Kreisky was the featured speaker. Our leaders had received permission to use the hall by declaring that we were holding a rehearsal of a choral society. They told us that if the police came, we must immediately begin singing Beethoven's "Ode to Joy." So we practiced.

I tell you, the sound we made was indescribable. I bit my lip, I bit my knuckles, I practically ate the sheet music, but nothing could prevent me—and everybody else—from dissolving into hysterical laughter.

The socialists called a general strike. But in 1934 over one-third of the workforce in Vienna was out of work. How could you go on strike when you weren't working in the first place? The equally foolish government called in the army, which shelled the workers' houses. The socialists fought back. Hundreds were killed and wounded. And so the two forces in Austria that needed to be allied against the Nazis were divided for all time by anger, bitterness, and mourning.

Dollfuss would exile the Nazi leaders, and Hitler would welcome them and set them up with a powerful radio transmitter in Munich from which they harangued and threatened us. They would tell atrocity stories about how German burghers were being butchered by Bolsheviks in Czechoslovakia, and about how the "thieving, lying, murderous" Jews had caused the economic depression which had thrown millions out of work. I refused to listen to the Nazi radio, so I never once heard Hitler screeching.

Nazi students instigated fights and riots to disrupt university life. They beat up students and professors who spoke out against Hitler. They threw stink bombs into the auditorium, making it impossible to assemble there. The police in turn tried to break up student demonstrations with tear gas. If we had any doubt what it would be like in Austria if the Nazis came to power, there were German authors who came to lecture at the Konzerthalle and warn us: Erich Kästner, a hero of mine, author of *Emil and the Detectives*; and Thomas Mann, the Nobel laureate, author of *The Magic Mountain*, tall and severe and so grim up there at the podium that my heart froze to look at him.

"I don't know what this evening means to you," Mann said to the anti-Nazi crowd gathered in Vienna to protest the escalating violence, "but it means more to me."

Some people we knew wore white socks to show that they were Nazi sympathizers. In addition to Rudolf Gischa, there was my old morning math student "Fräulein Einstein," and Elfi Westermayer and her boyfriend Franz Sehors. I thought they had gone temporarily insane.

You see, I cultivated blindness the way my grandmother grew cactus in Stockerau. It was the wrong plant for this climate.

The Austrian Nazis began to assassinate socialist leaders. On July 25, 1934, they murdered Chancellor Dollfuss.

Martial law was imposed. The streets seethed with policemen, armed guards who stood watchfully at the gates of the many embassies in our neighborhood. Once, as I walked home from my law classes, two men walking ahead of me were suddenly cut off by a policeman on a motorbike who demanded to see their papers and made them open their briefcases. I turned the corner onto Argentinierstrasse, where a young man was being frisked. His girlfriend—just about my age—was being interrogated.

Truthfully, I would have enjoyed being detained myself. It would have been an exciting event for me to talk about with my friends. But no one noticed me! If anyone even glanced my way, it was without concern. Something about me said "silly," "innocent," "unimportant." So I walked freely through the alarmed, dangerous town, a twenty-year-old law student who looked fourteen and posed no threat to anyone.

A new chancellor, Kurt von Schuschnigg, came to power after Dollfuss's death. People did not love him so much, but they respected him and thought he might be able to extricate us from Hitler's aggressive plans.

Pepi and I took long walks through the city, read to each other, and dreamed of the socialist paradise. Meanwhile the German Army invaded the supposedly demilitarized Rhineland, and then the Nazis instigated a civil war in Spain. The Italians, who were supposed to be Austria's allies, instead allied themselves with Hitler so they could be free to attack Ethiopia.

And then my father died.

It was June 1936. He stopped at the doorway to the restaurant at the Hotel Bristol, looked around to make sure everything was perfect—the tables spotless, the waiters standing at attention—and fell down dead.

The news came to us with such force and suddenness that we were helpless to respond. Our pillar, our rock, had crashed.

Mama sat in our parlor, her eyes vacant, her hair unkempt, her face blurred behind a veil of tears. Mimi sat silent and devastated, holding the hand of her boyfriend, a fellow student and friend of mine named Milo Grenzbauer. Our darling little Hansi couldn't stop crying.

I went back and forth from the kitchen, serving coffee to the visitors who came to pay their condolences. Our concierge, Frau

Falat, was there. My cousin Jultschi came with her fiancé, an arrogant, handsome Czech tailor named Otto Ondrej. Jultschi hung on him, clutching his hand, wiping her eyes with his handkerchief.

Pepi came with his mother. She sat next to Mama, talking about how hard it was to be a woman alone, and meanwhile not very discreetly inquiring of the other guests about how much money my father had left.

In the kitchen, Pepi stroked my hair and told me that everything would be all right.

I didn't believe him. I felt suddenly much more vulnerable to politics than ever before. How could we withstand these tumultuous times without our father to protect us? At the Munich Olympics that summer, the German athletes saluted their ugly little Führer and every victory of theirs felt to me like a personal attack against the Hahns of Vienna.

To support our family, Mama decided to open her own dressmaking business. She would cut out pictures of elegant suits and make them up for her customers to order, in the fabrics they wanted and with the trimmings they requested. According to a custom of the time, she was obligated to ask all the other dressmakers in the neighborhood whether it was all right with them for her to set up shop. Without exception, they said "yes." Given such a vote of confidence, how could Mama doubt that she was held in high esteem by our neighbors?

My contribution to my family's support was to take on as much tutoring work as I could manage and to study without ceasing for my final state exam. Once I had become a doctor of law and could make a good living, I thought, our political problems might solve themselves.

But it was hard to concentrate. I went to my classes in a fog of despair and grief. I would sit in the library with a book open and unread, my mind at a standstill. One day Anton Rieder, my old crush from high school, sat down next to me. He had been fatherless since we were kids. He knew the feeling—the loss of direction, the insecurity, the premature aging.

"You are still beautiful," he said.

"And you were always gallant."

"I've enrolled at the Consular Academy. I'm going there not because I am so eager to be a diplomat, but because they have given me a scholarship."

"But it will be wonderful for you, Anton. You will be able to travel, maybe even go to England or America."

"Come with me."

"What?"

"I know you go with Pepi Rosenfeld, but believe me, he's too smart for his own good—his brains will always get in the way of his conscience. He's not fine enough for you. I have always been in love with you; you know that. Leave him and come with me. I have nothing. Now your father is dead, and you have nothing. We'll be perfect together."

He reached across the library table and took my hand. He was so handsome, so earnest. For a moment, I thought: "Maybe. Why not?" And then of course all the reasons why not spilled onto the long oak table, and Anton could not fail to see them there; and like a wise young diplomat, he rose and kissed my hand and took his leave.

WE HAD A visit from a new neighbor—an engineer named Denner, a nice-looking, gregarious man. He had recently lost his wife to tuberculosis after a long, miserable illness. He had two daughters: Elsa, age eleven; and Christl, fourteen. Since he often had to travel on business and leave the girls to fend for themselves, he was looking for a tutor to keep them involved in their studies. The concierge had recommended me highly, and I readily accepted the job. So now, every day, I came from the university and spent the afternoon with these delightful girls.

The Denners lived on the ballroom floor of our house, in a large space that defied subdivision, where people with "von" in their name had once gathered to dance to baroque music. The windows were enormous. They reached from floor to ceiling. The floor was wood and seemingly endless. To see those two children polishing that floor was enough to break your heart.

"Who's coming to the ball?" I cried as I watched them scrubbing and rubbing. "The Hapsburgs have been deposed. The Bourbons are out of town."

"Father likes us to do our part to keep up the former glory of our country," Christl groaned.

Each girl had a puppy with a Russian name, in honor of Frau Denner, who had come from White Russia. Elsa's puppy behaved well and slept in her lap. Christl's dog wanted to chase pigeons and leap into the arms of visitors and slobber over them lovingly. So it was with the girls themselves. Elsa had things under control. Christl's life was an adventure.

Christl was taking a business course, but she couldn't manage the bookkeeping, couldn't write a neat letter, and couldn't concentrate. I sat with her while she plowed through her homework; I walked with her and her dog in the yard of our building. Soon she was coming to me with every sort of adolescent problem. She was tall and vivacious, with light-brown hair and almost violet eyes, and she was beset by boys. They stood in the street and sang to her, followed her home, sent flowers, bought treats for the dog, anything to get her attention.

When she was fifteen and I was twenty-three, Christl fell in love. His name was Hans Beran. Everyone called him Bertschi. "He's a bit of a fool," said Herr Denner, "but at least he doesn't throw his money around like the rest of these young people."

Bertschi gave Christl a hard time. First he wanted her desperately. Then he was too shy to accept her affections. Then he decided she was too beautiful for him and he simply couldn't bear the jealously of the other boys. Then he phoned very late at night and said that he couldn't live without her, that she must meet him at the Café Mozart so he could tell her how much he adored her.

Every time I came to their house, Christl would greet me breathlessly at the door and whisper wildly: "I have to speak with you—in private!" And she would bundle me into the shadows of the hallway and tell me what marvelous stupid thing Bertschi had done now, and how she had to write a letter to him, and how she couldn't possibly do it without my help.

"Oh, please, Edith, please. If you write the letter it will come out perfect. Please, please!"

How could I resist her? I could never resist a little sister.

When she passed the final exam at the business school, her father gave a party. He hired a boat and invited his guests for a moonlight cruise on the Danube. Toward the end of the evening, a waiter presented me with a bouquet of red roses. There was no card, and I wondered who could have sent them.

My mother, sitting in the parlor, appliquéing pretty birds on my new yellow blouse, knew immediately. "The flowers are from Herr Denner," she said. "Because when his girls needed a substitute mother, someone to listen to them with a caring heart, you were there." Mama grinned. "So you see, you must become a mother, Edith—because obviously you have a talent for it."

■ ■ ■

THE NAZI BULLIES roared that Chancellor von Schuschnigg was determined to restore the Hapsburg monarchy and if that happened, Germany would be forced to enter Austria and destroy this idea by military might. That was a direct threat, a preface.

The chancellor fended them off for a while but soon saw that no one would help him and resistance was useless. On March 11, 1938, as Pepi and I were walking through a working-class neighborhood—holding hands, leaning on each other's bodies, a warm column of love in the cold, darkening night—someone leaned out of a window and said, "Von Schuschnigg has resigned."

That was complete silence in the street.

Pepi held me. I whispered into his neck: "We have to get out."

"We'll wait and see," he said.

"No, no, we have to get out now," I said, pressing myself against him.

"Don't give way to hysteria. It could all be over in a week."

"I'm afraid . . ."

"Don't be. I am here with you. I love you. You are mine. I will always take care of you."

He kissed me with such passion that I felt my whole body grow warm and light. What did I care if politicians disappeared and nations prepared for war? I had Pepi, my genius, my comfort, the rock who had replaced my father.

The next day was the golden wedding anniversary of my mother's parents. The whole family was planning to go out to Stockerau to celebrate. We had presents, cakes, wine, and toasts prepared.

But we never made this happy journey, because the German Army chose that same day to march into Austria. Flags were flying.

Martial music played. The Nazi radio station—which had become the *only* station—roared with victory, and thousands of our friends and neighbors and countrymen gathered on the boulevards to greet the Wehrmacht with wild joy and tumultuous cheering.

On April 10, 1938, more than ninety percent of the Austrians voted "yes" to union with Germany.

A socialist friend, whose father had been executed by Nazi assassins, wanted to organize protests against the Anschluss and tried to recruit me for the underground. He told me that I could get a different name, belong to a cell, and deliver messages.

For the first time, I saw the practical wisdom of political activism. "Yes," I said, pressing his hand as a promise. "Count me in."

But Pepi said no. He told me it was irresponsible for me even to think of such a thing, because now I had a widowed mother and young sisters who depended on me. What would happen to them if I were arrested?

So I told my friend that he would have to work without me. Like a good little girl, I did what Pepi Rosenfeld said.

FOUR

■

The Trap Set by Love

ONE OF THE first things the Nazis did was to distribute 100,000 free radio sets to the Austrian Christians. Where did they get these radios? From us, of course. Right after the Anschluss, the Jews were required to turn in their typewriters and their radios, the idea being that if we could not communicate with each other or the outside world, we would be isolated and more easily terrorized and manipulated. It was a good idea. It worked well.

The man the Germans appointed to eliminate the Jews from Vienna was Adolf Eichmann. His policies became a model for making the whole Reich *Judenrein*—"cleansed of Jews." Essentially he made us pay as much as possible to escape. The rich had to sign over everything they owned; the less rich had to pay such exorbitant amounts for tickets out that families were often forced to choose which of their children should go and which should stay.

Gangs of thugs in brown shirts owned the streets. They drove around in trucks, flashing their guns and their swastika armbands, hooting at the pretty girls. If they wanted to pick you up or beat you up, they did so with impunity. Anybody who resisted was beaten or killed or taken away to Dachau or Buchenwald or some other concentration camp. (You must understand that at that time, the concentration camps were prisons where opponents of the Nazi regime were detained. Von Schuschnigg was in a concentration camp; so was Bruno Bettelheim for a time. The inmates were made to work at hard labor and lived in dreadful conditions, but they often came back from these places. Not until the 1940s did the words "concentration camp" come to stand for monstrous cruelty and almost certain death. Nobody even imagined there would one day be a death camp like Auschwitz.)

How can I describe to you our confusion and terror when the Nazis took over? We had lived until yesterday in a rational world. Now everyone around us—our schoolmates, neighbors, and teachers; our tradesmen, policemen, and bureaucrats—had all gone mad. They had been harboring a hatred for us which we had grown accustomed to calling "prejudice." What a gentle word that was! What a euphemism! In fact they hated us with a hatred as old as their religion; they were born hating us, raised hating us; and now with the Anschluss, the veneer of civilization which had protected us from their hatred was stripped away.

On the pavements, protesters had written anti-Nazi slogans. The SS grabbed Jews and forced them at gunpoint to scrub off the graffiti while crowds of Austrians stood around jeering and laughing.

The Nazi radio blamed us for every filthy evil thing in this world. The Nazis called us subhuman and, in the next breath, superhuman; accused us of plotting to murder them, to rob them blind; declared that *they* had to conquer the world to prevent *us* from conquering the world. The radio said that we must be dispossessed of all we owned; that my father, who had dropped dead while working, had not really worked for our pleasant flat—the leather chairs in the dining room, the earrings in my mother's ears—that he had somehow stolen them from Christian Austria, which now had every right to take them back.

Did our friends and our neighbors really believe this? Of course they didn't believe it. They were not stupid. But they had suffered depression, inflation, and joblessness. They wanted to be well-to-do again, and the fastest way to accomplish that was to steal. Cultivating a belief in the greed of the Jews gave them an excuse to steal everything the Jews possessed.

We sat in our flats, paralyzed with fear, waiting for the madness to end. Rational, charming, witty, dancing, generous Vienna must surely rebel against such insanity. We waited and we waited and it didn't end and it didn't end and still we waited and we waited.

The restrictions against Jews spread into every corner of our lives. We couldn't go to movies or concerts. We couldn't walk on certain streets. The Nazis put up signs on Jewish shop windows warning the population not to buy there. Mimi was fired from her job at the dry cleaners because it had become illegal for Christians to employ Jews. Hansi was no longer allowed to go to school.

Uncle Richard went to the café where he had been going for twenty years. It now had a Jewish side and an Aryan side, and he sat on the Jewish side. Because he had fair hair and didn't look Jewish, a waiter, who did not know him, said he had to move to the Aryan side. But on the Aryan side, a waiter who did know him said that he had to go back to the Jewish side. He finally gave up and went home.

Baron Louis de Rothschild, one of the wealthiest Jewish men in Vienna, tried to leave the city. The Nazis stopped him at the airport and put him in prison, and whatever they did to him there convinced him that he ought to sign over everything to the Nazi regime. Then they let him leave. The SS took over the Rothschild Palace on Prinz Eugenstrasse and renamed it the Center for Jewish Emigration.

Everybody talked about leaving.

"Maybe we could go to a kibbutz in Palestine," I suggested to Pepi.

"You? My adorable little mouse? Doing farmwork?" He laughed and tickled me. "You might get blisters on your pretty fingers."

I stood in line for days at the British consulate, trying to get clearance to work as a housemaid in England. Every Jewish girl in Vienna seemed to be applying.

An Asian gentleman approached me and my cousin Elli with a bow and a smile. "If you are interested in seeing the glories of the East . . . the Great Wall . . . the Imperial Palace . . . I am author-ized to offer you fascinating work in one of several Chinese cities," he said. "We arrange passports, transportation, and lodging. I have a car nearby. You could be out of Austria by tomorrow." I am sure there were some who went with him.

My cousin Elli got a job in England. I got clearance for a job— but no job.

One afternoon Hansi did not come home. Mimi and I went out hunting for her. When we returned without her, Mama began to weep. A pretty seventeen-year-old Jewish girl had disappeared in a city crawling with anti-Semitic thugs. We were sick with terror.

Around midnight Hansi returned. She was pale, shaking, grim, older.

She told us the Nazis had picked her up and taken her to an SS office and put a gun to her head and ordered her to sew buttons on dozens of uniforms. In the room next door, she saw Orthodox Jews, devout men with long beards, forced to do ridiculous gymnastics by their tormentors, who found the show hilariously funny. Hansi had cried out in protest. Some lout had threatened to beat her if she didn't shut up and sew. At the day's end, they let her go. She had been wandering the streets ever since.

"We have to get out," she said.

It was easier to get a ticket out if you were married, so Milo and Mimi decided to tie the knot.

"Let's get married, Pepi," I said.

He grinned at me and wiggled his eyebrows. "But you promised your father you would never marry a Christian," he joked. In truth, he was a Christian now. His mother, Anna, in an effort to protect him from the Nuremberg Laws—which denied Jews citizenship in the Reich—had taken her twenty-six-year-old son to church and had him baptized. Then she had used her connections to have the family name erased from the list of the Jewish community. So when the Jews of Vienna were counted—and they were counted constantly by the precise Colonel Eichmann—Josef Rosenfeld was supposedly no longer on the list.

"It won't do you any good," I told him. "The Nuremberg Laws are retroactive. Everything they say applies to people who were Jews before the Laws went into effect, in 1936. So people who became Christians in 1937 don't count."

"Do me a favor, darling," he said. "Don't tell that to my

mother. She thinks she has saved me from all this foolishness. I'd hate to burst her bubble."

He kissed me, making my head spin. Somehow my proposal of marriage was forgotten.

I refused to let the political situation keep me from my studies. I had taken both state exams and passed with high grades. One last exam, and I would be a doctor of law, qualified to serve not just as a lawyer but also as a judge. I felt that if I earned my degree, if I was trained, qualified, certified, I would have a much easier time emigrating.

In April 1938, I went to the university to pick up my final exam papers and to receive the date for my doctoral exam. A young clerk there, actually someone I knew, said: "You will not be taking the examination, Edith. You are no longer welcome in our university." She gave me my papers and the transcript of my grades. "Good-bye."

For almost five years, I had studied law, constitutions, torts, psychology, economics, political theory, history, philosophy. I had written papers, attended lectures, analyzed legal cases, studied with a judge three times a week to prepare for my doctoral exam. And now they would not let me take it.

My legs buckled. I leaned on her desk for support.

"But . . . but . . . this last exam is all I need for my degree!"

She turned her back on me. I could feel her sense of triumph, her genuine satisfaction in destroying my life. It had a smell, I tell you—like sweat, like lust.

GRANDMOTHER HELPED THE maid carry some heavy mattresses into the yard for an airing and got a hernia. She had to be operated on, and during this operation she died.

Grandfather couldn't quite believe it. He always seemed to be turning around, expecting to find her there, always reminding himself with a heavy sigh that she was gone.

Right after Grandmother died, the world held a conference at Evian-les-Bains, a luxurious spa in the French Alps near Lake Geneva, at which the fate of the Austrian Jews was up for discussion. Eichmann sent representatives of our community to plead with other countries to pay the Nazi ransom and take us in. "Don't you want to save the urbane, well-educated, fun-loving, cultured Jews of Austria?" they asked. "How about paying $400 a head to the Nazi regime? Too much? How about $200?"

They couldn't get a cent.

No country wanted to pay for our rescue, including the United States. The dictator of the Dominican Republic, Trujillo, took a few Jews, thinking they might help bring some prosperity to his tiny, impoverished country. I have heard that they did.

ON NOVEMBER 9, 1938, I did not go to work at the Denner house, because my sister Hansi had received a ticket to emigrate to Palestine. With a feeling of joy mixed with grief, we were taking her to the railway station. In her knapsack and the one suitcase the Nazis allowed her, she had bread, hard-boiled eggs, cake, evaporated milk, underwear, socks, shoes, sturdy trousers, heavy shirts, only one dress, and only one skirt. Femininity and its pretty paraphernalia had declined in importance. Like fruit and flowers, femininity spoiled quickly and cost too much relative to its small utility in wartime.

Mama and Mimi and I were crying, but Hansi was not. "Come soon," she said to us. "Get out of this damned country; get out as fast as you can."

The train came and took her away. She leaned out the window with the other fleeing young people. She waved. She didn't smile.

Mama had emptied the bank account to pay the Nazis the enormous price they demanded for Hansi's ticket. There was, Mimi and I knew, virtually nothing left to ransom us. "But you have men who love you," Mama said, holding us close. "They will save you. Hansi was too young to have a man."

Walking home from the station, we heard a strange rumble in the darkening streets. On the horizon we saw the orange glow of a fire. A building on the other side of the city was burning. The sidewalks were unnaturally empty. Nazi vehicles roared by, full of excited young men, but there were no pedestrians.

Mimi and I, our senses sharpened to danger in these past months, broke into a run, dragging our mother along with us. At our house, we found the concierge, Frau Falat, waiting for us, her face drawn and worried. "They've been attacking all the Jewish shops," she said. "One of the synagogues is burning. Don't go out any more tonight."

Milo Grenzbauer arrived, out of breath from a long spring through the streets. "May I trouble you, Frau Hahn?" he asked courteously. "I need to stay at your house. A friend of my brother who is in the SA says that the Nazis are grabbing all the young Jewish men and taking them I don't know where—Dachau, Buchenwald. He told me and my brother not to be found at our home tonight."

He sagged into one of the leather chairs. Mimi sat at his feet, trembling, holding on to his knees.

Outside, the streets had begun to roar with the sound of shouting men, screeching brakes, and crashing windows. Around ten o'clock, our cousin Erwin, a medical student, joined us. He was sweating. His face was white. He had come home late from the laboratory, encountered a mob outside the synagogue, and turned around and headed for our district just as the synogogue began to burn. He had seen Jews being beaten and dragged away.

Pepi arrived right after him. Of the three young men in our house, he was the only calm one—clean, dapper, unruffled.

"Mobs get tired and go home after a while," he said. "You'll see. Tomorrow morning, they'll all have a terrible hangover and we'll all have a lot of broken windows and they'll sober up and we'll fix the windows and life will return to normal."

We sat gazing at him, astonished. Was he crazy?

"You always keep up such a lovely front, Pepi," said my mother, greatly amused. "You will make a splendid lawyer."

"I don't like to see my sweet little girl upset," he said. He rubbed the worry from my forehead. "This furrow in her lovely brow must disappear."

He threw his arm around me and pulled me down next to him on the sofa. At that moment, I adored Pepi Rosenfeld. I felt as though his good nature, his fearlessness, would ultimately lead us all out of this inferno.

And then his mother, Anna, arrived, screaming. "Are you an idiot?" she bellowed at him. "I have bribed half the officials in the city to make you a Christian and get you off the list of the Jewish community! And now, tonight, when the Jews are being carted away and their shops are being torched, what do you do? You come right into their hiding place and sit in their parlor! Get away from these people! These are not your people! You are a Christian, a Catholic, an Austrian! These people are foreigners! Everybody hates them! I will not have you spending another minute in their company!"

She turned to me, her eyes wild. "Let him go, Edith! If you love him, let him go! If you hold on to him, they will drag him away and put him in prison, my only boy, my son, my treasure . . ." She began to sob.

My mother, ever sympathetic, offered her a brandy.

"Now, Mother," Pepi said, "stop making a scene, please. Edith and I will soon be gone from here. We're planning to go to England, possibly to Palestine."

"What?! Is that what you are plotting behind my back? To desert me? To leave me, a poor widow, alone on the eve of war?"

"Now stop this 'poor widow' nonsense," Pepi admonished her. "You are no such thing. Herr Hofer is your husband, and he will take care of you."

Having her secret revealed like that drove Anna wild. "If you abandon me, if you take your little bitch Jewess and run away, I will kill myself!" she screamed. And she ran for the window, and climbed onto the sill as though to throw herself out.

Pepi leaped up, grabbed her, and gathered her big, bulky body into his arms, patting her heaving back. "There, there, Mother . . ."

"Come home with me," she wailed. "Get away from these people! Leave that girl—she will be the death of you! Come home with me!"

He looked at me across the broad, shaking expanse of her back, and in his eyes I finally saw what he had been putting up with all these weeks since the Anschluss, why he had never quite agreed to leave. I understood that daily, Anna had been in a state of hysteria, pressuring him, screaming, crying, threatening suicide, that she had entrapped him and held him immobile with an iron chain that she called "love."

"Go," I said softly. "Go home with her. Go."

He did. And the rest of us sat up together for all the rest of Kristallnacht, listening to the sound of our lives shattering.

■　　■　　■

MY SISTER MIMI married Milo Grenzbauer in December 1938. They went to Israel on an illegal transport in February 1939. My mother sold the leather chairs to pay for their tickets. We might have been able to raise the money for a third ticket for me—but to be honest, I couldn't face the thought of leaving Pepi.

Events crashed into each other with such speed and violence that we felt as if we were caught in an avalanche with no time to recover before the next mountain collapsed. In March 1939, one year after the Anschluss, Hitler—appeased by Chamberlain—took Czechoslovakia. "If the goyim won't defend each other," said my mother, "how can we expect them to defend us?" Then my grandfather had a stroke. Uncle Richard hired a nurse to take care of him, and we all tried to visit him in Stockerau as much as possible. But then the Nazis arrested Uncle Richard and Aunt Roszi too.

They spent six weeks in prison. To get out, they gave the Nazis everything they possessed: real estate, bank accounts, bonds, dishes, silver. Then they left immediately, heading east. Russia swallowed them. My mother waited and prayed for word of them, but none came.

One day a young man in uniform knocked on our door. I must tell you, they had a certain way of knocking, these Nazis, as if they resented the door, as if they expected it to disappear beneath their pounding fists. My body could always tell when they were knocking. My skin crawled. My stomach tightened. The Nazi told Mama that Grandfather's house and shop were being taken over by "good" Austrians, and that he had to go live in a room with relatives.

That was it. No more Stockerau.

Grandfather had been living in that house for forty-five years.

The dishes, the chairs, the pictures, the pillows, the rugs, the telephone, the pots and pans and spoons, the piano, the gorgeous knitted lace doilies, the Puch motorbikes, the sewing machines, the letters we had written him that he had saved in his big wooden desk, the desk itself—all of it, every stick and memory, was stolen; and the thieves sold it to his lifelong neighbors for a very good price.

Mama sent me to take care of him. The stroke, following on Grandmother's death, had slowed him; but the loss of his home, *his place,* now crippled him beyond repair. I led him to the toilet; I massaged his feet. Whatever I made for him to eat on his special diet, he would thank me and then say, sweetly, almost apologetically, "Your grandmother made it better."

"Yes, I know."

"Where is she?"

"She's gone."

"Ah, yes, of course, I knew that, I knew that." He looked at his old hands, worn, callused, scarred from all their work. "When can I go home?" he asked.

He died one morning.

I saw his house again, in later years. I believe it was still being lived in. Donaustrasse Number 12, in Stockerau.

COMPARED WITH GRANDFATHER'S eviction, ours was a triviality. Our concierge stood weeping in the doorway, holding an eviction notice from our noble landlord. "What could he do?" she said. "The regime demanded this."

So Mama and I moved to 13 Untere Donaustrasse, in Leopold-stadt, the Vienna ghetto, to the flat of Milo's widowed aunt,

Frau Maimon. Two other were ladies already boarding with her—sisters, one a spinster, the other with a husband in Dachau. We lived, five women in a flat intended for one, and we never argued; we never failed to excuse ourselves when we could not help violating each other's privacy.

Mama and I supported ourselves by sewing. Not couturier tailoring, of course, but mending and recutting old clothes to fit the new times. We did a lot of "taking in," because our Jewish neighbors in the ghetto were growing thinner.

My cousin Jultschi, however, was growing fatter.

She sat with me in the park, crying her eyes out, her skin blotchy and broken out.

"I know I shouldn't have gotten pregnant in such terrible times," she wept. "But Otto had been drafted and we were afraid we would never see each other again and we were so overcome. It just happened, and now I don't know what I'm going to do. Maybe they'll leave the child alone. What do you think, Edith? I mean, it has to be of some help to at least have a father who is not a Jew, who is a soldier of the Reich."

"Maybe it will help," I said, although I did not really believe that.

"I tried to get a job as a maid in England. I thought they would just think I was fat. But they knew right away that I was pregnant." Her large melting brown eyes fixed on me. "I have to not be pregnant, Edith, with Otto going off to war and all these laws against the Jews. I have to go see a doctor."

I got in touch with our old friend Kohn. He had just finished his studies and opened a practice—and now the Nazis had revoked his license. He looked awful.

"Did you hear about Elfi Westermayer?" he said bitterly. "She didn't even finish her medical studies and she's taking patients. Apparently all you need to practice medicine in this country now is a membership card in the Nazi Party."

He agreed to see Jultschi, but in the end he would not give her an abortion. "I cannot perform this operation safely," he explained. "I have no surgery, no place at the hospital, no access to drugs. God forbid, you could become infected. . . . There might be terrible consequences." He held her hand. "Go home. Have the child. It will be a comfort to you in the days to come."

So Jultschi went home to her husband. He was packing his gear, getting ready to go off to conquer Poland. He kissed her, promised to return, and left her to wait alone for her baby.

Mama and I descended into poverty with astonishing speed. Denied the ability to make a living, working for customers who paid us in groschen (now re-counted as pfennigs by the Germans), we began to barter our possessions for things we desperately needed.

Mama had a decayed tooth that was killing her. Our Jewish dentist was no longer allowed to practice, but with Pepi's help, Mama found an Aryan dentist who would pull the tooth. He wanted gold. Mama gave him a gold chain. He wanted more. She gave him another. He wanted more. She gave him her last. Three gold chains for one tooth.

I tried to collect the installments for sewing machines and motorbikes that had been rented through my grandfather's franchise. But nobody who owed a Jew money felt obligated to pay anymore. Most of them laughed in my face.

Mama's younger sister, Aunt Marianne, had married a man named Adolf Robichek and settled in Belgrade, where he worked for a Danube shipping company. The Robicheks sent food packages to us with the ships' captains, and we shared our good fortune with Frau Maimon and the two sisters. These packages became a lifeline for us.

Did the rest of the Austrians understand what was happening to the Jews? Did they understand that we were being dispossessed, that we were beginning to go hungry? By way of answer, let me tell you a story.

Once, after the Anschluss, I was stopped by a policeman for jaywalking. He ordered me to pay a stiff fine. "But I am Jewish," I said. That was all he needed to hear to know that I was penniless and could not possibly pay, and he let me go.

So you see, when they tell you that they did not realize how the Jews were being despoiled, you must never believe them. They all knew.

CHRISTL DENNER'S LOVE life, always frantic, now became tumultuous because of Nazi politics.

We were talking in the bathroom, because the other rooms, with their palatial windows, were all freezing.

"Let me tell you, Edith, this is such a stupid situation that only the SS could have created it. The Nuremberg Laws on race say that you are not a legitimate Aryan unless all your grandparents on both sides are Aryan, right? So if you have even one Jewish grandparent, you are considered Jewish and deprived of all your privileges as a citizen, right? Well, guess what. Bertschi's father is a Czechoslovakian Jew."

"Oh, my God," I said, appalled.

"So," she continued, "my father helped Bertschi's father buy illegal papers 'proving' that he too was an Aryan three generations back. A good idea, right?"

"Excellent," I said.

"The result of this was that Bertschi's father was immediately drafted."

"Oh, my God!"

"In the army, they discovered Herr Beran's true identity and put him in jail. But meanwhile they had drafted Bertschi, who now appeared to be satisfactorily Aryan because of his father's false papers. But then, in short order, the army discovered that Bertschi's father was in jail, but not *why* he was in jail, so they slapped Bertschi with a dishonorable discharge and sent him back to Vienna. And, listen to this, Edith, you won't believe this—"

"What? What?"

"While Bertschi was returning to Vienna, his entire unit was blown up by a bomb set by the French Resistance."

I felt sad for the unit, thrilled for Bertschi, and delighted to know there actually was a French Resistance.

"Now they have figured out that Bertschi is half Jewish, so the Gestapo is after him."

"Oh, no . . ."

"But I have a plan. My father has bought me a formerly Jewish shop. I am to sell souvenirs: coffee cups with maps of Saint Stephen's imprinted on them, replicas of Nymphenberg statuettes, music boxes that play Wagner. Of course I need a bookkeeper to help me run my shop. So I have hired Bertschi."

She smiled. Her dog put his head in her lap and gazed up at her adoringly.

"Oh, Christl, that's so dangerous. They'll come after you . . ."

"They already have," she said. "I must report to Prinz Eugenstrasse tomorrow."

"You must not go!" I cried. "You're an Aryan, you can get out, you have papers, you must leave the city, leave the Reich!"

"My father has been assigned to work in the antiaircraft unit in Münster, in Westphalia," she said. "I'm not going anywhere."

I thought of Hansi, the SS, their brutality to women.

Christl smiled. "Just lend me your yellow blouse with the appliqued birds, and everything will be all right."

The next day, Christl Denner put on the blouse my mother had made for me. It fit her perfectly. She applied her reddest lipstick and darkened her lashes. As she headed down the street, her skirt swinging, her hair shining, she looked as if she were going to a dance.

She walked into the Gestapo headquarters. Every man in the place emerged from behind his desk to have a better look at her. The Nazi Captain tried to be severe.

"You have a man working for you, Fräulein Denner, one Hans Beran . . ."

"Yes. My bookkeeper. He is traveling in the Reich. I had a postcard from him."

"When he returns, we want to see him."

"Of course, Captain. I'll send him right over."

She gave him a big smile. He kissed her hand. He asked Christl if he could buy her a coffee. She agreed.

"You what?! You went out with an SS man?"

"How can a woman turn down a simple invitation for coffee?" she explained. "It would be rude. It might raise suspicions. When the captain suggested a future meeting, I simply told him that I was promised to a brave sailor on the high seas and could not possibly betray his sacred trust."

She grinned as she gave me back my blouse. She had the flair of a Hollywood heroine, my friend Christl.

In the basement of her shop sat Bertschi Beran, the luckiest of men.

■   ■   ■

PEPI VISITED ME every day. He was working as a stenographer for the court, and after work he would go out and have a bite and then come to us, a forty-five-minute walk. He would arrive at seven P.M., put his watch on the table so as not to forget the time, and leave precisely at nine-fifteen so as to arrive home at ten, the hour his frantic mother expected him.

Our long-delayed, frustrated love affair could find no place, no corner, and we had begun to starve for each other. Even in the coldest weather, we walked outside and found a bench or a doorway where we could kiss and cling together.

One afternoon we crept into his flat, terrified that the neighbors would see us. He had bought some condoms and hidden them from Anna (who snooped into everything) by putting them in a box marked UNDEVELOPED FILM! DO NOT EXPOSE TO LIGHT! We were wild with excitement and couldn't wait to get at each other. But no sooner had we begun to undress than we heard men shouting in the hall outside; that horrible Nazi banging on some unfortunate Austrian's door; the lady of the house crying, "No! No, he's done nothing! Don't take him!"— and then the heavy steps of the captors as they dragged their prisoner away.

Our passion died of fright. We could not revive it that evening. Pepi walked me back to the ghetto.

He was not fired from his job at the court. He just stopped showing up for work one day, and his colleagues there assumed that, like all the other Jews, half-Jews, and quarter-Jews, he had been arrested or was doing his best to get out. He couldn't receive Jewish rations because now, with his mother's machinations, he was not registered as a Jew. If he had tried to acquire Aryan rations, he would have been drafted.

So Pepi was trapped in his mother's apartment. He lived on what his mother brought him. She swore to the authorities that she was a big smoker, and so she received cigarettes, which she brought home him to him. He went out during the day to sit in a park where he would not be noticed. He occupied himself by writing laws for the new "democratic" Austria that he felt sure would exist after the elimination of the Nazis. Can you imagine? My brilliant Pepi, pretending not to exist, rewriting the Austrian penal code, for fun.

In 1939, when the Germans attacked Poland, bringing France and Britain into the war, we had a moment of hope that Hitler would soon be beaten, that our decision to stay in Vienna might work out for the best. But soon enough, we understood that the widening war had cut off all escape.

The old and the sick saw no way to save themselves. The aged widow of the great German-Jewish painter Max Liebermann killed herself just as the Gestapo came to collect her. My mother's uncle, Ignatz Hoffman, an eminent physician, had married a young woman and spent some very happy years with her. Before the Gestapo came for him, he took poison. "You must run now, my love," he said. "Run like the wind. You cannot have an old man to burden you." He died in her arms.

We heard that a mysterious Nazi woman helped Uncle Ignatz's wife smuggle out her possessions before she herself escaped.

All the Jews of Polish origin were being sent back to the land of their forefathers, and so the two gentle sisters kissed us and packed and left. We sent them packages in care of the Jewish community in Warsaw, but of course the packages were returned because it was illegal to send anything to Jews. So we took the advice of a wily neighbor, wrote the address in Polish, and like magic the packages arrived. I too became wily. I never mailed two packages from the same post office.

We began to lose touch with all our relatives and friends. They were drifting away like stars without gravity, through whatever hole opened in the wall of Nazi conquest.

My aunt Marianne Robichek wrote that she and her family were heading west toward Italy. Uncle Richard and Aunt Rozsi sent a postcard from China. Hansi, Milo, and Mimi sent messages through other relatives that they had made it to Palestine. My cousin Max Sternbach, a gifted artist who had graduated from the art school that would not accept Hitler, disappeared across the Alps, headed—we hoped—for Switzerland.

I borrowed Christl's lilac blouse and had a formal picture taken of myself for Pepi's birthday. Somehow I had the feeling that we would need pictures of each other, if we were separated. He said we would never be separated, but so many people were. Look at Otto Ondrej, locked down on the Eastern Front. He had never even seen the little son whom Jultschi had named for him.

Now all my hopes centered on the defeat of Germany. If only France would hold fast . . . if only Italy would ally itself with England . . . if only America would enter the war, I thought, then the Nazis would be destroyed.

In June 1940, while Pepi and I were walking along the Danube Canal, someone on the far bank called out joyfully, "France has fallen!" The whole city erupted with cheering . . . and I actually vomited in the street. I couldn't breathe, couldn't walk. Pepi half-carried me home. His mother had some pills to keep herself calm. Now that I was as hysterical as she, Pepi stole a few from her, put them into my mouth, and watched while I swallowed them.

When Italy declared war on France and Britain, a clear indication that Mussolini thought Hitler would win the war, I took the pills of my own volition, for I felt now that all was lost. We were trapped in the fascist empire.

Pepi refused to despair. His punctuality regulated and calmed our lives. His small gifts from the Aryan side—coffee, cheese, books—reminded us of better days gone by. And then, in an unforgettable act of romantic abandon, he pressured his mother into giving him some money, and he took me to the Vachau.

We had three glorious days in a fairy-tale wonderland. We floated on the crystal blue river. We climbed up to the ruin of the Durenstein castle, where Richard the Lionhearted was held prisoner and Blondl the troubadour sang of his escape. We locked the door of our hotel room and fell on the bed and rolled in each other's arms. People would ask me why I had married a man so much older than I, for Pepi looked old for his age and I looked young for mine. I said: "Because he is the world's greatest lover!"

The Nazis vanished like evil dwarfs under a magic spell. We wandered along the charming paths where Bertrand Russell had walked before us, pronouncing this place the enchanted garden of Austria, and we knew nothing but our delight in each other. Politics, poverty, terror, and hysteria all disappeared into the thin sharp mountain air.

"You are my angel," he whispered. "You are my magic little mouse, my darling girl . . ."

That was the only reason I stayed in Austria, you see. I was in love, and I couldn't imagine life without my Pepi.

WHEN ABOUT 100,000 of the 185,000 Viennese Jews had somehow made their way out, the Nazis decided that all other

Jews remaining in Vienna had to be registered, so we were forced at gunpoint to line up in the square. All the F's had to appear on one day, all the G's on another day, and all the H's on April 24, 1941. Mama and I stood in line from early morning on. When people fainted, we helped to pick them up and tried to carry them out of the sun. A unit of Gestapo men cruised by in a truck. One of them jumped out and yanked at my mother and me.

"Get in the truck," he said.

"What? Why?"

"Don't ask stupid questions, you Yid bitch, get in!"

We were pushed up into the truck. I held Mama's hand tight. They took us to an SS office and put a paper in front of us.

"You are both needed for agricultural work in the Reich. Here. Sign this. It's a contract."

Instantly, my training as a lawyer came flooding back. I turned into a litigator. I argued as though I were inventing the art of argument.

"But this woman should not even be here," I said, pushing Mama behind me. "She's not a Viennese, she's not a Jew, she's just an old maid we once employed, who was visiting and decided to keep me company."

"Sign the paper."

"Besides, look at her! She can't possibly be any good for work. She has bone spurs in her feet, arthritis in her hips. She's an orthopedic mess, I tell you. If you need workers, go find my sisters. My sister Gretchen is beautiful, only twenty-two years old, and an athlete. Yes sir, the best! If she hadn't been Jewish, she would have been on the Olympic girls' swimming team. And my sister Erika is as strong as two horses. You'll be able to hitch her to a plow, I tell you. They're both back in that line; you must have missed them. How could you miss two such strong and robust young women and seize upon this old crone? Is there something wrong with your eyes? Perhaps you need an exam . . .''

"All right, all right, shut up!" the Nazi yelled. "Let the old woman go. Go, go, Mother, get out of here!" They pushed Mama into the sunny street.

I signed their paper. It was a contract obligating me to spend six weeks doing farmwork in the north of Germany. If I didn't show up at the train station tomorrow, the paper said, I would be treated as a wanted criminal and hunted down without mercy.

My mother and I slept in each other's arms that night.

"Six weeks," I said. "That's all. Six weeks and I will be home. By then America will have entered the war and conquered Germany, and it will all be over."

I took a knapsack and one suitcase, as my sister Hansi had done. Mama packed nearly all the food in the house for me.

Pepi came with his mother to the train station. He looked so sweet, so sad. All his adorable debonair patter had abandoned him. He took my hands and put them in the pockets of his coat with his hands. My mother had great dark circles around her eyes. We were silent, we three. But Anna Hofer would not shut up. She was babbling about rations and fashions, full of joy that I was leaving.

Suddenly, Mama put her arm around Anna and before she could protest, turned her around, allowing Pepi and me one last moment. The salt tears in his kiss stayed with me. I tasted them in my dreams.

As the train whistle blew, I whispered to Mama that she shouldn't be sad, that I would see her in six weeks.

FIVE

■

*The Asparagus Plantation
at Osterburg*

At FIRST, IT felt like an ordinary journey. I rode in a compartment with several women, and by the time we arrived in Melk, I knew how long they had been in labor with each of their children. A whining frightened girl clung to me. I finally managed to get rid of her. We had a keeper, a bustling German. She looked efficient in her Nazi uniform, but during the long, sleepless night, she wandered through the train in her dressing gown, not really knowing what to do.

At the Leipzig station, we were herded into a room where we were guarded by two policemen and ordered to remove any lipstick or other makeup. We had to ask permission to use the toilet. We then continued the journey on a local train. By now, our womanly chatter had ceased. After a few hours of being treated like prisoners, we had *become* prisoners, watchful, silent. I stood the whole time, looking out the window at Germany, at the painfully clean villages and tidy little gray houses, all of a uniform design. The countryside, still spotted with winter's resilient snows, brimmed with mud.

"That mud is where I am going," I said to myself.

At Magdeburg, we had to haul our luggage up the steep steps. A very slow train took us to Stendahl. We stood on the platform, freezing.

The farmers came—plain, rough people determined to behave in a superior manner, still a bit uncomfortable with all this new power. They looked us over critically, as though we were horses, then divided us into groups. The smallest farmer took two girls. A few others took eight or ten. I went with the largest group—I think there were about eighteen of us—to Plantage Mertens in Osterburg.

It was a big farm on six hundred morgens of land. (A morgen, about two-thirds of an acre in Germany, was a measurement invented by medieval farmers, who estimated that this was how much land you could plow in a *Morgen*, a morning.) The farm had five heavyset horses; a large house, which I never entered; some barns; and barracks for us, the workers. Frau Mertens, a woman in her twenties whose husband had gone to war, expected Jews to be what Goebbels's radio broadcasts had promised—ugly, crude, ratlike miscreants who would surely try to steal everything she possessed. She seemed pleased that we said *"Bitte"* and *"Danke"* and appeared meek and exhausted.

The next day we started working in her fields.

Never in my life had I done work of this nature. If only I had not cut gym, I might have been stronger, but it was too late for regrets.

We worked from six until noon, then from one to six in the

evening, six days a week, with a part day on Sunday. Our task was to plant beans, then beets, then potatoes, and to cut asparagus. To cut asparagus we would reach into the ground, feel for the tender white stem, cut it with a knife, pull it out, and fill up the hole— thousands of times a day. Soon every joint and muscle throbbed and burned. My bones ached. My head ached. Herr Fleschner— we called him Herr Verwalter, literally "Mr. Overseer"—was a thin man with dull eyes and a nervous expression. He wore a cap and, under a vest and a jacket, a clean white shirt. He literally stood over us in the fields.

I had been told at Prinz Eugenstrasse that I would stay at Plantage Mertens for six weeks. On the train, I heard two months. But at the farm, when I said "two months" to Herr Verwalter, he burst out laughing. I remember, he had a high-pitched cackle like one of the lesser devils in hell.

"It is the role of certain races to work for certain other races," he would proclaim as he watched us work. "That is the decree of nature. That is why the Poles work for us Germans and the French work for us and you work for us today and tomorrow the English will work for us as well."

I was supposed to shovel out a ditch. The loose earth on the sides kept caving in on me. The overseer shouted: "Faster! Faster!" I tried to go faster. "Idiot!" he yelled. "Stupid useless Jewish fool! What good are you?" I burst into tears. However, I could have filled that ditch with my tears and drowned in them for all the sympathy they evoked.

In my bed at night, I berated myself for behaving in such an undignified manner before such a despicable person. I swore to myself that it would never happen again, and it didn't. In the following weeks, the overseer found me to be one of his better workers, fast and efficient. He now turned his wrath on an unfortunate Romanian woman. "You old crow!" he screamed. "You dried up stupid useless Jewish fool! What good are you?" Repeatedly, he pushed her face down in the dirt.

On occasion, Frau Mertens, looking clean and fresh, would walk out into the fields to see how things were going. She had a colonial largesse about her. By way of greeting, she said "Heil Hitler" to us, with a smile. We would straightened up from the muddy earth and stare at her. No one said a word. She seemed disappointed.

There were five rooms and a kitchen in our brick-and-timber barracks. My room had four inmates: Frau Telscher, aloof and quiet; Trude and Lucy, both eighteen; and me. No one believed that I was twenty-seven and—almost—a university graduate. Across the hall lived a group we called "the Elegant Six," women from Vienna's upper class. Next to them lived six other women, among them the poor Romanian; a pretty, high-strung dark-haired girl named Frieda; another girl who was two months' pregnant; and a woman who had once worked as a maid in homes like those owned by "the Elegant Six." The former maid loved to watch these pampered women stumble through the rutted fields with the rest of us. But her joy soon ended. Nothing can make backbreaking labor a pleasure for long, even the satisfaction of a victory in the class struggle.

We each had an iron bed with a straw mattress, blue-and-white checked sheets, and a single blanket. I wore everything I could to bed because it was so cold—two pair of pants, two shirts, my nightgown, my bathrobe, two pair of socks. I wrote to Mama and Pepi and pleaded for them to send me an eiderdown, a warm feather-filled quilt.

It quickly became apparent that the Germans were interested in using our strength but not in preserving it. We received a ration of "flower coffee"—made not from coffee beans but from flowers, or maybe acorns. We each had half a loaf of bread, which had to last us from Sunday to Wednesday. At midday, we had a cold soup made from broken asparagus that couldn't be sold, or a mustard soup with potatoes, and maybe a hard-boiled egg. At night, we had a milk soup; on lucky days, it contained some oatmeal. We were always ravenous. Like the Ancient Mariner, surrounded by water and dying of thirst, we were surrounded by bounty and aching with hunger. I began to live for little packages from home that might contain bread or a little cake or that greatest of treasures, some fruit jam.

Frau Fleschner, the overseer's wife, supervised us. She had a child, a four-year-old named Ulrike, who played around the farm, a spot of sweet innocence in a harsh environment. Frau Fleschner smoked constantly. She loved her authority. She lined us up outside and read aloud the "Rules for Jewesses Who Are Coming to Work at the Asparagus Plantation."

"All inmates must adhere to the rules and be responsible to Frau Fleschner—that is, me," she said.

"Every inmate, in the morning when she leaves her bedroom, has got to make her bed, clean her washstand, and make sure that her place in the bedroom is cleaned.

"The oldest girl in the room must be responsible for the cleanliness and order in the bedroom." She pointed to me. "That is you." She continued reading.

"Meals will be taken in the dining and common rooms. Food may not be taken into the bedrooms.

"There are special rooms for washing and ironing.

"Smoking is prohibited.

"It is not allowed to leave the camp and the environs. It is therefore not allowed to visit nearby towns and villages, or cinemas, theaters, etc.

"All personal purchases have got to be shown to the manageress of the camp—that is, me—and will be made through her agreement."

With a sinking heart, I realized that I would have to ask her for everything—a toothbrush, a sanitary napkin, salt.

"It is possible to take walks on Saturdays from 1900 to 2100 hours and on Sundays from 1400 to 1800 hours. These walks must be made in groups of at least three persons.

"And of course, it is not allowed to use certain streets or to take part in any activities in the city of Osterburg. You walk. You walk back. That's it."

The local police visited often. They threatened us with jail should we become disruptive. We listened obediently, and when they left, broke down in gales of laughter. We could barely crawl into bed at night! Who had the strength to be disruptive?

Regularly the police posted notices to alert us to some activity, previously considered normal, which had now become a crime. Going to a dance hall, attending the cinema, drinking a beer in a café—all became crimes for us Jews. And the worst crime of all, said Frau Fleschner, pointing to the notice, was *Rassenschande*, racial disgrace—specifically, sexual relations between Germans and Jews. You could go to jail for that, she said.

Being sick never worked as an excuse at the asparagus plantation at Osterburg. For example, the pregnant girl wanted to go home. She cried and pleaded. The doctor declared her fit for work. She willfully threw up in the fields every morning. An official from the work department, stuffed into his Nazi uniform, finally gave her permission to leave, but not for home—for Poland.

The high-strung Frieda made the mistake of telling Frau Fleschner that she had a toothache. She was taken to a dentist. He pulled *ten* of her teeth! After one day, they put her back in the fields, spitting blood. She was twenty-one years old.

All through the early spring we cut asparagus. We crawled through the rows, digging, weeding, cutting. My fingers ached as though they were broken. My back would not straighten. We had started out working fifty-six hours a week, but now we were up to eighty hours. All the local farmers met and agreed to stop cutting the asparagus on one certain day, which meant we had to work mightily to cut as much as possible before that date. We were up at four in the morning and in the fields until after six at night. I organized my own campaign of sabotage. When I shoved my knife into the earth, I would cut and destroy as many of next year's young shoots as I could.

Once, after I had worked twelve hours in a driving rain, my knees swelled rheumatically, my clothes rotted, and I gave in to self-pity. "Wouldn't it have been better just to die quickly in Vienna than to die here by inches in this mud?" I wrote to Pepi.

Immediately, though, I felt ashamed to be complaining, and sought socialist dogma to belittle my own suffering. "Isn't this the way it is for ninety percent of the people in the world?" I wrote. "Don't they have to toil from early morning? Don't they have to go to bed hungry and cold?"

You see, shame was still a useful psychological tool for me. I still had pride.

After the harvest, when the workload lessened, some of the girls were sent home. Six of us—considered the "best workers"—remained.

Warm weather came. The fields rustled in the breeze like a sweet green sea. My body had grown stronger, somewhat adjusted to my labors. I was seized by thoughts of love.

"I want to press myself against your lips," I wrote to my darling. "But you are so far away! When will I feel you again?"

I picked poppies and marguerites and put them in everyone's hair. I became the camp comforter, affecting gaiety, waltzing with Trude and Lucy among the sugar beets. At lights-out, I recited to my young roommates my favorite lines from Goethe's *Faust,* which I had posted on my little cupboard:

Cowardly thoughts, anxious hesitation,
Womanish timidity, timorous complaints
Won't keep misery away from you
And will not set you free.
To preserve all your power despite everything,
To never bend and show yourself to be strong,
Brings the might of the gods to your aid.

Exhausted from encouraging everybody, most of all myself, I would fall asleep in the sun, at lunchtime, with my head on a sheaf of barley.

THE MAIL WAS our greatest comfort. We lived for our packages. The Nazis kept the mail coming regularly at that time. They knew that every package sent to us made our relatives in Vienna poorer and simultaneously relieved our captors of the cost of feeding us too well. The *Ostarbeiter*—the Polish, Serbian, and Russian workers—were not allowed to write home at all because the regime was afraid they would tell people how badly they were being treated and future labor deportations would be resisted.

I wrote to Mama, Pepi, Jultschi, the Denner girls, the Roemers, and the Grenzbauers all the time, sometimes three times a day. Often I said nothing but incoherent babbling or sophomoric expostulating. Sometimes I made precise agricultural records: how many rows of asparagus I had harvested, that the rows were two hundred meters long, that this kind of pest ate the frothy leaves and this kind of grub destroyed the roots, that this was the tool for weeding and that was the tool for chopping. I described how the Serbian prisoners were traded like farm equipment, how Herr Verwalter had swiped the tobacco that Pepi had sent me (which I had intended to give to the French prisoner who helped us all so much), how I had learned to sit down in the rows and inch along on my behind to save my knees.

To Pepi I tried to write the truth. To Mama I resolutely and consistently lied.

I told Pepi I was sick with the flu; I told Mama I was strong and healthy. I told him that Frau Hachek, an old acquaintance, was in the camp. To Mama I said nothing of this, for she might write to Frau Hachek and discover that I had chronic bronchitis and an unidentifiable rash, that my teeth were turning brown, that I needed more food. When Frieda, Trude, Lucy, and I walked to work, the German children hooted at us: "Jewish swine!" In town, the shopkeepers would not even sell us a beer. I wrote to Mama that Osterburg was a friendly town.

I read Nordau and Kästner and *Faust* and *The Idea of the Baroque*. I tried to learn a little French from our fellow captives and a little English from a book we called "McCallum," because it was clear to me that my body, now thin and hard, was being sacrificed in this ordeal and only my mind might be preserved.

We were completely cut off from the world. We never saw a newspaper, never heard the radio. I wrote to our old friend Zich, now a soldier in the Wehrmacht, hoping to learn something. I even wrote to Rudolf Gischa, my Nazified former beau in Czechoslovakia.

I begged Pepi for news. "Is it true that Crete has been taken?" I asked him at the end of May 1941. I couldn't believe it. To me, Crete was a site in Greek mythology. In my mind's eye, I saw the Germans shooting bazookas at one-dimensional sandaled warriors with curlicue beards and decorative, spindly spears.

I could not make the war seem real for myself. Even though I had heard about the Nazi bombing of cities in Spain, I couldn't imagine an air attack on unarmed civilians. Remember, there were still horses on the roads of rural Germany at that time. Very few people understood what modern war would be like.

One day, as we went into the asparagus fields at six A.M., we saw black clouds gathering on the horizon. We knew it was going to rain, and so did the overseer. "Faster, faster," he muttered, a worried man with a quota. It began to pour. The earth softened. The knives began to slip. We expected him to say, "All right. Enough." But he didn't.

He stood with an umbrella shielding him, and we put our faces down toward the earth and kept harvesting the asparagus. When the rain was coming down in torrents and the asparagus was beginning to swim like rice in Burma, he finally let us go into the shed.

We assumed that now he would call for the wagon and send us back to the hut, but no.

"We shall wait for the worst of the rain to pass," he said. "Then back to the fields."

Frieda, the girl who had lost ten teeth, began to wail: "Why is the asparagus so much more important than human beings? Why are we living at all when the whole purpose of our life is such misery?"

The overseer, miraculously moved by her outburst, let us go back to the hut.

You see, even the inhuman ones were not always inhuman. This was a lesson that I would learn again and again—how completely unpredictable individuals could be when it came to personal morality.

The Frenchman who worked with us, Pierre, was called Franz (short for Franzose or Frenchman) by the Germans because they couldn't pronounce his name. A winegrower from the Pyrenees, he wore a white patch on his clothes with "KG" (for *Kriegsgefangener*—prisoner of war) stamped on it. He led the horse and the plow out onto the fields and we followed him, usually on our knees, sowing, weeding, with me shouting out French words so he could correct my accent.

"Egless!" I would call.

"Non, non, église!"

"Palm de turr," I would call.

"Pommes de terre!" he corrected me.

With my box camera, I took a picture of him, then sent the film back to Vienna for Pepi to develop so Franz could send it on to his wife and children.

Pepi was jealous! Like so many Germans, he believed that the French possessed some erotic advantage over other men and would surely seduce us.

"Time to give up these stupid stereotypes," I said to my brilliant boyfriend. "Franz is far too exhausted, too emaciated, and too lonely for his family to have any erotic designs on anybody."

Actually, it was the Germans who tried to seduce us. The overseer made crude jokes with Frieda, trying to tempt her with his power. Werner, a local boy who hoped to sign up for twelve years in the army, took every opportunity to grope young Eva, the daughter of the vengeful maid. Otto, the SA man from the neighboring farm, battered us with vile suggestions and vulgar jokes.

The farmers had grown proud and haughty. They ate better than anyone else in Germany now. And, like Volkswagen and Siemens, they had slaves. All they had to do was feed the local Nazi power elite, and they could have all the slaves they wanted.

"The city people call us shit farmers," Otto sneered, "but now they will pay, you watch!" He charged like a bandit for a chicken or a hog, and he loved it when the city people competed to meet his price.

Rumors of growing hardship in Vienna came to us in between the lines of our loved ones' letters. I knew what Mama did not have because she always sent exactly that thing to me. When she was cold, she sent mittens she had knitted from some yellow yarn she had found. When she was hungry, she sent me tiny cakes.

I had collected a few reichsmarks worth of pay, and I sent the money home to Pepi with instructions for him to buy soap for Mama, some writing paper for me, and even a gift for his mother, whose favor I was still trying to win. At harvesttime, I bought apples and potatoes from the farmers, kilos of beans for pickling, asparagus, and potatoes, and I sent them home to Pepi and Mama and the Roemers and Jultschi, knowing that this bounty would be shared.

The Jews of Polish origin had already been sent back to Poland. Now, in the summer of 1941, we heard talk that the German and Austrian Jews would be sent there as well. These deportations— or *Aktions*, as we called them—filled us with dread. We did not know what Poland meant then, but we knew it wasn't good. We thought of it as a kind of uncivilized wilderness, where Germans went to colonize and subjugate the local peasantry. If Mama went to Poland, I thought, she would have to be a maid for German colonists—do their dishes, scrub their floors, iron their clothes. I could not bear to imagine her in such circumstances. My mother, a maid? Impossible!

Frau Fleschner and the overseer assured us that as long as we worked here, our families would not be deported. I had the feeling that they tried to look out for us more and more as time went on. One Sunday, the six of us went out for a walk. While we were away, the police came snooping. The overseer said we had gone far out into the fields to work and shouldn't be bothered. When we arrived home, he grinned and said, "Say thanks, ladies. I pulled you out of the shit again."

AN ENCAMPMENT OF Polish slave laborers sprawled on the outskirts of the farms. These men moved boulders for the farmers, rebuilt their houses, cleaned the pig shit out of their barns. The Poles would call to us as we went on our way to work with our hoes and spades.

"Don't pay any attention," I said to my young comrades.

But a lively dark-haired girl named Liesel Brust, eager to know more about this place where so many Jews were now going, inched a little closer to one of the men and asked: "What is it like, Poland?"

"It's beautiful," he answered. He was young. He smiled. His front teeth were gone.

"And Warsaw?"

"Glittering palaces, museums, operas, libraries, universities full of professors—just the kind of thing that a pretty little Jew girl like you would love. Come inside, sweetheart, and I'll tell you more about Warsaw."

I pulled Liesel away from him.

"I met a Chinese man who talked the same way to me in Vienna," I warned her. "If I had gone with him, I would be in a brothel in Kowloon at this moment. If you go into that Polish camp, you will never return, I promise you that."

I thought I was talking about a bunch of sex-starved prisoners on the German plains. How could I know then that I might as well have been talking about Poland itself?

The harder I worked, the thinner I became, the closer I came to losing hope and imagining death, the more I was overwhelmed by tenderness for every living thing. I made no distinctions among people anymore; I held no grudges and appreciated everyone. We found mice in the hut. Instead of killing them, we left crumbs for them to eat. An impaired chick was hatched in the egg house. I brought it back to our room and fed it carefully for three days before it died.

I wrote to Pepi that there were two spirits at war in my breast. The first felt that there would be no end to this suffering, that we would all die here in the mud. The second believed that a miracle would happen: the RAF would drop a bomb right on Hitler and Goebbels, the Nazis would disappear, I would be a free woman again, and we would get married and have many babies.

I MADE A true friend in Osterburg, Mina Katz. An adorable, lighthearted girl of eighteen, blond and graceful, she was somehow immune to depression and always saw the bright side. She came from a large, impoverished family and brought nothing with her to the labor camp except an inferiority complex. She could have been a fine scholar if only fate had given her an education.

Mina and her older associate Frau Grünwald had been working for a Jewish-owned delivery company. It had been taken over by a Nazi woman, Maria Niederall, who needed the two Jewish employees to teach her the business. As time went on, this woman grew fond of them and wanted to keep them working for her. However, the Gestapo had other plans. Mina and Frau Grünwald received regular packages from their former employer—sumptuous assortments of food, soap, and clothing that only a well-connected Aryan could have provided.

Like a candle in the fields, Mina carried a glow of good nature about her. She giggled. She sang silly love songs. She invented stories. She brought little gifts to everyone. We all loved her. She and I began to work side by side at every task, cutting the asparagus canes, binding the huge stacks of hay, and pulling the new potatoes out of the damp black ground. We tossed the potatoes into twenty-five-kilo baskets, then hauled them to a waiting wagon, each of us carrying one handle of a basket. We wore wooden shoes. We told each other about our sisters and our schools. We worked without thinking of our work, so quickly that one girl dubbed us the "racehorses" of the bean fields. While wrestling beets from the ground, while mulching tiny bean shoots, I began to teach Mina what I knew—economy, law, politics, literature. She drank it in. This education in the fields nourished both of us and kept us going.

In July we baled hay. The sweat ran down our faces. We burned. I smeared mud on my arms and Mina's arms. I wrote home asking for any kind of skin cream, but of course, there was none to be had, not because it had disappeared from Vienna but because the Jews were not permitted to buy anything anymore, except what their meager rations allowed. You see these spots on my face? They appeared in later years. They are little black reminders of the blazing sun in Osterburg.

Sometimes, in the wild riot of my thoughts, I had visions of peace, of a perfect rural community, like those in socialist literature, where love of life would lock out war and hatred.

One day when I was coming out of the bean fields, I saw a group of people taking a rest in the shade of a chestnut tree at the edge of a neighboring farm. There were some old women, Germans with weathered faces and hands like iron. There were some young Jewish girls—"H's" from Vienna, like me—and some German boys, too young for the Wehrmacht, wearing wide-brimmed hats; and a few Frenchmen. No one looked like anyone's boss; no one looked like anyone's slave. They were all just sitting in the shade, drinking from a pitcher of water.

"Come sit down for a moment, Edith," one of the girls called. I joined them. A young Frenchman laid before us on the grass a battered photo of a little girl.

"Elle est très belle," I said.

Tears cut pathways through the dirt on his face.

So much for my vision.

IN AUGUST THE rains came, again untimely. The harvest, which had started out so well, was now ruined and there was not enough food. We hoped that after the corn harvest, we would be able to use our few marks of "pay" to buy extra food from Frau Mertens. Realizing that if it was bad with us, it must be awful in Vienna, I received permission to go to the post office with a sack of potatoes.

"You can no longer send potatoes to Vienna," said the postmistress very loudly, so that her boss in the back room could hear.

"Why not?"

"Not enough potatoes to feed the Germans. The Jews will have to eat the rain."

I turned away from her. She grabbed my arm and whispered into my ear, "On the outside of the package, say it is clothing. Then it will go through."

We now could see that our letters were being opened and read. I was terrified of what I had written, of what my mother or Pepi or Christl might write. We heard about denunciations and deportations. Suddenly there was so much to hide. If my mother wrote to me and said, "Remember, darling, I am saving my fur coat for you," maybe somebody would read that letter and come and steal the fur coat and hurt my mother. If Pepi wrote to me that he stayed in the little park near the old café and read his paper until the evening, maybe the Gestapo would read the letter and go and find him there.

"Destroy my letters!" I wrote to him. *"Read them and put them in your heart and then burn them!* I will do the same with yours. And when you write, use abbreviations. Never mention places or people."

We began to call the Gestapo "PE," for Prinz Eugentrasse, where they had their headquarters. We said "going to school" to signify reporting for deportation, since people being deported were often assembled at school buildings.

By now I had begun to beg Pepi to marry me, hoping that if he did, we would be able to emigrate like Milo and Mimi, or at least that we might be happy together. "A married woman with a ring on her finger!" I thought. "Able to have children! What unspeakable joy!" I treasured the notion that even if we couldn't get out, I would be safer married and sharing Pepi's invisibility. He said he loved me. He spoke of his passion. But in response to my proposals, he said nothing, neither giving me hope nor ending it.

We all thought about converting to Christianity. What would have once seemed unthinkable, a shameful betrayal of our parents and our culture, now seemed like a perfectly reasonable ploy. I thought of the Marranos in Spain, outwardly converted Christians, waiting for the terror of the Inquisition to end so they could follow their true faith again. Perhaps I could pretend to be a Christian too. Surely God would understand. And it might help. Why not try it?

I took myself into the town of Osterburg and stared at the statue of Jesus in front of the local church, trying to will myself to love him. It was wartime. Men were at the front. And yet I saw no candles in the church, no kneeling worshipers praying for the safe return of sons and husbands and fathers. The Nazis had done a wonderful job of discouraging faith in anything but the Führer.

I wrote to Pepi for instructions on how to convert. What papers did I need? What affidavits? What signatures? I read the Parables. I found pictures of the Holy Family. I waxed poetic when I wrote to my lover: "Look how beautiful the mother is! How content and sweet! Look how proud the father is, how delighted with the child, the gift he has been given! How I wish we could have a family as happy and close as this one!"

Somehow what had started out as praise of the Holy Family had evolved into a celebration of the family Pepi and I might have, if only he would marry me . . . if only he would say he wanted me . . . if only he would leave his mother—and if only I would get my menstrual periods again.

For you see, I had lost my periods. They had gone, disappeared. "You should be happy," I said to myself. "Think of the convenience." But in truth, I was in despair. At night, I lay on my straw bed, trying not to think about the pain in my back, trying to force my stiff fingers to make a fist, and I prayed: "Come back! Come back!" But they did not.

■   ■   ■

I SAT ON an animal trough, writing letters, the laundry flapping around my head. Trude sat down beside me.

"Stop writing, Edith; you are always writing. Listen to me. How long has it been?"

"Since June."

"Me too. Liesel and Frieda and Lucy too. I wrote home and told my mother and she asked the doctor and the doctor said it comes from overwork. What does your doctor say?"

"Dr. Kohn told my mother I must be pregnant," I answered.

We laughed until we wept.

From Vienna, Pepi wrote obliquely in his new code that it was silly for me to think of converting now, that the time where such a gesture might have proved useful had long since passed.

Frau Mertens lent us to her neighbors the Grebes, who were a little shorthanded. Now we were just like the other prisoners of war, the Serbs, the Poles, the emaciated Frenchmen—except that we were not *really* like them, because we had no country.

I clung to the belief that I would be able to go home in October. What was there to do on the farm in the winter months? We were seasonal workers, were we not? The prospective return of cold weather terrified me—the rheumy damp, the frozen mornings. How would we survive here?

I thought about my mother, with her dark hair and her perky little gait, the marvelous sweet cakes that fell like the food of the gods from her sugary fingers, her wry ironic commentary on the racist fools who were destroying the earth. I was twenty-seven years old, and I still dreamed of her sweet embrace, her gentle voice. *You must become a mother, Edith, because obviously you have a gift for it.* I thought about home, the warm cobbled streets, the music. My hands cracked the asparagus canes and tossed the potatoes into their bins, and my mind sang waltzes to itself and danced with my true love.

"Come back, Edith," said the overseer. "You are in Vienna."

He was right. I had learned to fill myself up with memories and lock out Osterburg, a fabulous partitioning of the mind that preserved the soul. When the local police arrived and told us we must wear a yellow *Magen David* at all times, I imagined that such a silly thing could never happen in Vienna, which I still put on a pedestal as a model of sophistication. And then Trude received a letter saying that all Jews in Vienna had to wear the six-pointed Jewish star as well.

I couldn't believe it. Was it possible? Had Vienna descended to the level of an ignorant rural backwater? The idea horrified me. You see how long it takes for us to abandon treasured assumptions.

The police told us we must write to Vienna for the yellow stars, and that when they arrived, we must wear them at all times. But if we had done so, no shopkeeper in town would have waited on us. So we didn't wear them. Our supervisors on the farm seemed to care not at all. I believe that in their way they had began to want to keep us content enough to go on obediently working for them, even more than they wanted to please the police.

PEPI WROTE THAT Jultschi's husband, Otto Ondrej, had died on the Eastern Front.

Poor Jultschi, the weakest among us, the most beset by tragedy, was alone again. I could not bear to think of her, and yet she did not leave my mind. "My funeral clothes are still in Vienna," I wrote to Pepi. "Tell her to take them."

Lest I have any doubt that my youthful certainties had changed forever, Rudolf Gischa wrote to me from the Sudetanland.

"I was surprised to learn that you were still alive," he said frankly. (Why? Was there a new policy? Were they getting tired of having us work for them? Were the Jews expected to be dead now?) "I feel sorry for anyone who is not a German," he said. "It is my greatest joy to know that I am privileged to create the great empire of the Reich for the German Volk according to the principles laid down by our Führer. Heil Hitler!"

One of the girls who had been allowed to leave, Liesel Brust, was more courageous than most of us and had always tried to get to know the foreign prisoners. Now she sent me from Vienna a coded letter with a large package of men's underwear and asked me to leave it by a certain boulder in a certain field on a certain night and then to tell the French prisoners, who were in rags, where they could find it.

I had never done anything like this—an act of political sabotage! To be caught meant banishment to one of the proliferating concentration camps, but to refuse meant such dishonor that I could not even bear the thought of it. I waited for my roommates to fall asleep. Softly, softly I slid open the window and eased myself out. It was a hot night, cloudy and thick with tomorrow's rain. Under my shirt, the package shifted and crunched. It seemed to me a thunderous sound. I took a deep breath and then raced across the open fields and plunged into the corn. The sharp stalks sliced at me. My heart pounded. I did not once dare to look back, for fear of seeing someone behind me. The boulder bulged in the distance at the end of a bean field. I crouched as low as I could, ran, left the package, and took one look around me. I saw no one, no light in the farmhouse, no patch of clear sky to let a star shine through. I heard distant thunder. My hands were slick with sweat. I lowered my head and sprinted back to the workers' hut.

Trude was sitting up on her bed, her eyes wide with terror

at my absence. I put one hand over her mouth, the other over mine.

The next day Franz pulled me behind his horse and plow.

"Where is the underwear?"

"I left it."

"It wasn't there."

"I left it exactly where Liesel said."

"*Merde!* Someone else took it."

I gasped. Maybe I had been seen! Maybe the authorities had opened and read Liesel's letter! We would be arrested! I imagined the barracks at Dachau. All that day and the next and the next, I waited for the Gestapo to come.

They never did, though, and we never found out who had taken the underwear.

I was put into a new room. I slept under the window. In the night I awoke and discovered that my face was wet. It wasn't tears. It was rain. I rolled away from the broken window and went back to sleep. So the bed got wet—so what?

AS THE TIME for my return to Vienna approached, I tried to tell the truth of my heart to Pepi. I told him how much I regretted that we had not left when we could, what a terrible mistake it was, how we had no one to blame but ourselves. "We cooked this soup," I said, "and now we must eat it, you and I. I promise you that I will always be a good comrade, whatever may happen. Count the days which are still between you and me. Another fourteen days. Then I will be with you."

Mina turned toward me in her bed and raised herself up on one arm. The moon lit her face. "Tell me," she said. "Tell me how it will be."

"I will come in at the Western Station," I said. "I will step off the train and not see him right away. But then he will see me, and he will come to me without calling my name so that all of a sudden he will just be there, suddenly, like magic—that is how he always appears. He will have flowers for me, and his wicked smile. We will go home together through the Belvedere and over the Schwartzenbergerplatz. We will go to his room and make love for three days, and he will feed me oranges."

She fell back on her mattress, groaning. She had never had a lover.

We packed our suitcases. Nine of our friends, among them Frau Grünwald and Frau Hachek, received tickets for home. They were transformed by delight and anticipation, as they put on their city clothes for the journey. We could not wait to be them.

When we returned from the beet fields, Frau Fleschner assembled those of us who were left in front of the hut. We eagerly awaited her announcement, sure that she would tell us the day, the time, the train.

"You are not going to Vienna," she said. "You are going to Aschersleben to work in the paper factory there. Consider yourselves lucky. Remember that as long as you are working for the Reich, your families are safe."

Mina began to cry. I put my arm around her.

"Please tell Mama," I wrote to Pepi on October 12, 1941. "I can't write to her. When will we see each other again? Life is so hard now. I don't know anything about what is happening in Vienna! For today I can't write anything more. I kiss you. Your desperate Edith."

SIX

∎

The Slave Girls of Aschersleben

WE STOOD IN the center of the *Arbeitslager*—the work camp—at Aschersleben, wearing our cleanest work clothes, our least muddy shoes, and the yellow star marked *"Jude"* which we had been required to wear for the train ride and which we could now never take off. We were brown as the autumn leaves.

The girls stared at us, astonished, just as we stared at them. Because you see, they were beautiful. They had manicured hands, lovely hairstyles. They wore stockings! The workhouse itself seemed beautiful to us; it was a bright three-story building with a kitchen, a shower room, dayrooms, windows with curtains, and pictures on the walls. I thought: "This place is going to be wonderful compared with Osterburg!"

A big girl named Lily Kramer brought us a cup of acorn coffee.

She had a university degree. Her spectacles sat low on her long nose.

"They let you dress like that in Osterburg?"

"It was a farm."

"Well, here, you've got to look as though you're going to business," she said. She leaned forward and spoke very quietly. "They like to make it seem that we are real workers, earning real wages, so that they won't have to think about who we really are, and in case visitors see us, they will not be disturbed or upset."

"Are there many visitors?" Mina asked eagerly. She always seized upon the positive, that girl.

"No," answered Lily. "There are no visitors. Are you by any chance interested in chamber music?" We squinted at her. "How about drama? Schiller?" Was she crazy? "Too bad."

She sighed and drifted off, like Yelena in *Uncle Vanya,* weary to death of the fools who surrounded her.

We settled in. The girls came and went constantly in their pretty dresses, all marked with the compulsory yellow star. At six in the morning, the curling irons were heating up for the day's coiffures. Initially I thought the girls were just trying to keep up appearances. But soon I realized it was more than that. They were trying to attract a protector. Not necessarily a lover, for by this time—October 1941—an Aryan could be imprisoned for consorting with a Jew. No, the slave girls of Aschersleben were just trying to find someone who would want to have them around and keep them employed so they and their families would be allowed to remain in the Reich.

In later years, I saw pictures of the paper factory of H. C. Bestehorn in Aschersleben. It had an attractive front entrance, a courtyard, and windows adorned with boxes of flowers. I never saw that side of Bestehorn. We came every day from our barracks, guarded by our pretty, young, mean-spirited camp commander, Frau Drebenstadt, and went through the back door straight into the factory. I counted eighty-two of us, but there might have been more.

Trude, Mina, and I were assigned to the stamping machines, old green Victorian monsters that punched out cardboard boxes for products like macaroni, tapioca, cereal, and coffee—none of which we got to eat.

I stood at one machine. With my left hand, I pushed four cartons under the blades. The blades came down. I turned the cardboard. The blades came down. I pulled the cardboard out with my right hand and pushed in four more sheets with my left hand. The blades came down. I stood in one place and pushed the cardboard in, turned it, pulled it out, pushed it in, from six-thirty in the morning until eleven forty-five and then from one-fifteen to five forty-five. The blades came down like rockets. Pang! Pang! Pang! The roar of the motors, the beating of the blades, and the swishing of the cardboard were incessant.

Our department head, Herr Felgentreu, a confirmed Nazi, proud of his job, waited for the engineer, Herr Lehmann, to set the machine timer, then synchronized his stopwatch. "You!" he barked. "Start now!" I worked like crazy. Push, turn, push, pull, push turn push pull push turn *Pang! Pang!* as fast as I could, snatching my fingers back from the knives. Ten minutes flew by. Suddenly he shouted "You! Stop!"

I was sweating. My heart was racing. The tips of my fingers burned from pushing and pulling the cardboard. Felgentreu counted how many boxes I had stamped out, then multiplied by six and came up with a quota for the hour. Then he multiplied by eight and came up with my quota for the day: 20,000 boxes.

"But it's impossible, sir," I protested. "One cannot work eight hours at the same rate that one works for ten minutes."

He wasn't even listening. He was walking away. I started to run after him. Herr Gebhardt, our supervisor, reached out and stopped me. The forewoman who worked under him put her finger over her mouth, signaling me to keep me quiet. I saw that it was the only finger besides her thumb that remained on her right hand.

That first day, I produced 12,500 boxes. This wasn't backbreaking labor as in the fields, but when the whistle blew I was so tired that I could barely walk.

For the evening meal, we received two pieces of bread and a cup of coffee.

The second day, I was told that if I fell short of my quota again, I would have to stay late to make up what was missing. At the last whistle, I had produced 17,000 boxes. They kept me working. By then I was so weary and so hungry that it took me several more hours to reach my quota. As I was finally leaving the factory floor, an Aryan worker shoved a broom at me and ordered me to sweep up. "No, Edith," said Herr Gebhardt. "You go and have your dinner."

The bulk of our food came at lunchtime in a brown ceramic bowl, a kind of improvised mixture of potatoes, cabbage, and celery, "arithmetically equidistant between vegetable and liquid," said Lily, our resident intellectual. That was a fair description.

In addition to the factory work, I had kitchen duty one week out of every month. I cleaned the tables, peeled potatoes, washed the pots. Standing before the kettle of boiling potatoes, ladling one into every brown ceramic bowl, I thought: "I could slip one into my pocket. It would burn, but who cares?" The Nazi cook was watching me. She knew exactly what I was thinking. What girl had not succumbed to notions of potato theft in this place? Frightened, I put the potato in another bowl and *dreamed* that it was in my pocket.

At our dinner of bread and coffee, Mina whispered, "Do they mean to starve us, Edith?"

"I guess we'll have to try and fill up at lunch," I answered. "Meanwhile, we'll write home and ask for food."

"The Jews haven't got enough food for themselves at home," Trude whispered. "When my sister was married to an Aryan, she and her children received plenty of food. But she had to give food to my parents because their Jewish ration stamps bought them so little."

"Where does your sister live?"

"I don't even know *if* she lives. Her husband threw her out. He told the Gestapo she was dead and kept the children."

"But how could she bear to let him keep the children?" Mina cried.

Our normally calm, well-behaved Trude grabbed Mina angrily. "Don't you understand that she was lucky that he just *said* she was dead and didn't hand her over to the Gestapo himself? When will you stop being such an idiot, Mina?"

At first glance, the rules at Aschersleben seemed just like the rules at Osterburg. But then you saw that there were differences. A ramrod heartlessness had set in.

"One may go to the toilet only on the floor on which one lives," said the rules. "Otherwise one must pay a fifty-pfennig fine. One may wash only on specific days. One may not shower after eight o'clock. The beds must be made according to the prescribed system, corners turned under, then under again, blankets unwrinkled. Nothing may stand on the cupboard. One may not leave the home except for Saturday from 2 to 6 and Sunday from 9 to 11 and 2 to 6, and one may not go out without the yellow star. Jewesses may not go into stores. They may not buy anything."

Mina showed me the bread rations that her former boss, Maria Niederall, had sent. "What shall we do with these?" she asked. "Frau Niederall thinks we can buy bread with them."

"I'll send them to Pepi," I answered, "and he'll buy bread and send it back to us."

But, you may ask me, wouldn't the bread be stale by then? Stale, hard, and even moldy? The answer is yes, of course. Now try to imagine how little such considerations had come to mean to us. We gratefully ate bread that was fourteen days old. We wrapped it in damp rags to restore some moisture and gnawed on it like mice.

On Saturday, I got "paid." Twelve reichsmarks and 72 pfennigs. More than 6 reichsmarks were deducted for room and board. Several more were deducted to recompense Bestehorn for the extra power I had used to make my quota. I ended up with 4 reichsmarks and 19 pfennigs. Since there was nothing to spend it on, I tried to go to the post office to send this tiny bit of money home to Mama. The guard at the door would not let me pass.

"You need permission from Frau Drebenstadt."

"But she's off today."

"You should have gotten permission last week."

"But if Mama doesn't hear from me, she'll think something terrible has happened!"

"And if I let you out with that letter, the factory manager will think I have allowed you to steal something."

"What could I steal? There's nothing in the factory but cardboard."

"Get back inside," he said. He was an old man, but he carried a stick and he was much too frightened not to be cruel. "I warn you."

One night Trude had an upset stomach. Since all the toilets were occupied, she used a toilet on the next floor. When she came down, Frau Drebenstadt was waiting for her and, without a word, repeatedly slapped her face. Trude was too shocked to cry.

"Your pay will be docked fifty pfennigs," Frau Drebenstadt said. "Mail privileges are suspended for a week."

That made Trude cry. The mail meant everything to us. When it was cut off—a punishment called *Postperre*, used for many infractions—we felt completely lost.

OUR FOREWOMAN HAD been working at Bestehorn all her life. She was an unattractive woman, bent over, with swollen red elbows, but her eyes held a smile for us. She waited until Herr Felgentreu disappeared around the corner of a machine, then:

"Listen to me, Edith. If you stack the cardboard carefully, you can shove in five pieces instead of four." She showed us how. "If the blades break, tell me, and I'll get the engineer to replace them. Don't let anyone else see you." She hurried away.

I tried it. Production increased by twenty percent in a few seconds. A miracle! Immediately the eight of us working on those machines began to push in five sheets of cardboard. After fifteen minutes the forewoman passed by and with her eyes told us that Felgentreu was coming our way. We went back to stacks of four.

Around four o'clock, when our bosses were having tea, the forewoman bumped me with her bony hip. This was a sign that she would take over for fifteen minutes while I went on a break. Every day she gave one of us a break like that.

There was no more "reason" for her kindness than for the cruelty of the camp commander who had slapped Trude. It was the individuals who made their own rules in this situation. No one forced them to behave in an unkind manner. The opportunity to act decently toward us was always available to them. Only the tiniest number of them ever used it.

In November, despite my careful planning and pacing, they gave me a new daily quota: 35,000 boxes. My spirits sank. I was sure I would fail, and that if I failed, Mama would be sent to Poland. However, Mina had a different attitude.

"In honor of your new quota!" she said brightly, presenting me with a red ribbon. "You are clearly one of 'Bestehorn's best'! Mazel tov!"

Our old friend Liesel Brust wrote that she was working in the Jewish Ration Center in Vienna, that she had seen our families, that everyone was all right. That letter gave me strength. I wore the red ribbon in my hair and attacked the machine with renewed vigor.

Then they raised the quota to 3,800 boxes per hour. I made it because I always took five pieces of cardboard instead of four and worked like lightning. Naturally, I broke the blade. Felgentreu docked my pay for the extra cost and yelled at me. I hung my head in contrition, a performance at which I now excelled. However, in a few days I was loading in five sheets again. Gebhardt saw me—I know he did. However, he said nothing.

The skin on my fingertips wore through, rubbed to a bloody mess by the cardboard. I would have been happy to use gloves, but you couldn't run the machine wearing gloves; they slowed you down and increased the likelihood that your fingers would be chopped off. So I just bled.

"We must keep working!" I said to my friends. "As long as *we* keep working, *they* are all right."

In late November, we saw two of the third-floor girls standing at the barracks door wearing their city coats and holding their suitcases. They were going home.

"Oh, lucky you!" Mina cried. "Are you getting married? Are you getting divorced? We heard that a girl from the Nordhausen *Arbeitslager* went home because she was pregnant. Are you pregnant?"

The girls laughed. Pregnancy had become a dark joke by then, because so few of us were still menstruating.

"Our parents are being sent to school," one girl explained. "We are going back to be with them."

Soon three more people were selected to be sent back to Vienna to accompany their parents to Poland. Bestehorn, however—apparently short of labor—would not let them go, so their mothers and fathers had to journey east without them. On the one hand, it comforted us to know that the company would fight to keep its workers. On the other hand, I lived in terror that such a circumstance would one day separate me from Mama, and that she would somehow be sent without me.

"You must tell me the minute you hear anything!" I wrote to her. ("I will need a few days to get permission to travel from the Gestapo," I wrote to Pepi. "So please please tell Mama she must let me know immediately if she's going to school!")

I WENT TO work in the dark and returned in the dark, so I couldn't tell when the day ended and soon lost track of time. I would put the wrong dates on my letters. I wrote to Mama twice a day, sometimes even more, and sent a cry of questions into the dark.

Who is at war against whom? I wrote to Pepi during one of the many mail suspensions. *I can't keep it straight. We never see a news-*

paper. There's one little radio in the dining area, but we have no time and no strength to listen. We know nothing except rumors. When will this war be over? When will our liberators come? How is it in Vienna? Do you have enough food? Tell Mama to stop sending me food, because I am sure she does not have enough for herself. Can you go out? Are you able to walk in the streets? Can you work at anything? Is your mother able to support you? Burn my letters! Read them and then burn them!

Between the lines, he could read: *Do you remember me? Do you still love me?*

Rumors drove us wild with worry. We heard that the Nazis, in their zeal to "purify" their race, were actually killing the retarded, the insane, and the senile with poison gas. "Oh, this is too much; this must be somebody's propaganda," Lily and I said to each other. We heard that people in the concentration camps were literally dying from overwork, that sadistic guards conceived inhuman tortures for those who couldn't keep up: made them carry heavy stones for no purpose, made them stand all night in the rain, cut their rations in half.

And we heard awful things about conditions in the Polish ghettos. One girl received a letter from her boyfriend in the Wehrmacht. "Stay in Aschersleben!" he warned. In the Polish city where he was stationed, he said, the ghettos were crowded; there was no food, no work, no space to breathe. People were falling sick and dying from lack of care. And every day, more transports brought more Jewish people, from all the countries Germany was conquering.

When the Gestapo heard about this letter, they burst into the barracks, dragged the shrieking girl away, and ransacked her cupboard and tore her mattress off the bed, looking for other letters. From their reaction, we all understood that what the soldier had written must be true. Poland must be worse than Aschersleben.

"Tell Z not to write to me!" I wrote hysterically to Pepi. "We must not be caught corresponding with the military! It is forbidden!"

DECEMBER 1941 BROUGHT the grimmest Christmas of my life so far. Yet we were all obsessed with giving gifts. I asked Pepi to buy an umbrella for Mama—"the most elegant and modern," I insisted—or maybe some earrings or a pretty box for her face powder. I wanted to believe that she was still my beautiful Mama, with earrings and face powder and any need at all for an elegant umbrella. Fantasies; we all had them.

One girl, whose father had been sent to Buchenwald, asked her boyfriend at home to buy a shaving kit for him, then wrapped it beautifully and attached a card that said, "To my dear father for Christmas, from your loving daughter." She left it in a cupboard, imagining that when he came out of the concentration camp, she would give it to him.

One of the unluckiest girls among us had come from Poland to study medicine in Vienna in 1933. Can you imagine worse timing? She had long ago lost touch with her family and received nothing from anybody, so I gave her a loaf of mama's bread. It was hard as a rock.

"Wonderful!" she wept. "Just like my mama's bread. Someday I will ask my mother to bake a loaf of bread for you too, Edith!"

We believed in the future, you see. We all still believed.

My friend Mina planned her gifts as though she were Santa Claus and Pepi Rosenfeld were all the reindeer in the North Pole.

"Now look here, Edith, I've saved up eight reichsmarks. So if we send this money to your Pepi, he should be able to buy a small box of herb tea for my mama, and a nice new pen for my papa, and a box of candies for my brothers and sisters. They love sweets! They still have teeth only because the Nazis won't let them have sweets, so you see, in its way, this regime has done the Katz family a big favor."

She actually made me laugh.

"Frau Niederall will surely send us something wonderful for Hanukkah. My papa used to give each of us kids a box of worthless coins on Hanukkah—we thought they were the greatest treasure— and we would play *dreidel* games and make bets and eat *latkes*. Oh, it was so much fun, Edith, such a pleasure to be Jewish. Someday when you and Pepi are married and I am the godmother of your children, I'll teach them *dreidel* games and we'll sing all the wonderful Yiddish songs my father knows."

"I'm afraid to hope for so much happiness, Mina."

"Don't be silly. Hope is God's gift to the world. Look at what wonderful luck I personally have had so far, just because I kept on hoping. Frau Niederall bought the Achter Delivery Company. She kept me and Frau Grünwald when she could have tossed us out. She taught me how to dress nicely, how to dab perfume here and here, how to write business letters and greet customers. I call her Auntie, that's how much I love her! When you meet her, you must call her Frau Doktor."

She reached under her bed, her face shining. "Look, I have a Hanukkah present for you," she said, "to give you hope." She brought forth a piece of wood into which she had burned a French saying which our friend Franz had used to cheer us, in Osterburg:

La vie est belle, et elle commence demain.
"Life is beautiful, and it begins tomorrow."

A few Jewish families were still living in Aschersleben in the late fall of 1941, among them Frau Crohn and her daughter Käthe, a sweet, smart woman about my age. When we girls from the *Arbeitslager* went out on Saturday or Sunday, the Crohns invited us for "coffee." I cannot tell you how much these visits meant to me. They brought back a feeling of home, civilized life, Jewish community in a world of hatred.

One Sunday, we were returning from the Crohns' house. I remember a girl named Ditha was there, and a girl named Irma, and another named Clair. We walked on the Breite Strasse, a street forbidden to Jews. Some local boys called out flirtatiously, "Hey, there go the lucky stars!" Somehow they did not understand the humiliation and persecution those hateful patches symbolized. We took their friendliness as a good omen.

Mina and I scrounged everywhere for something to bring the Crohns as the holidays approached and finally, by trading and promising, managed a tiny bottle of cognac. Frau Crohn served it right away, in little glasses she had somehow hidden from the neighborhood looters, who had taken everything else. We toasted the Americans, who had just entered the war after the Japanese attack on Pearl Harbor.

When all the Jews in this North German area were ordered to prepare for deportation to Poland, I went to Käthe's house to help her pack. I remember that she was not allowed to take a knife or a scissors. Käthe gave me one of her books—*The First Born* by Frischaner—and wrote inside: "In memory of many sunny hours."

She was taken with more than a thousand others from Magdeburg to the Warsaw ghetto. I wrote to her there. It struck me as very strange that my good friend did not write back.

In late November, in the freezing dark before dawn, Herr Wittmann, one of the company managers, marched into the barracks Frau Drebenstadt, frightened, made us stand at attention.

"You will not go to work today," he said. "Stay here. Pull the shades. Turn out the lights. Richard Bestehorn, a distinguished business leader and freeman of the town of Aschersleben, has died, and there will be a funeral procession in the courtyard. Under no circumstances should you attempt to watch. If you appear in the courtyard, you will be arrested."

He left. We gathered at the window and peeked out. Two French prisoners were sweeping the yard in front of our barracks. They decked the building with pine branches and black mourning crepe.

"Why don't they want us out there?" Mina asked. "We could certainly help those Frenchmen, who are not doing such a wonderful job."

"We are too despised to join the 'master race' in their solemn assemblage," said Lily with her usual smart bitterness. "Besides, if they don't see us, they can pretend they never knew we were here."

I thought at the time that Lily was just a cynic, but of course she turned out to be a prophet. I understand now that everything was done so that the Germans would never see us; or, if they saw us, would not have to admit it; or, if they had to admit it, would be able to say that we looked fine and would never be irritated by a sense of guilt or pricked by a moment of compassion. I remember reading what Hermann Göring had said to Hitler: These moments of compassion could be a big problem. Every German probably has one favored Jew to pull out of the bunch, some old doctor, some pretty girl, some friend from school. How would Germany ever become *Judenrein* if all these exceptions were made? So the policy was not to tempt anybody to behave decently, and all the while to keep us in the deepening dark.

Under such circumstances, no kindness went unnoticed. Herr Gebhardt never said one word to me, but I knew he helped me in little ways for which I will always be grateful. Even the slippery, eel-like Wittmann had a soft spot for one girl. Her name was Elisa. She was beautiful, stately, well educated, a lady. Before she was sent back to Vienna, he called her into his office and said: "If you need anything at all, just ask me. I will help you."

I stood at my machine. The cardboard slid, my fingers bled, and I tried to teach Mina the theories that might make our work meaningful. Taylorism in America; Keynes in Great Britain; Marx, Lenin, and Trotsky. Some days I couldn't remember any of it. "Either you come here stupid," I wrote to Pepi, "or the work makes you stupid."

I told Mina the stories of all the books I was reading. A biography of Marie Antoinette—too proud and beautiful, my cautionary tale. A biography of Isadora Duncan, so wild and free, an inspiration. I told Mina the story of *Chaim Lederer's Return* by Sholem Asch, *The Gooseman* by Jacob Wasserman, and *The Legends of the Christ* by Selma Lagerlof.

"Think of our forewoman as Veronica," I whispered. "Veronica wiped the brow of Jesus as he was carrying his cross to Golgotha, and his face remained imprinted on her cloth. Our faces will be imprinted on the hearts of those who are kind to us, like a blessing."

SINCE AMERICA HAD entered the war, and we took this as a sign that we would soon be free, we decided to celebrate

Hanukkah, the festival of freedom, in December 1941. One of the new girls, a coloratura soprano, sang for us. She knew arias, *Lieder*, and also some Yiddish songs that only a few girls like Mina understood. The sound of the old language, *just its sound,* filled our hearts with happiness.

We found some candles and made a kind of menorah. But then, to our horror, we found that not one of us knew the prayer—not one. Can you imagine? To be so bereft, so ignorant of our own culture, our own liturgy! This was the legacy of our assimilated life in Vienna. We turned to Mina. She covered her face with her hands. "I can't remember," she moaned. "Papa always said the prayer. Papa . . ."

We stared at the flickering lights, not knowing how to empower them. Lily suggested that we should just hold hands and close our eyes and say together: "God help us." So that's what we did.

God help us. God help us. God help us. *Lieber Gott hilf uns.*

AFTER HANUKKAH, WE got a new camp commander, Frau Reineke, and they raised the quota to 44,000 boxes per day.

A girl we knew announced with great delight that she was going home to get married. So once again, I proposed to Pepi.

Of course I will marry you. But it's not possible right now, he answered.

Why is it possible for her and not for me? If we can't save each other, at least we could warm each other! I dream of the day when we will live together. Where do you think? In a little villa or in a small castle? In an apartment in the center of town or in a cottage like my grandparents' house in Stockerau? I'll cook and clean and bathe the children and go to work in the court.

Listen to me, Edith, this is foolish talk. We will not be able to marry. Surely you understand how much is against it. (Did he mean Hitler?

History? His devoted mother?) *I will love you forever. Now you must forget me.*

A girl we knew named Berta had a boyfriend at a labor camp at Wendefurt near Blankenburg. He received permission to visit her, but as a Jew he was no longer allowed to use the train. So in the freezing cold, in the snow, he trudged to Aschersleben. Berta's joy when she saw him broke my heart, for I knew that Pepi would never have made such a gesture for me.

One Sunday, I walked with Trude and Mina. The snow was blinding. All white and pure lay Germany in its Christmas mantle. You couldn't see what lay beneath. I was overwhelmed by my insignificance, feeling myself a black dot on their vast landscape. "I cannot go on," I said to my friends and turned back, despairing.

Now, as I stood at my machine in the factory, every story escaped me. Isadora Duncan, Marie Antoinette, Marx, Keynes, Asch, Wasserman, Lagerlof—gone. All I could think about was the truth of our situation. I was a slave, and Pepi did not want me. Pang. Pang. Pang.

I stopped working. The blades crashed and broke. My legs gave way. I sank to the floor. The other girls didn't dare look at me. Herr Gebhardt picked me up and led me to a chair. And then our forewoman came over and put her arms around me and spoke to me with so much tenderness and concern that my misery lost its grip and I could go on working again.

That's all it takes, you see—a moment of kindness. Someone who is sweet and understanding, who seems to be sent there like an angel on the road to get you through the nightmare. Veronica.

Upon reflection, sinking into her straw that night, Mina concluded that Pepi was just having a panic attack. "Pay absolutely no attention to his letter," she said. "Go on writing to him about how you long to kiss him and taste him and all those other romantic things you always say, and it will all turn out wonderful."

So I wrote to Pepi that he should breathe hope from my letters, that next year we would surely have peace. "Spend your holiday in joy," I wrote to him. "Imagine how I would kiss you if I were there with you under the lights of the Christmas tree."

I TOLD THE people at home that the work no longer presented any problem for me. It wasn't a complete lie. You can grow accustomed to anything, to having "Sara" as your assigned middle name, wearing a yellow star on your coat, working endless hours, eating little, sleeping instantly the minute you can.

We made a million boxes for red compote and millions more for artificial coffee and artificial honey, for macaroni and spaghetti, for chewing tobacco. Every time a German opened one of those boxes, he touched us.

It was late January 1942. The Nazis would soon resolve at Wannsee to murder all the remaining Jews in Europe, but we knew nothing of such plans. We only knew that now we could not go into town at all, the rations had been reduced again, and the mail had stopped again.

The girl whose father had been sent to Buchenwald received a letter from a friend of his. "This is the song that we sing together on our way to work in the morning," wrote the friend. Our coloratura taught us all the Buchenwald song, and we hummed it whenever we had the strength to hum.

O Buchenwald, I can't forget you,
Because you are my fate.
Those who have left you are the only ones

Who can measure how wonderful freedom is.
O Buchenwald, we don't complain and moan,
Whatever our fate may be.
We want to say "yes" to life
Because the day will come when we will be free.

The song gave me courage. I went to Frau Reineke, our new camp commander, who was middle-aged and a mother, and who we hoped would prove more considerate than her predecessor.

"Please, ma'am, even though the mail has stopped, may we have the packages our families have already sent for us? We know our mothers are taking the food out of their own mouths to help feed us. And we know that now the food is spoiling, getting stale, becoming rotten."

She looked at me with cold eyes and turned me down. From then on, we no longer received food packages.

But there are, thank God, other kinds of food. Pepi must have raided a school trash bin, for he sent us some frayed paper copies of *Don Carlos,* by Friedrich von Schiller. Lily was ecstatic.

Every night with the last of our light and the last of our strength, we sat and read that eighteenth-century play as though we were girls in a drama class. Another girl came to protest that we were making too much noise. She ended up becoming our audience.

I played King Philip, the tyrant who has his own son, Don Carlos, murdered rather than liberalize his policies and let his subjects live in freedom. Do you think there was a single one of us who did not identify with the son, who did not hear his words and remember Evian-les-Bains?

I have no one, no one [cried Mina as Don Carlos],
In all this great and far-flung earth, no one. . . .

There is no place—not one—not one
At which I may disburden myself of my dreams.

We all understood that King Philip was the progenitor of Hitler.

The welfare of citizens blooms here in cloudless peace! [I declared,
     playing the angry defensive monarch.]

The peace of cemeteries! [sneered Lily, playing the progressive Mar-
     quis of Posa.]
Thousands have already fled from your lands, poor but happy.
And the subjects that you have lost for the faith's sake were your most
     noble ones.

We thought of Thomas Mann, Freud, Einstein. I thought of
Uncle Richard and Aunt Roszi, Mimi and Milo and our little
Hansi. Were they all not Austria-Germany's most noble subjects,
fled abroad, poor but happy?

It seems incredible, but in hindsight I believe Schiller himself
was sending us a message, a warning about the Final Solution
through his old play.

Said the king to the Grand Inquisitor:

Can you create a new religion which will
Support the bloody murder of a son? . . .
Do you agree to sow this notion
Throughout all Europe?

And the answer was yes.

We were Germany's children. A new religion demanding our
"bloody murder" had been promulgated throughout Europe, with

the cooperation of the church. Had we Viennese not witnessed the way Cardinal Innitzer, the head of Austria's Catholics, greeted Hitler with the Nazi salute after the Anschluss?

I did not realize it then, but through art, we might have understood reality.

On January 18, 1942, I got my menstrual period again for the first time in almost a year.

IN FEBRUARY, I came down with scarlet fever. So did a young, chunky girl, Anneliese, who had once led a privileged life.

For two weeks, I lay sweating and running a fever in the Bestehorn infirmary. I was wild with anxiety. I couldn't be sick! If I were sick and no use to Bestehorn, they might send Mama to Poland! I said I was well when I wasn't. I tried to get out of bed. The nurse locked us in. She brought our food and disappeared. If we got better, fine. If we didn't, so be it.

Actually, scarlet fever was the best thing that could have happened to me, because I was exhausted and terribly weak. I needed food and prolonged rest, and that was exactly what I got: six weeks of food and rest. I am sure the scarlet fever saved my life.

By the time I could work again, it was the middle of March. I found the barracks emptier. Mama had been writing cheerful letters; she and a man named Max Hausner were in love, and I had been delighted and hoped she would marry him. But now her letters became fragmented, disjointed, as though she couldn't organize her thoughts.

Pepi told me that his aunt Susie, the wife of his father's brother, had been deported; and that Wolfgang's parents, Herr and Frau Roemer, were also being sent east.

In Aschersleben, the attrition continued. Berta, whose boyfriend had walked so far to see her, went out without her star and was immediately arrested and sent to a concentration camp.

We heard that girls who had left to get married were being deported with their husbands. A girl who had a love affair with a French prisoner was sent to a concentration camp, and the Frenchman was executed.

Our old friend Zich was killed on the Western front.

Then a package that Mina had sent to her family came back. She was told that her mother and father and her brothers and sisters were being deported and she had to join them.

We knitted her a sweater from scraps of wool in various colors. I worked on one sleeve; Trude knitted the other.

The day Mina left, the last light at Bestehorn went out for me. I wrote asking my mother to take care of her; I pleaded with Pepi to see if something could be done to keep her in Vienna. But what could be done, really? A few days before she went away with her family, Mina wrote to me that she had visited my mama and Anneliese's father too, and both of them had given her something for the journey.

"Don't lose touch with Auntie," she wrote, meaning Maria Niederall, her former boss. "Don't be sad, dear girl; there is still the possibility that everything will turn out well, so don't give up hope. Don't take Aschersleben too seriously. Of course, I will write to you when I can, but don't worry if you don't hear from me. Remember that I am always thinking of you with love. Your Mina."

I had no way of knowing that Hitler had ordered all Jewish workers to be sent to concentration camps, that we were all to be replaced by slave laborers from conquered countries. But I felt the darkness closing in. I felt ignorant of what was happening and terrified of what lay ahead.

I burned all of Pepi's letters except one. It was dated May 26, 1942, and I think I kept it because, with its boundless sympathy, it kept me: "My dearest little mouse! Be courageous and believe as strongly in the future as you have believed so far. My poor child, if I could only assuage your hunger! Please be kissed a thousand times and embraced by your Pepi."

MAMA SENT ME TELEGRAMS: "I WILL HAVE TO GO SOON. COME QUICKLY. COME RIGHT AWAY."

In Aschersleben, I went to the police. "My mother is leaving! I must go with her!"

They gave me no answer.

I pleaded with the supervisor to send me home. I went to Frau Reineke. "My mother cannot go without me," I wept. "She is old; I am her only child—please."

IN VIENNA, MAMA begged the Gestapo to let her stay until I arrived.

"How old is your daughter?"

"She is twenty-eight."

"Then she is old enough to travel by herself after you."

"Please."

"No."

"Please, sir!"

"No."

I WENT BACK to the police. But they would not give me the papers I needed to travel with, and Jews were no longer permitted to travel without special papers. I felt the door closing between my mother and me, and I was the one locked out.

SHE LEFT LETTERS for me with Pepi. "Tell Edith I tried my hardest. I hope she isn't too dejected. She will come on the next train. God will help her and me so we can be together again."

And then she wrote: "The Jewish community here tells me to leave Edith where she is. Maybe it is better that way. She must stay, even though it is dreadful for me."

HER LAST LETTER: "It is 12:30 at night," she wrote to Pepi. "We are waiting for the SS. You can imagine what I feel like. Herr Hausner is still packing for me, because at the moment I am just not capable of doing anything. Please, please help Edith do her packing. Please look after my last few things that I have left. There is a suitcase to be collected from Herr Weiss, who is being left here because he is seventy-five years old. It is full of things Edith will have to take with her. May you stay well. May we meet again in health and happiness.

"Oh, my dear Pepi, I am so sad. I want to live. Please don't forget us.

"Kisses again. Klothilde Hahn."

MY MOTHER WAS deported on June 9, 1942.

The Gestapo in Aschersleben refused to let me travel to Vienna until June 21.

SEVEN

■

Transformation in Vienna

SIX OF US were leaving Aschersleben for Vienna. Our travel permission stipulated that we must report to a certain place on a certain day for *Umsiedlung*—"relocation"—in the east. But every rumor we had heard suggested that we should not keep this appointment.

"But how?" asked a girl named Hermi Schwarz, as we packed for the journey. "They'll see the yellow star and grab us right away."

"I'm not wearing mine," I whispered. "If I wear the star, I'll never have a chance to see my cousin Jultschi and to hear how Mama was before she left. I won't be able to spend any time with my friend Christl or with Pepi." I was imagining the warmth of their welcome, a few days of love.

"But we can't even get on the train without the star," Hermi said.

"True," I answered. "But we can get off the train without it."

We met in the dark of the early morning, the last Jewish slave girls of Aschersleben. We embraced and whispered good-bye and, so as not to attract attention, agreed to travel in groups of two, each pair in a different compartment. Hermi and I rode together. It was a pleasant train, full of families on vacation. For a people at war, I thought, the Germans seemed awfully carefree. In my isolation, I had not yet learned that they had been winning victory after victory and, in June 1942, fully expected to conquer all of Europe.

About an hour into the journey I made my way down the train corridor to the lavatory. I shimmed past chatting policemen, murmuring "Excuse me." I held my coat over my arm and my handbag over the place where the star was sewn. Once inside the lavatory, I tore the loose stitches and dropped the star into my handbag. On the way back, I met Hermi in the corridor. She was on her way to the bathroom to do exactly the same thing.

You will ask why we did not think of Berta, our friend who had been sent to a concentration camp for doing this. I will tell you that we thought of nothing but Berta, that every uniformed man who passed the window of our compartment filled us with terror. But we tried to appear calm, and we exchanged pleasantries with the other passengers. One of them said she was going to Vienna to visit her daughter. I wished her a happy visit. I turned my face away so she would not see that I was fighting back tears, thinking of Mama.

At the station, my dear friends melted into the Austrians the way flesh melts into dust. Does anyone remember them? Did anyone see them at the end?

I stood absolutely still. I had a sense that the holes where I had sewn the star onto my coat were forming a vivid Jewish outline for everyone to see. I expected the Gestapo to spot me and arrest me.

Pepi came out of nowhere, took me in his arms, and kissed me. For a split second, I lost myself in love again and believed he would save me. And then I saw his mother—the penciled eyebrows, the jowls, the double chin. She charged at me, grabbed my arm, and held me tightly, walking fast, hissing into my ear: "Ah, thank God you didn't wear the star, Edith; we wouldn't even have been able to say hello to you if you had been wearing the star. You must go directly to your cousin, take a nap, have a meal, then go tomorrow as soon as you can to Prinz Eugenstrasse because they are waiting for you. So is your mother—for sure, she is in the Vartegau in Poland. She wants you to join her for sure."

"She wrote to you! Mama!"

"Well, not since she's been gone, no, but I am absolutely sure she's there. You must join her right away. Don't even think of not reporting to school because they will hunt you down and find you, and your mother will be punished, and so will all the other people you know. You wouldn't want to put people you love in mortal danger, would you, Edith? Look at you—you're so thin! Make sure your cousin gives you a nice hearty meal."

Pepi finally pried her off my arm. He was white with anger. She hung back, frightened by his fierce glare. He walked beside me, carrying my bag in one hand, holding my hand in the other. Our shoulders touched. Pepi Rosenfeld had always been the perfect size for me. Anna hustled after us, torn between trying to hear what we were saying and not wanting to walk on the same street with a Jew.

We went to Jultschi's building. She was sitting on the steps with her little boy, Otto, an adorable child with huge, tender, dark eyes and big ears just like his father. With a cry of happiness, I started to scoop him up. I wanted to throw myself into Jultschi's arms.

"Ah, come in, Fräulein Ondrej," Jultschi said politely, shaking my hand. "How nice to see you again." One of her neighbors came down the steps. "This is my husband's cousin from Sudentenland," she said.

The neighbor smiled warmly.

"Welcome to Vienna. Heil Hitler!"

I had heard the phrase before, but only now did I realize that it had become a common greeting among ordinary people.

"Tomorrow five P.M., at the Belvedere," Pepi whispered. "I love you. I will always love you."

His mother pulled him away.

I sat down in Jultschi's kitchen. She was making tea and talking the way she always had—an outpouring, an explosion. I fell asleep at the table.

LITTLE OTTO TODDLED about with a smelly diaper and sticky fingers. I washed him in the sink and played the game of stealing his nose and then putting it back, making him howl with laughter. He seemed to me the most beautiful, angelic little child in the world. Jultschi sat at her machine and sewed. The covering noise of the machine made it possible to talk, she said. You couldn't be too careful. People listened and denounced. Their neighbors disappeared.

"Every week the Nazis bring me pieces of wooden cases that I must glue together. I think they hold medals or revolvers. I have a quota. I live on Otto's pension, which is not so bad. But of course, I am a Jew and so my little Otti is considered a Jew as well.

According to the Nuremberg Laws he would have to wear the yellow star, but he is under five years old so they don't bother him yet. Pepi has helped me with the application to have him declared a *Mischling*—that's what they call an officially recognized mixed-race person. Then they may give him more to eat and let him go to school and let me go on living here outside the ghetto. They leave a small remnant of us here, so our neighbors will see us and not be bothered about the deportations. How long do you think you'll stay? Two days? Three?"

"Actually, I thought I would stay for the rest of the war," I said, tickling Otti's toes.

Jultschi uttered a little scream. I laughed.

"Don't be funny, Edith. There's a time to be funny, and this is not it."

"Tell me about Mama. And her Herr Hausner."

"He's a darling man. His first wife died. They sent him to an *Arbeitslager* at the beginning, then they let him out so he could go to Poland. You know, back in February, we heard they took twelve thousand Jews out of the German factories and sent them east because there were so many prisoners from occupied countries to replace them. Oh, Edith, this *Blitzkrieg* makes me so nervous; nobody else in Europe seems to have an army—only Germany. What's going to happen when they conquer England?"

"They won't conquer England."

"How do you know?"

"Now that our little Hansi has joined the Jewish Brigade, the British army is invincible."

She laughed at last. She made her sewing machine roar.

"Now, remember, you mustn't talk about the Jews, Edith. Nobody speaks about them anymore. You mustn't say the word. People hate to hear it."

At the back of the Jewish ration station, Liesel waited for me, all confidence and smiles as always. She gave me rations for bread, meat, coffee, cooking oil.

"If you give me your rations, how will you eat?"

"There's food here. I take enough. Give the coupons to your cousin and Pepi. Let them buy for you. Come back every day. I will always have something for you to eat. But don't come at the same time two days in a row. And change the way you look. Keep changing."

I did not dare walk in my old neighborhood—someone there might recognize me. So I wandered through the Kohlmarkt, past Papa's old restaurant, past the place where I had first heard the radio, which was now being used to destroy my world. I sought a feeling of nostalgia. But toward Vienna, at that moment, I felt only rage. In this, my own city, I had become a hunted fugitive. If I was seen by someone who knew me, I might be denounced. If I did not go to the people who knew me, I would starve.

Pepi met me the next day in the park. He brought with him the things my mother had left for me: a suitcase with six summer dresses, and a little leather packet of jewelry that included my father's gold watch chain. He gave me a pawn ticket which my mother had received when she pawned her old fur coat.

"Do we have to meet here?" I asked. "I thought I could go back to your house."

"No, that's impossible," he answered. "Mama always prepares lunch for me and then I have to have my nap in the afternoon; otherwise I am no good for anything. I'll always meet you late in the day and we'll eat supper here together."

He reached for me. I pulled away.

"Are you completely without feeling?" I cried. "How could

you fail to know that I was expecting to stay with you? Why do you think I defied the Gestapo and became a fugitive? So we could have supper in the park?"

He started to say something. I slapped him in the mouth.

"For fourteen months, I was so lonely, so desperate, and the only thing that kept me going was the thought of you! Why have you not arranged to be alone with me? Do you love someone else?"

"No!" he whispered hoarsely. "No."

Inflamed by my desire, he pulled me to him. Proper Viennese Aryans glared at us, shocked that we should kiss in public.

"I will find a place," he said.

I WENT TO see Maria Niederall at the Achter Delivery Company on Malvengasse in the Second District. An office assistant named Käthe recognized my name. "It's Edith, Frau Doktor!" she called. "Mina's friend!"

From the back of the store, there emerged a tall, dark-eyed woman. She looked me up and down, then flashed a big grin. "Come on in," she said. "Käthe, bring coffee and sandwiches."

Frau Doktor wasn't beautiful, but, oh, did she have style! A sporty dresser, elegant as Dietrich, she had long fingernails, long legs, chestnut hair wrapped in waves and curls against her face. She wore real gold earrings, and on her bosom a special swastika honor badge to show that she had joined the Nazi Party early in the 1930s. She had married a lawyer with a doctorate like the one I had not been able to receive. So she was the wife of the Doktor— thus, Frau Doktor. She watched me eat, noticing my famishment and how my battered hands shook from tension. "Looks to me as if you need a vacation," she concluded.

"I thought I would have a few days with my boyfriend. But his mother won't let me in the house."

"And he obeys her?"

"In all things."

"Is he a man?"

"He's a lawyer and a scholar."

"Ah, well, that explains his docility. Did you sleep with him?"

"Yes."

"Then he belongs to you, not to his mother. Käthe, bring some of those gooey cakes."

I ate every crumb, then wet my pinky and mopped up the last essence of the icing from the flowered china plate.

"My girl Käthe here has an uncle in Hainburg with a big farm—lots of food and fresh air. I'll arrange for you to be his guest for a week so you can get your strength back."

"But, Frau Doktor, how will I travel? They so often have a *razzia*—a raid—on the train. They'll find me."

"You will travel by night. You will have a party membership card with your picture on it just in case anybody checks. But nobody will check, I'm certain. Have some more coffee."

"I was hoping you would have heard from Mina."

"Nothing," Frau Doktor said. Suddenly her eyes glistened with tears. She shook them away. "I could have helped her, you know. She could have stayed in Austria."

"She wanted to be with her family," I explained. "If I could have been with my mama, I would have gone as well."

She took my hands in hers. "You have to soften up these hands," she said, and rubbed sweet-smelling lotion into the cracked and callused palms. The feel of her strong fingers on my wrists, the smell of the cream—it was such an urbane comfort, so civilized. "Take this cream with you. Put it on your hands every day, twice a day. You'll soon feel like a woman again."

The next evening, to Jultschi's vast relief, I boarded the train for Hainburg, in a beautiful area near the Czech border, famous for its spectacular birds, misty forests, and luxurious farms. I had in my handbag whatever papers Frau Doktor had given me. But I did not trust them. I sat rigid in my seat. Mentally I rehearsed what I would say if the Gestapo found me.

I got the money for the ticket by accumulating my pay since Osterburg. The Nazi Party card I stole from a complete stranger somewhere on the train from Aschersleben. Then I pasted in my own picture. I have no family or friends left in Vienna. They are all gone. No one helped me. No one helped me. No one.

In the midst of this anxious reverie, I arrived in a fairy tale by the Grimm brothers, lit by a gentle summer moon. Käthe's boisterous uncle was waiting for me with a horse and buggy. He was fat and hairy and friendly, and so was his horse. The uncle had been told that I suffered with an intestinal ailment and needed some fresh air and good food to recuperate. As we clip-clopped through the lovely town, he told me all the marvelous things his wife was going to feed me. Pork chops and skewered chickens, dumplings and sauerbraten, pickled cucumbers and potato salad.

"Sounds delicious," I murmured, feeling sick.

I slept in a large bed under a pile of quilts. On the dresser there was a little shrine—fresh flowers and miniature Nazi flags surrounding a framed portrait of Adolf Hitler. The Führer watched me sleep.

At the breakfast table, looking at the eggs and bread and bacon and smelling the porridge, I became nauseated. I ran outside, gasping. Later on the robust farmer took me and his other guests for a hayride in the blooming countryside. The other people at the farm—a man, his wife, and their two pale-eyed grandchildren— had come from Linz, on a trip supported by Hitler's "Strength Through Joy" program, which encouraged citizens to visit sites and shrines throughout the Reich. Our host rolled out a lavish picnic for us.

I nibbled, breathing deeply, thinking: "Get your strength back. Heal your body. Use this chance."

The farmer had begun to talk about the greatness of the Führer. What a man he was! A lover of little children, a patron of the arts! What a future lay before us all because of his inspired leadership! *Lebensraum*—space to breathe, to move outward. The green fields of Russia, the "empty" plains of Poland. Had we seen the newsreel of Hitler marching triumphantly through Paris? What glorious days for Austria, finally united with her brethren in Germany, finally enjoying the world leadership which the demonic Jews had snatched from her by duplicity and cunning.

He lifted his glass of beer. "To the health of our Führer! Heil Hitler!" And they all cried with one voice, there by the babbling brooks among the breathtaking forests and the warbling birds, sated by their delicious meal, as content as cats in the sunshine: "Heil Hitler!"

I rushed to an embankment of bushes and retched helplessly. I could hear the Nazi farmer whispering behind me: "Poor girl. A friend of my niece Käthe. Sick as a dog. Some kind of stomach trouble."

In less than a week, I was back in Vienna. The farmer's wife packed up bread and ham and cheese and country *Stollen* for me. I laid the package down on Jultschi's table. We watched little Otti gnaw at the cake with his tiny new teeth. That at least was a pleasure.

■ ■ ■

CHRISTL MET ME in a café. She was prettier and stronger than ever, but a line of tension had stiffened her mouth. She was still hiding Bertschi wherever she could. A number of boys who had courted her and her sister had been lost in the war.

"Remember Anton Rieder, the one who studied to be a diplomat?"

"No. Don't say it. No."

"He died in France."

I wept for Anton. Maybe we could have saved each other.

Christl feared for her father, who was working with the Wehrmacht as an engineer on the Russian front. "The radio ridicules the Russians," she said. "Tells us every day how inferior they are, how Bolshevism has left their people starving and made them stupid. But my mother was a Russian. And she bore the pain of her illness like Athena. And I think we will have more trouble from the Russians than our Führer knows." She threw her arm around my shoulders. "What will you do?"

"I don't know. I guess I will have to go to Poland."

"Stick with this Niederall woman," Christl said. "She's well connected. As a reward for her early support of the party, she got the shop that belonged to that nice Achter family—they at least were wise enough to get out of here early on. Unlike you, my brilliant friend."

She gave me a playful shove. I didn't laugh. As Jultschi said, there was a time to be funny and now was not the time.

FRAU NIEDERALL SAT at her highly polished dining table, pouring real coffee from a delicate porcelain pot.

"The way you ate the other day, I was sure you would love the meals at Käthe's uncle's farm. But I hear you could hardly keep down a mouthful."

"I'm sorry. I don't mean to appear ungrateful."

"You appear to be sick. Under ordinary circumstances, I'd send you right to hospital. Tell me, did you have an Uncle Ignatz Hoffman, a physician in Floritzdorf?"

"Yes. He killed himself."

"I knew him," she said. "When I was a little girl I lived in that district, and I became very ill and your uncle saved my life. After he died, his wife needed help to take their things out of Austria."

"Ah! So you were the one . . ."

I leaned toward her, eager to understand who she was, why she had become a Nazi.

"As a young girl, I went to work for Doktor Niederall. I was not so good at shorthand, but I was excellent at other things. He found me a nice apartment and kept me there. That's all most men want, you know, Edith—they want a woman waiting, in a comfortable room, with a good meal ready and a warm bed. For years, I was his open secret. But he could not divorce his wife, whom he hated, and who hated him, because the Catholic laws of our God-fearing country forbade divorce.

"The Nazis said they would change the divorce laws. So I supported them. And they repaid me. I am at last Frau Doktor. Too late to have children, I am sorry to say, but not too late to enjoy the respect that comes with legitimacy."

Is it not amazing that such a fine woman would align herself with monsters just to acquire a wedding band?

■   ■   ■

CHRISTL GAVE ME food. I slept in the back of her shop. In the night, the watchman came by with his light. I hid behind a wall of boxes, afraid to breathe, thinking: "If they find me, my friend who has hidden me will go to a concentration camp. I have to find someplace else to stay!"

I ran into Uncle Felix Roemer on the street. He passed me, I walked on a way, and then I turned and followed him into an alley. The Gestapo had come to his flat and demanded to see his papers, but he said he didn't have his papers because he was trying to emigrate to South Africa and had sent them there. And the investigator had believed him. Not all the SS were as bright as Colonel Eichmann, you see.

I stayed only one night with Uncle Felix. To stay longer was too dangerous. If the neighbors noticed this old man harboring a young girl, they might take a second look. I lay listening to his harsh old man's breath as he slept, and I thought: "If we are caught, they will send him to a concentration camp. He will never survive it. I have to find another place to stay."

My mother had written me that my cousin Selma, the daughter of my father's oldest brother Isidore, had been assigned to a transport. When her boyfriend heard about this, he ran away from the *Arbeitslager* at Steyr and returned to Vienna, so he could go to Poland with her.

This story inspired me. "Come with me to Poland," I said to Pepi. "At least we'll be together there."

He did not agree, but he used this idea successfully to threaten his mother. "Edith must have a place to stay!" he insisted. "If you don't help us, I will go east with her."

Alarmed, she gave him the key to another flat in their building that belonged to a vacationing neighbor. I slept there several nights. But I could not wash there or use the toilet or turn on a light—people would have thought burglars had broken in and would call the police. I don't think I ever even undressed in that place. Anna came in the mornings. She would beckon me to the door, look around to make sure that nobody was around, then push me out, saying: "Go. Go quickly."

I was a wreck.

I wandered like a derelict, in a trance of worry. Where would I sleep tonight? Where was Mama? If I gave up and went to Poland, would I find her? Where would I sleep tonight? Distracted, I wandered into the path of a young man on a bicycle. He swerved so as not to hit me.

"Watch where you're going!"

"I'm sorry."

He smiled. I remember him as a wiry little fellow, wearing shorts. "Well, no harm done," he said. "But now that I've spared your life, that surely entitles me to walk with you a bit." I was terrified of him, but he didn't know that. He just kept chattering on. "The damn Nazis have ruined Vienna with all their checkpoints and road blocks and such. If you ask me we'd be better off with Von Schuschnigg, wherever he may be, but if you say I said that, I'll deny it. Come on, let's stop for a cold drink; what do you say?"

"Thank you, I have to go, but thank you . . ."

"Oh come on, half an hour . . ."

"No, really . . ."

He looked hurt and maybe a little angry. That frightened me terribly. So I sat with him for a while and he talked and talked. Finally he let me go on my way.

"Here's something to remember me by," he said, and handed me a little Saint Anthony's medal. My eyes filled with tears. "Oh, my, now don't go on like that, it's not a proposal of marriage after all, just a good-luck charm . . ."

I kept that medal for the rest of my life.

TO HAVE A proper wash, I went on "ladies' day" to Amalienbad, the public baths off Favoritenstrasse in the Tenth District. This was a working-class area where no one was likely to know me. Far from the center of the city, the bathhouse served the many Viennese who had toilets but no bathtubs at home. No guards stood at the doors. There were no signs prohibiting Jews. No one asked any questions or demanded to see any papers.

I washed in the shallow pool and soaped and rinsed my hair under the spray and sat for a bit in the dense fog of the steam bath, feeling safe enough to dose off.

Suddenly I felt a hand on my shoulder. I jumped, started to scream.

"Shhhh. It's me. Remember me?"—a tall heavy girl with delicate misted spectacles and a big smile.

It was Lily Kramer, the cultural leader of the Aschersleben *Arbeitslager*. I was so happy to see her that I could not stop hugging her. Lily said that her father had made it out to New Zealand, and she herself was hiding with the governess who had helped to raise her, who lived in this neighborhood.

"How do you stand the tension?" I asked.

I expected her habitual cynicism. Instead, I got Schiller. " 'Man is a greater thing than you have thought him,' " she said, quoting the lines of the Marquis de Posa, the role she had played in *Don Carlos*. " 'And he will burst the bonds of lengthy slaughter, and will demand his consecrated rights.' I believe that, Edith. I believe that the world will rise up against this tyrant Hitler and send him to hell."

I have no idea to this day whether my friend Lily made it through the war. But I must tell you, at that moment, I saw absolutely no reason to share her optimism.

"FIND ME A room," I said to Pepi in the park that night.

"There is no place," he protested.

"The best-connected young man in Vienna, the lawyer-without-portfolio for everyone who needs official correspondence, cannot find a place for his old girlfriend?"

"Why didn't you stay in Hainburg? They were ready to board you, but you . . ."

"Because I could not stand to listen to all the Nazi talk! When my mama might be starving in some ghetto in Poland! When my friends are all scattered—maybe dead, God forbid! Mina and Trude and Berta and Lucy and Anneliese and Frau Crohn and Käthe and . . ."

"Shh, my darling, my little mouse, shh, don't cry."

"Tell your mother to move in with her husband Herr Hofer in Ybbs, and let me stay in your apartment with you!"

"She's afraid that if she moves, they will find me!" he said. "You don't know what it has been like here. They won't let me work because I am a Jew. But if I go out, they don't know why I am not working and they think I am a deserter from the army. I tried to work as a chimney sweep because I would be hidden in the chimneys and my face would be obscured by the soot, but still someone recognized me and I had to disappear again. I tried to learn bookbinding, but I have no gift for these artistic things. I am afraid to show myself in the street for fear that someone who knew me will wonder why I am still here and report me. Everyone is afraid, Edith. You don't understand what it can mean to be involved with a person like you who is wanted by the Gestapo."

He looked pale and bald and delicate in the moonlight—like a child, not like a man. I felt so sorry for him. I felt so tired and hopeless. I had come back to Vienna for him, because I was sure in my heart that no matter what he said in his letters, when he saw me, he would want me again, and we would live in hiding in this city for the rest of the war. But it was a vain and stupid hope. The focus of my life had been my love affair with Pepi Rosenfeld, and the Nazis had destroyed that. They had made him afraid of me.

I WALKED THE streets all through July. I sat in the cinema, just to sit in the dark, to rest. One day I saw a *Wochenshau*—a newsreel—of Jews being herded into a camp. "These people are murderers," said the announcer. "Murderers finally meeting with the punishment they deserve." I ran out of the cinema. The streets were blazing. I walked and walked past the tramway. Someone called to me with a tone of warm surprise: "Fräulein Hahn!"

"No," I said. "No!"

I didn't even look at whoever had called to me. I ran onto the tram, sat down, and rode somewhere, anywhere.

I knocked on Jultschi's door. She took me in, but she was weeping. "I have a child here, Edith," she said. "I have applied for papers for my child. They will come and check and see who is staying here with us. Please. You've got to find another place to stay."

I stayed in Christl's store again. I stayed several nights with Herr Weiss, my mother's aged friend. I sought out Jultschi's father, once a man-about-town, a bon vivant, always making deals. Now he was paying someone a fortune for permission to hide in a tiny room. He could not help me.

I knocked on the door of my old friend Elfi Westermeyer. Her mother answered. She had met me often when Elfi and I were both members of the Socialistische Mittleschülerbund.

"Hello, Frau We . . ."

"Get out."

"I thought I might have a few words with Elfi."

"Get out."

"Just a moment of her . . ."

"If you ever try to get in touch with Elfi again, I will call the police."

She shut the door. I ran from there.

At the back of the Jewish ration shop where Liesel Brust gave out her lifesaving food rations, I met Hermi Schwarz, the girl who had ridden home with me from Aschersleben.

"I can't live this way anymore," she wept. "No one wants me. They are all afraid. And I am so afraid to hurt them. Tomorrow I'm going to school. Maybe I'll find a better life in Poland."

I boarded the tram and sat by the window. Despair seized me. I began to weep. I couldn't stop. All the nice Austrians came over to comfort me. "Poor girl. She must have lost her boyfriend in the war," they said. They were quite concerned.

It had been almost six weeks since I had gone underground in Vienna. I had exploited all the goodwill that was available to me, and although there was surely more, I no longer felt comfortable endangering those who were kind to me. I had been unable to find a job that might support me or a room to live in. Like Hermi, I was at the end of my rope. I decided that I would pay one last visit to Frau Doktor, drink one last cup of coffee, thank her for her help, and take my place on a transport to the east.

"I HAVE COME to say good-bye," I said.

Frau Doktor did not answer. She picked up the phone.

"Hansl," she said, "I have a girl here. She has lost all her papers. Can you help her?"

The answer was clearly yes, for she immediately told me to go right away to Number 9 Fleischmangasse in the Fourth District. "When you get there," she instructed, "tell him the truth." I went right away, with no more conversation.

The sign on the door said JOHANN PLATTNER, SIPPEN-FORSCHER—OFFICE OF RACIAL AFFAIRS.

In those days, many people looked for a *Sippenbuch,* a record book explaining the lineage of their parents and grandparents on both sides, to prove they had been Aryan for three generations. For this they needed the help of a *Sippenforscher,* an authority on racial matters. That was where Frau Doktor had sent me.

I thought: My God, I have been betrayed. But Mina's voice came to me: "Go to Auntie. You can trust her."

Plattner's sons led me to his office. When I saw him, my heart contracted in my chest. He was wearing a brown Nazi uniform with a swastika on his arm.

"You are lucky to find me at home," he said. "Tomorrow I go back to North Africa. Now. Tell me exactly your situation."

There was no turning back. I told him. Exactly.

"Do you have any good Aryan friends?"

"Yes."

"Find a woman friend who looks like you, who has similar

coloring, someone who is about the same age. Ask her to go to the ration book office and give notice of her intention to take a holiday. They will give her a certificate entitling her to receive rations during her holiday, wherever she should be. Then she should wait a few days. Then she should go to the police and tell them that while she was on vacation rowing on the old Danube River, her handbag fell into the water, carrying all her papers, including her ration card, to the bottom. Use exactly this explanation. Don't say there was a fire, or the dog chewed up the papers, because they will demand a remnant. Only the river will keep the secret. The police will then give her a duplicate. Are you committing this to memory, Fräulein?"

"Yes."

"Your friend should then give you the original ration card, as well as her birth certificate and her baptismal certificate. You will assume her name, take her papers, and immediately leave Vienna and go to live somewhere else in the Reich.

"Under no circumstances—mark me, now, under no circumstances—should you ever apply for a *Kleiderkarte*, a ration book for clothing. These are held in a national registry, and if you apply for one, the authorities will instantly know that somebody else with the same identity already has one.

"Buy a season ticket, a *Streckenkarte*, for the railway—this will have your picture on it and will be an acceptable identification.

"Use this ticket plus your friend's personal data, and that should cover you."

"Yes, sir," I gasped. "Thank you, sir."

"One more thing," he added. "We are short of labor in the Reich, as you probably have guessed, with your background. Very soon, all the women in the country will be asked to register for work. This could get you into trouble, because your friend will be asked to register as well as you. So you ought to go to work for the Red Cross, because that is the only organization which will be exempt from the registration."

He turned away. The interview was over. I had never listened so hard to anything in my life. Every word was printed on my mind.

He did not wish me luck. He did not ask for money. He did not say good-bye. I never saw him again.

He saved my life.

PEPI ARRANGED A rendezvous with Christl. He spoke for me, explaining Plattner's plan. Christl did not hesitate for one second.

"Of course you may have my papers," she said. "I'll apply for the vacation ration card tomorrow."

And that was it.

Do you understand what it would have meant if Christl Denner had been discovered aiding me in this way? She would have been sent to a concentration camp and possibly killed. Remember that. Remember the speed with which she assented, the total absence of doubt or fear.

Frau Niederall invited me for dinner along with some teachers, members of the Nazi bureaucracy, mostly people involved in the dissemination of ration cards. She deliberately led the conversation to the subject of rationing, so that I would hear their explanation of the system, with all its tortuous ins and outs.

Christl got herself a little tan by sitting on the terrace, so that she would look as if she had been out sailing. A delicate sprinkling of freckles danced on her nose. On July 30, 1942, she reported to the police that she had gone on vacation and lost her papers in the river. They immediately gave her a duplicate set. And of course the officer invited her out for coffee and she went, and of course he wanted to see her again, but she told him the story about the brave sailor on the high seas, or maybe the one about the brave doctor in the Afrika Korps, or whatever.

She gave me the original papers—her baptismal certificate, her vacation ration stamp book. Then she and Elsa went to visit their father at Osnabrück. I was supposed to leave Vienna immediately, but I didn't know where to go. I didn't know Germany—I had been only to little towns like Aschersleben and Osterburg. I was so frightened that I could not summon even one simple idea.

I went to the cinema to think.

In the newsreel they showed some pictures of Goebbels opening the "Great German Art Exhibition of 1942" in Munich, at a new, low-slung, ugly building that Hitler thought was beautiful; it was called Das Haus der Deutschen Kunst, "The House of German Art." Loud military music played as the works of art flickered by. There was a terrifying picture of the war on the Russian front, with German soldiers crawling across the great steppes into the flames and chaos of battle. There was a bust of Hitler by Pagels— that style of sculpture so well liked by the Nazis, in which all soft, human expression is distorted by a mien of ferocity and cruel determination. There was Ernst Krause's group portrait of the members of the *Leibstandarte* SS Adolf Hitler, holders of the Knights Cross and the Iron Cross. The most detested men in Europe had been made as handsome as movie actors and were set before us in glory as though they were indomitable heroes of a righteous cause. I saw *The Judge*, one of Arno Breker's ghastly relief sculptures. This one depicted a grim-faced Germanic avenger about to draw his sword.

But also . . . but also, you see, there were two white marble statues: *Mutter mit Kind* by Josef Thorak, a mother nursing her baby; and *Die Woge*—"The Wave"—by Fritz Klimsch, a woman lying outstretched, leaning on one arm, one knee bent, her hand on her knee.

I looked at the statue, and something happened to me. How shall I explain this to you? It was a kind of epiphany. *The Wave* washed over me. I heard the statue speak to me. *"Komm, Edith, komm zu mir."* I heard the voice of *The Wave* calling like my mother's voice, and in it I heard love, security, kindness, blessing. It was a fantasy, of course; but it happened, I swear to you—it happened to me in my time of greatest fear and confusion, when I was about to un-become myself. This white marble statue spoke to me about peace and freedom and the promise of life. I felt that in the next minute she would leave the screen, her marble skin would warm and become flesh, and she would embrace me and tell me that I would be safe.

"I have decided to go to Munich," I said to Frau Doktor.

I was never in my life more confident of any decision.

I BOUGHT THE Munich newspaper, *Münchner Nachrichten*. In the "Rooms for Rent" section, a women in the little suburban town of Deisenhofen offered a room in exchange for sewing and mending. I thought: This is perfect for me. It is a sign that Munich is the right choice.

Frau Doktor sold my mother's Persian lamb coat and gave me the money. I left the jewelry with her, not as payment—neither of us would ever have considered such a thing—but for safekeeping. I hugged her close to me, blessing her with all my heart.

I went to my cousin Jultschi's house and picked up my suitcase with the six dresses Mama had made for me, and the shoes and underwear, the little nightgowns she had left. I kissed my poor cousin, feeling as sorry for her as she felt for me, and I kissed our darling little boy.

I went to Pepi's house. Anna was there, happy to see me dressed for departure. She talked about how a niece of hers had just this morning gone to travel in the Reich on vacation with the "Strength through Joy" program, how she had packed her up with cakes and sausages. I was sitting there quietly waiting for Pepi, and she didn't even offer me a sandwich for the journey.

Finally he came. He had brought me a present. It was a book of poems by Goethe which he himself had bound—rather clumsily—in a dusty blue paper cover. Deep inside the binding were my true identity papers, the ones that said I was Edith Hahn, a Jewess and a resident of Vienna. With this were my last exam papers, and my grade transcripts from the university.

"Someday maybe you will need these," he whispered. "To show someone what a brilliant law student you were in your previous life."

He walked me to the train station and put me on the night train for Munich. He did not kiss me good-bye. The time for kisses was over.

There was no *razzia*, no search of passengers' papers by the police, on the train. This was good luck—no *razzia* on the train from the *Arbeitslager*, when I could have been arrested for not wearing the star; none on the train to Hainburg, when I could have been arrested just for being on a train; and none on the train to Munich, when I was first carrying papers that said I was Christina Maria Margarethe Denner, twenty years old, an Aryan Christian. I rode all night in a compartment with other people, pulled my coat over me, and slumped down so that, whoever I was now, I should not be noticed.

During that long terrible ride to Munich, I finally swallowed the bitter pill of my lover's rejection and poisoned myself with it. I murdered the personality I was born with and transformed myself from a butterfly back into a caterpillar. That night I learned to seek the shadows, to prefer silence.

In the morning, I stood in the station and looked around at the Germans. They seemed just fine—healthy, pink, well-fed. Swastika armbands and Hitler's picture were everywhere. Red and black and white banners fluttered from the walls and the roofs, and martial music was playing. There were so many pretty, laughing women; so many confident, decorated soldiers. You could buy every sort of flower and wine, and wonderful things to eat. A holiday place, this Munich, with high spirits and happy people.

I thought: *Now I am like Dante. I walk through hell, but I am not burning.*

EIGHT

∎

The White Knight of Munich

ℐN FACT, I had journeyed not into hell but to a corner of heaven, to the little town of Deisenhofen outside of Munich and the cheerful home of Herr and Frau Gerl. When she opened her front door and saw me, she gasped. I understood what must have alarmed her. She saw a tiny, thin, exhausted girl, with haunted eyes and a timorous voice, too nervous to say her own name properly.

"Margare . . . the . . . D . . . D . . . Denner. But everybody calls um . . . um . . . me Grete."

"Do you know what I think?" she said. "I think you must go right to bed and I'll bring you coffee and cake. Now do as I say, there you go."

Every time I go to bed at night in my apartment in Netanya, it is a little bit like going to bed at Frau Gerl's house that first morning after the train ride to Munich. Safe at last—safe enough to shut your eyes and sleep.

Frau Gerl was a humorous, imaginative woman, a nurse by profession. Her husband worked for the courts, I believe. She had met him the way she met me—through a newspaper advertisement. They had a little boy, about four years old. As Protestants in a Catholic town, they lived in some isolation from their neighbors. That suited me fine.

Instead of paying rent, I sewed for Frau Gerl three days a week. I made skirts out of her husband's old robes, remodeled his shirts to fit her, made little outfits for her son, mended the sheets. I told her that my mother had died and my father had married a young woman, only a few years older than I was, and that this new wife hated me and made my life in Vienna a misery, so I had fled and applied for employment with the Red Cross. She believed me. She called me her *Dennerlein*. Her only rule was that she didn't want any boys coming to visit. I was happy to comply.

"Before the war," she told me, "I worked for a Jewish lawyer, taking care of his mother. But then the government said I could not work for them anymore. The old lady cried to see me go. And then the lawyer was arrested. And then I was arrested too."

We were sitting in her sunny kitchen. I was sewing. She was mashing potatoes.

"They accused me of having an affair with my employer. 'Where does he keep his gold?' they asked. How should I know, I said, do I look like a miner? 'You were a servant! You must have seen!' I was a nurse. I said, I saw bedpans."

She laughed. But by now the potatoes were liquefied.

"They brought my employer to see me in prison," Frau Gerl continued. "Ah, that poor man, he had been so abused by them. And you know what he did, Grete? He fell down on his knees before me and begged my forgiveness that my association with his family should have landed me in this terrible place."

"What happened to him?" I dared to ask.

"Gone," she said. "Disappeared. The whole family."

Sitting in Frau Gerl's kitchen those first few weeks in Deisenhofen, I heard stories I could not believe.

"The SS men are often quite attractive—racially they are just perfect, you know—but everybody is afraid of them, so nobody wants to be their friend and they are very lonely."

I sighed regretfully—ah, the poor SS!

"So the government has taken pity on them and persuaded the girls from the Hitler Youth to sleep with them and have racially perfect babies who are raised in government nurseries like pine trees."

I burst out laughing.

"Oh, this cannot be, this must be somebody's propaganda . . ."

"It's called *Lebensborn,*" she said, rolling out her dough with authority. "When you go to Munich, you will see the office."

A GOOD MOOD animated the city of Munich in August 1942, making it throb and dance, because the Germans were winning the war. People on vacation thronged to national sites like the beer hall where Hitler had made his *Putsch* against the Bavarian authorities in November 1923, and the House of German Art, home of my "magic statue."

I walked through the bustling streets, shrinking into my clothes but wildly curious. There were exhibits, operas, band concerts. I saw SS men from the Baltic countries. They didn't speak a word of German, but they still wore that uniform. What would happen to the Jews of Vilna, the city my father had called the Jerusalem of Europe, with such people in power? I saw Russian prisoners of war doing heavy construction work, guarded by a German with a rifle, their clothes marked with a red circle.

I saw a middle-aged Jew with a yellow star on his coat, scrubbing the streets. My heart twisted in my chest. If only I could touch him, speak to him. I walked past him without even daring to turn my head. And then I found myself staring at the offices of the *Lebensborn* program, just as Frau Gerl had said.

Along with my proven gift for going unnoticed, which I had discovered in Vienna in the days after the Dollfuss assassination, I was now wrapped in a further disguise called Grete. She was quiet, shy, very young, and inexperienced, with no ambitions, no opinions, no plans. She did not seek to meet people but was always ready to be polite and helpful.

This girl would sometimes attract the notice of young German soldiers on leave in Munich, lonely, with no one to talk to, and they would strike up a conversation and suggest a stop at a café.

Remembering how Christl dealt with the Gestapo, I would accept. To be honest, I desired primarily that someone should buy me a meal. I was living on the money that Frau Doktor had saved for me from the sale of Mama's fur coat, and it was running out fast. Every sandwich and every piece of cake helped.

Usually these boys wanted to talk about themselves. They would like me because I was such a good listener. Of course, I told them nothing about myself. That turned out to be surprisingly easy. People didn't want to know too much in those days. They had their own thoughts and secrets and troubles. It was wartime, after all. If a young soldier wanted to see me again, I would agree, make the date, and then not keep it. He never came looking for me, because he had no idea where to look.

Just about that time, the Red Cross summoned me for an

interview. It was in the large, expensive home of an upper-crust woman. She wore a maroon velvet dress. Her terrace overlooked the River Isar. She had Hitler's picture hanging in her parlor and a diamond swastika on a gold chain hanging around her neck. She asked me about my background.

With precision, I rattled off every detail I had memorized from the papers that Pepi had secured about Christl's grandparents. My grandfather on my father's side was born in such and such a city, studied in this school, worked at that job. My grandfather on my mother's side died of such and such an illness, attended this church, founded that company. The only gap in my knowledge concerned my—Christl's—mother's parents. Although Aryan papers had been found for the maternal grandfather, they could not be found just yet for the maternal grandmother. Still, since my—Christl's— mother was dead and her father had been an officer in the German Army, the Red Cross woman let it slide.

"You show admirable knowledge of your forebears, Grete. An impressive display. Most of our applicants are not so well informed."

My stomach tightened. "Fool! You knew too much!" I thought. "You'll give yourself away by knowing too much! Watch that!"

She said I would receive my assignment in a few weeks.

Gradually I learned to wear my disguise with greater comfort. I moved like a speck of dust on a bubble—invisible, yet vulnerable to destruction at any moment.

I went to the opera, *La Bohème*. I believe that Trude Eipperle was singing the role of Mimì. A soldier asked if he could say that I was his bride because military couples didn't have to wait in line for tickets. Of course, I agreed. We received our tickets right away. Then he took me to a crowded restaurant. I guess he must have been a high-ranking fellow, because when a waitress passed by with two plates full of food meant for other people, he took them right out of her hands and put them down at our table, and nobody protested.

Frau Gerl decided to buy me a dress. She had a few extra points on her *Kleiderkarte*—the ration card for textiles and clothing—and since I said I had used up my points (in fact, I didn't dare buy any clothing, because Johann Plattner had warned me not to), she gave her points to me. She took me to a shop that sold the traditional dirndl, a style popular then, because it recalled the Nordic tradition celebrated by the Nazi regime. I remember the dress exactly. It was red, and it came with a white blouse and a matching jacket. Frau Gerl stood behind me. I could see her in the mirror. How delighted she was at the fit, the cut, the style! I suddenly remembered my mother grinning in the same way, remembered the tape measure around her neck and her silver thimble and her shining eyes.

"Grete? Are you all right?"

I nodded, recovering quickly.

The store owner must have been caught up in Frau Gerl's enthusiasm because she sold that dress to us for fewer coupons than she might have.

I wore that dress when the Gerls took me to a beer garden that featured the Weiss Ferdl Cabaret. The place was packed with Germans high on their *Blitzkrieg*, out for an evening with their loved ones, feeling prosperous, enjoying their new apartments and their new businesses, so cheaply acquired—from where, they did not stop to wonder.

"The Nazis are such good-hearted, generous people!" exclaimed the comedian. "I hear they have stopped bathing themselves and have given over the use of their bathtubs to their geese, so that the geese will be nice and clean and fat when they are slaughtered for Christmas dinner!"

That comedian soon disappeared.

AUGUST 28, 1942. A Friday, steaming hot. I remember the date because it was Goethe's birthday. At the Maximilianaeum, a famous art gallery in Munich, I sat down before a lush, gold-toned landscape, probably one of those paintings by Schmid-Fichteberg or Herman Urban that the Nazis loved because they made Germany look like the Elysian fields. I tried to see what they saw, to think of their land in those bold heroic yellows and oranges and wipe away my memory of the exhausted girls crawling in the mud behind the emaciated Frenchman.

A tall man sat down next to me. He had thin, silky blond hair, bright blue eyes, and a thin hard mouth—an Aryan through and through. He wore civilian clothes and, in his lapel, a swastika pin, the sign of a Nazi Party member. His hands were strong and clean, a craftsman's hands. He looked down at me and smiled.

"This landscape we have here before us is a perfect example of the Bavarian *Heimat* style," he said. "But I am sure you already know that."

"No, I didn't."

"Well, in this style, the painter celebrates the Fatherland. The farmers are always healthy and strong, the fields and the cows are always very full and fat, and the weather is always beautiful." He glanced at my hands, looking for a wedding ring, and found none. "Just as you are, Fräulein . . . ?"

I did not answer. I inched away from him on the bench, to show that I had no interest in him. He was not in the least deterred.

"I work in Brandenburg-Havel," he said. "We have all sorts of farmers thereabouts, but none quite so handsome and robust as those in the picture. Do you think perhaps someone is having a fantasy?"

I suppose I allowed him a little smile at that.

"You know, our Führer loves the arts. He buys two or three hundred paintings every year. If you can get a picture selected for exhibition in the House of German Art, your reputation is made. It also helps if your uncle is on the board of Krupp or your mother has tea with Frau Goebbels."

"Are you a painter?"

"Yes."

"Really! That is your profession?"

"My profession is to supervise the paint department at Arado Aircraft. My training, and my desire, is to be a painter. Did you hear that the Führer gave Sepp Hilz his own money out of his own pocket to build a studio? And Gerhardinger became a professor because the Führer ordered it. From an ordinary painter to a university professor, overnight."

"No, I didn't know any of this."

"Shall we walk through the gallery?"

"All right." He was so much bigger than I was that I found it hard to keep up with him. He talked and talked.

"Personally, I like the classics. The Führer prefers nineteenth-century Austro-Bavarian painters like Spitzweg. And Grützner. Me, I am a big fan of Angelika Kauffmann."

"Uh . . . who?"

"She was an eighteenth-century genius, and good-looking too, at least according to her self-portrait. Klopstock got her interested in German history, and she painted scenes from Hermann's victories." His face was animated. His eyes sparkled. "There's one Kauffmann picture of Hermann returning to the Teutoburg Forest. . . .

The pretty wife who has been home waiting while he was off fighting the Romans comes out to meet him, and the local girls are dancing. I love that picture."

He offered me his hand, "My name is Werner Vetter."

"Mine is Grete Denner."

"Would you like to join me for lunch?"

"If you keep telling me interesting stories about painters."

So he did. This Werner Vetter came from Wuppertal in the Rhineland near Düsseldorf. He knew a great deal about art, much more than I, and that impressed me. He had come to Munich for a two-week vacation. Seven days of it remained.

He asked me to contribute my food coupons (he was the only man I had met who did this) and then ordered sandwiches. Werner cut his with a knife and fork and ate it like a schnitzel. He caught me staring.

"My tante Paula taught me never to eat with my fingers," he explained. "I was about twelve at the time, but some things stick."

He looked so sweet and eccentric, this big man eating the sandwich with such delicacy, that I was quite charmed. On the other hand, he was a member of the party. On the other hand, he had such a friendly smile. On the other hand, he could be a plainclothes member of the SS. On the other hand, he knew so much about art. . . .

"Max Liebermann was a pretty good painter too," he said, washing his lunch down with a beer. "Too bad he was a Jew."

I agreed to meet him the next day. It was the first time I had ever agreed to meet any German twice. We ended up spending the rest of his vacation together.

When I think of the risk I took—he could have been anyone!— I am astounded, even now. But I liked Werner, you see. He was easygoing and entertaining. He loved to talk, so I didn't have to say much. And he seemed so typical of the Germans around me: committed to the Führer, confident of total military victory, scornful of the Russians, full of the latest gossip about Goebbels and his mistresses. During that week with Werner, I learned what I needed to know to successfully pretend to be one of them. It was Grete's training period.

And then, of course, there was the fact that he made me feel like a woman again, the way he held doors open for me and handed me up the train steps every evening. I felt that I had wandered into one of those *Heimat* paintings, that I was turning gold and orange like the idealized cornfields. It was a strange, surreal feeling. One month you're a starving, hunted, undesired liability. The next month you're a Rhinemaiden on a tourist holiday and the king of the Vikings is paying you compliments and trying to persuade you not to catch that last train to Deisenhofen before the evening blackout, so you can stay the night with him.

HE TOOK ME to Nymphenburg, the summer residence of the Wittelsbachs, Bavaria's ancient rulers. We wandered through the vast gardens, the baroque pavilions. We admired display cases full of porcelain figurines—seventeenth-century dandies with cascading wigs and gold-buckled shoes, graceful performers in the costumes of the *commedia dell'arte*.

Werner made fun of it all. He had the workingman's contempt for the aristocracy. He struck mocking poses as a courtier, making people laugh. He lifted me up onto pedestals so that I could imitate a cherub and hug the Wittelsbach coat of arms. I did not dare to think of Mama, slaving I supposed as a maid or a seamstress in some ghetto. I tried to concentrate on being Grete, an Aryan tourist, and to feel completely entitled to my "vacation." But when a policeman passed, I panicked and quickly slipped behind my tall companion.

We went to the English garden, with its endless lawns. He stretched himself out on the grass in the late-summer sun, his head on my knees.

"I have three brothers," he said. "Robert and Gert are at the front. My other brother got himself an easy job sitting on his behind doing work for the party. Gert has a cute little girl named Bärbl, my favorite niece."

We bought a floppy doll for Bärbl, with ochre pigtails and an embroidered mouth. We stopped for beer. Werner poured his down; I sipped mine. He found that enormously amusing, the way I sipped my beer. I made a mental note to try to learn to drink lustily, like a local girl.

"When I was a boy, my father left us," he said. "And my mother, well, my mother liked her beer a bit better than you do. So we boys were very poor and very wild. Mother kept herself clean enough—but not us, and not our house. Our house was a mess. I hate that.

"Tante Paula, mother's sister, would come and take care of us. One day she arrived and found my mother passed out, and she looked under the bed and saw all the stinking, empty bottles, and she simply picked us up—me and my little brother Gert—and took us home with her to Berlin.

"Her husband was a Jew named Simon-Colani, a professor of Sanskrit, a very smart fellow—you know, one of these real thinkers. I guess he thought I had some talent because he decided to send me to art school so that I would have a trade."

He has Jews in his family, I thought. We are not all monsters to him.

"But just because you were trained and talented didn't mean you could get work in the Depression," Werner continued. "I was so broke I had to sleep in the forest one summer. There were a lot of us, young fellows with no way to make a living." His voice was low, raspy. "The Nazis put us into a volunteer labor organization and gave us a place to live and a uniform. So then I began to feel a little better about myself, you know? I wanted to go back to Tante Paula and show her and my uncle how well I had done. And then he died."

I uttered a little cry. I had not expected this end to the story.

"So I went to his funeral."

I pictured a funeral like my father's, the Hebrew prayers, the men chanting, and this tall blond nephew with a Nazi uniform barging in. The whole idea took my breath away.

"Is that why you got a job that keeps you out of the war?" I asked. "Because you joined the party?"

"Ah, no, no—it's because I am blind in one eye. I had a motorbike accident and cracked my skull and severed the optic nerve. Look closely, you'll see." He leaned across the table to show me his blind eye. I leaned across the table to look. He leaned closer. I looked harder. He kissed me.

It was a shock, how much I enjoyed that experience. I was surprised at myself, and I must have blushed. Werner laughed at my embarrassment. "My God, you're a sweet girl," he said.

Werner and I went to see the Frauenkirche, the Peterskirche, the summer palace at Schleissheim. We went to Garmisch Partenkirchen, a beautiful resort area, and spent a whole day climbing in the hills, wading in the streams. I let him pick me up and carry me over rough terrain. Since we were alone, with no soldiers or policemen around, I felt somewhat more relaxed, which was a great danger—because I might forget myself and become myself. So I censored every word and look. Apparently Werner liked that. The self-limited me pleased him. He knew no other version.

Every afternoon we would gather with a crowd at a certain café to hear the broadcast of *Wehrmacht Bericht*, the war news, and update ourselves on the battle then raging at Stalingrad. Hitler had invaded Russia in June of 1941, and the Wehrmacht had been conquering one Russian city after another. But recently the Russians had begun ferocious counterattacks. And winter was coming. For the first time, in the crowd at that café, I saw a glimmer of concern in the Germans. Back at Frau Gerl's house, I had a letter from Frau Doktor saying that she—who had so much against the church—was going to mass every day and saying special prayers as a penance to save the Wehrmacht at Stalingrad.

Werner wasn't worried. "General Paulus is a military genius," he said. "He'll soon take the city, and our men will sleep inside, warm for the winter."

I walked along the third step of a lovely monument to raise myself up. He walked on the ground next to me, his arm around my shoulders. We came to a statue of a naked woman. He pulled me out of sight behind her and kissed me passionately. His embrace engulfed me—big, strong, a sensation of being completely buried and hidden. For me, in my situation, this was an undeniable comfort. I could hide in his shadow. His volubility made it unnecessary for me to say much. I felt protected with Werner, as though he completed my disguise.

As we were heading for the evening train, Werner realized that he had left his camera at the coffee house. The camera was very valuable; you couldn't buy one at that time. However, if we went back to get it, I would have missed my connection to Deisenhofen, and we would have had to spend the night. I was certainly not ready for that.

"You stay and look for the camera," I said. "I'll go home on my own."

"No. You are with me. I shall see you home."

"But it's more important to . . ."

I saw a glint of anger in his eye that scared me.

"Don't argue, Grete. Never argue with me, and never tell me what to do."

Simultaneously gallant and frightening—that was the essential Werner.

He wrote to me several times after his return to Brandenburg and sent me a little model of a sculpture called *The Innocent of the Seine*. For his birthday in September, I thought I might buy him some gloves.

"No, no, no," protested Frau Gerl. "You must send him a cake!"

"But I don't know how to bake a cake."

She smiled. "I do."

And that is how Werner Vetter in Brandenburg came to receive a cake from Grete Denner in Deisenhofen for his birthday, a gesture that he would not forget.

MY RED CROSS training began in October. The course lasted three weeks and took place in a very beautiful retreat in the forest at Locham in the city of Gräfelfing, where members of the Bakers' Guild would go on holiday. It was an old-fashioned wood and stucco building, with the fanciful insignia of the guild painted on the ceiling above the dining area. The forest in autumn was like heaven. So many things about Germany were like that: beautiful settings, bizarre behavior.

I did not become close to the other women working at the Red Cross. I kept to myself and did what was necessary. I said "Good morning" and "Good evening." In the morning, real nurses taught us the rudiments of anatomy and instructed us in the preparation of dressings and bandages. But then in the afternoon, representatives of the Frauenschaft, the women's auxiliary of the Nazi Party, came to instruct us in our real mission: to boost the morale of the wounded and spread the propaganda of German invincibility.

"You must make sure that every single soldier in your care knows that, despite the cowardly British air attack last May, the Cologne cathedral is still standing," said the sturdy, uniformed instructor. "You must also tell everyone that there has been no bombing in the Rhineland. Am I clear?"

"Yes, ma'am," we all said.

In fact, the Rhineland was being crushed by Allied air attacks.

"You are herewith invited to participate in the Germanizing of Vartegau in occupied Poland by settling and raising large families there. Conditions are excellent. You will receive an estate with plenty of cheap labor. The Poles now have come to understand that they are *Untermenschen* and that their destiny is to work for German superiors."

I did not think that many of the Red Cross girls would take all this seriously, but it turned out that thousands of Germans did go and enjoy their time as conquerors in the Vartegau. Later on, when the war had been lost and they came streaming back, destitute, with their hands out, very few of their countrymen wanted to help them.

You will wonder how it was possible for me to endure the same kind of "tomorrow the world" talk that had sent me running away from Hainburg. The answer is simply that I had run out of places to run away to. Surrounded by a population that had been completely sold on monstrous ideas, I simply retreated down, down,

down, trying to live in imitation of the German writer Erich Kästner, whom I had always admired and who responded to the Nazi years with what was called "internal emigration."

The soul withdrew to a rational silence. The body remained there in the madness.

"Remember," said our Nazi tutor. "The Red Cross nurses are nearest and dearest to Hitler's heart. He loves you. And you must return his love without reservation."

She made us swear a special oath to the Führer. We raised our arms. We said "Heil Hitler!" In my soul's fastness, I prayed: "Let the beast Hitler be destroyed. Let the Americans and the RAF bomb the Nazis to dust. Let the German Army freeze at Stalingrad. Let me not be forgotten here. Let someone remember who I really am."

WINTER WAS COMING, and I was waiting for my hospital assignment. As it grew colder, I thought I might make one last trip to Vienna. I wanted so desperately to talk to somebody; I needed to break the silence that was closing over me, to spend a few hours with people to whom I could speak honestly.

I told Frau Gerl that I had to go to Vienna to pick up some winter clothes—she never questioned this explanation—and I got back on the train. The trip felt somewhat safer now because I had a Red Cross ID with my picture on it.

The reception in Vienna broke my heart. Pepi seemed embarrassed at my sudden appearance; he didn't know what he was supposed to do with me anymore. Jultschi's life had deteriorated. She had very little work. Jewish rations had been cut. Little Otti had not been declared a *Mischling*, so now, like all Jewish children, he received no milk at all. He would not be allowed to attend school.

I tried to talk about the Red Cross, Frau Gerl, and Munich, but she didn't want to hear.

"Go back," she said. "I don't want you here anymore."

I had expected to stay with her for three days. After only two, I returned to Deisenhofen, miserable and rejected. And there in Frau Gerl's front hall was a telegram from Werner, saying that he was arriving in Munich in the morning and simply had to see me. It's amazing to consider these turns of fate. If I had stayed three days in Vienna, I would not have returned in time to receive that telegram. But by chance I did—by chance.

Early the next morning, I went to Munich to meet Werner. In the train station, I took my hat off, fearing that he would not recognize me in my winter clothes. But he spotted me instantly. He shouted a greeting, scooped me up in his arms, showered me with kisses, and sat me down for breakfast in the café at the House of German Art.

"I decided on my way to work yesterday that I had to have you," he said, kneading my hand.

"What?"

"That's right. It has to be. You must be my wife."

"What?"

"So I took time off from work by telling the boss at Arado that my mother's house in the Rhineland was bombed and I had to go and make sure she was all right."

"Werner! You can go to prison for that! False excuses! Absenteeism!"

"But they believed me. Look at this face." He grinned. "This is a face you *must* believe. So, when will you marry me?"

"We're in the middle of a war! People shouldn't get married in wartime."

"I am madly in love with you! You do not leave my thoughts

for one minute. I sit in the bathtub, I think of you, and the water begins to boil."

"Oh, Werner, stop that . . ."

"I want to meet your father. I will go to Vienna to meet him. He will think I am wonderful, you'll see."

My mind was racing. I had thought to spend a day with a charming man, bandaging my wounded ego. I had never dreamed of this! What was I going to do? Werner was ready to jump on the train to Vienna and ask my father for my hand in marriage. Where was I going to get a father?

"Now, please, slow down. This is not rational; we have known each other only a few days."

"For me, this is enough. I am a man of action."

"But why didn't you write to me? Why did you endanger yourself by lying to the company?"

He leaned back in his chair, sighed, and hung his head. "Because I felt guilty. Because I told you a lie about being a bachelor. I'm married and in the middle of a divorce, that's the truth, and my little niece Bärbl that I spoke of—well, she is really my daughter Bärbl. So I thought that since I had not been honest with you at first, now I must see you in person face-to-face to tell you the truth. I love you, Grete. You are my inspiration. Come and live with me in Brandenburg, and as soon as the divorce comes through, we can get married."

My coffee sloshed onto the table because my trembling hand could not control the cup. I was terrified. He wanted me to meet his brother Robert and his sister-in-law Gertrude and the famous Tante Paula; he wanted to introduce me to his friends; it was endless.

We went into the museum. He pressed me and pressed me as we walked past those huge Nazi paintings and friezes, by Helmut

Schaarschmidt and Hermann Eisenmenger and Conrad Hommel, portraits of Hitler and Göring, skies full of fire and eagles, grim-faced soldiers with steel helmets, Arno Breker's stone god-men with their Parthenon stances, waving their mighty swords. Werner didn't even look at them. He was holding my hand and talking into my ear, telling me what a nice flat he had and what a good job he had and how happy he would make me. "Think of the bathtub! Think of the sofa! Think of the Volkswagen I am buying for us both!"

It went on and on for hours.

"The world is too unsettled," I protested. "What if you are sent to the front and killed in battle?"

Werner laughed heartily. "They'll never send me to the front! I'm half blind!"

"What if the Red Cross hospital is bombed and I am killed?"

"What if they send you to another hospital and some soldier sees you and falls in love with you as I have done, and I lose you? It would be unbearable! I would not be able to go on living!"

"Oh Werner, stop that. . . ."

"Tell me about your father."

He was a dedicated Jew, and if he knew I was even walking through a museum with the likes of you he would kill me and then have another heart attack himself and die again.

"Tell me about your mother."

She is in Poland, where your vile Führer has sent her.

"Tell me about your sisters."

They are in Palestine, fighting with the British to destroy your army, may God help them.

"Your uncles, your aunts, your cousins, your old boyfriends."

Gone. Maybe dead. So deep in hiding from your Nazi plague that they might as well be dead.

"I love you. I must have you."

No, no, leave me alone. Go away. I have too many people to protect. Christl. Frau Doktor. Pepi. You.

"You!" I cried. "I cannot be involved with you!"

Rassenschande, the scandal of racial mixing—a crime.

"Why not? My God, Grete, are you promised to someone else? Did you steal my heart and not tell me? How can this be?"

He looked hurt, destroyed by the idea that I might not want him. I recognized his pain because I had felt it myself. I threw my arms around him and whispered violently into his ear:

"I cannot marry you because I am Jewish! My papers are false! My picture is in the files of the Gestapo in Vienna!"

Werner stopped in his tracks. He held me away from him at arm's length. I dangled in his hands. His face turned hard. His eyes narrowed. His mouth tightened.

"Why, you little liar," he said. "You had me completely fooled."

He looked as grim and determined as one of the SS men in Krause's painting.

Idiot, I thought. *You have signed your own death warrant.* I waited for the sword of Breker's god-man to fall. I imagined my blood spreading on the marble floor, the horrific pounding on Christl's door.

"So, now we are even," Werner said. "I lied to you about being divorced, and you lied to me about being an Aryan. Let's call it square and get married." He cradled me in his arms and kissed me.

I think I must have become a bit hysterical then.

"You are a madman! We cannot be together. They will discover us."

"How? Are you going to tell someone else besides me about your true identity?"

"Stop joking, Werner; this is serious. Maybe you don't understand somehow, but they could imprison you for being with me. They will kill me and my friends and send you to one of their terrible camps. Why aren't you afraid? You must be afraid!"

He laughed. I was imagining him at the end of a Nazi rope, like the Frenchman who had taken up with a Jewish girl from the *Arbeitslager*, and he was laughing and carrying me into a room full of golden landscapes.

To this day I cannot understand what made Werner Vetter so brave when his countrymen were so craven.

"I'm really twenty-eight, not twenty-one," I said.

"Good. That's a relief because at twenty-one you might be too young to get married."

He stopped in an alcove next to a bust of Hitler.

"Do you cook everything as well as that cake you sent me for my birthday?"

I swear it was the spirit of my mama, appearing like an angel whenever I needed domestic advice, who must have told me to say yes.

Of course this was a bald-faced lie. To understand Werner Vetter, remember that it was perfectly possible for me to tell him that I was Jewish in Germany at the height of Nazi power, but it was essential for me to lie about being a good cook.

"Go back to Brandenburg," I whispered. "Forget about this whole thing. I will not hold you to any promise."

He went back to Brandenburg, but he did not think it over. He had made up his mind, you see, and when Werner did that, there was no stopping him.

You ask me whether I thought he would denounce me, whether the Gestapo would come knocking on Frau Gerl's door.

I did not think that. I trusted Werner. For the life of me I do not know why. Maybe it was because I really had no choice.

He sent me several telegrams saying that he had arranged for me to come and stay with the wife of a friend of his. Her name was Hilde Schlegel. She had an extra room and would take me in until his divorce was final.

I was afraid to receive any more of these ardent telegrams, afraid that they might bring me to the attention of the SS. I was afraid that my Red Cross assignment, when it came, would send me out to the territories in Poland, where I would need a national identity card which I could not possibly get. I was afraid that if I stayed in Frau Gerl's house, the Gestapo would begin to wonder who I was. After all, she had an anti-Nazi record. I thought that if I went with Werner, I would be better hidden: a little *Hausfrau* in a kitchen living with a member of the Nazi Party who worked for the company that made the planes which were dropping the bombs on London. A man with clearances. A trusted man who would never be challenged. Of course to be this man's wife was a better disguise than being single.

When I wrote to Pepi saying that I had become engaged to Werner, he became irate. How could I do such a thing? How could I even consider marrying a non-Jew? "Think of what your father would say!" he protested. "Think of how much I love you!"

Well, I had learned the hard way just how much he loved me. Had Pepi arranged for me to sleep securely for even one night in Vienna? His mother, with all her connections—had she even made me a cup of tea while I was hiding? Do you know that when Pepi heard what Frau Doktor had said about him—that he belonged to me because I had slept with him—he refused even to speak to her? This wonderful woman, who had helped me so much, who could have helped him too—he never even thanked her for what she had done; he never even went to meet her. He could have run away with me before the war. We could have been in England long ago; we could have been in Israel building a Jewish country; we could have been out of this nightmare. But no! Pepi couldn't leave because of his blasted bloody racist mother! That was how much he loved me!

And here was this white knight in Munich, who came to me fearless and adoring, and he offered me not just safety but love. Of course I accepted. I accepted and I thanked God for my good fortune.

Frau Gerl and her husband went into the woods and stole a little Christmas tree for me. It was illegal to cut down trees at this time, but they wanted to send me away with a present. On December 13, 1942, I came to Werner Vetter in Brandenburg with that tree strapped to my bag.

Leopold Hahn, my father.

Klothilde Hahn, my mother.

At the spa in Badgastein. *Left to right*, my cousin Jultschi, a hotel guest, me, another hotel guest, my sister Mimi, my little sister Hansi.

Pepi tying his shoe on a visit to Stockerau in 1939.

This picture, taken on the same visit, is the only one I have of Pepi and me together. He came to visit me when I was caring for my grandfather, who had suffered a stroke.

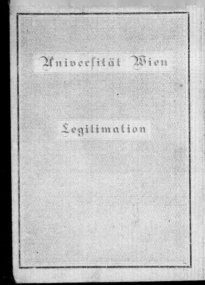

My student identification at the University of Vienna, 1933.

This picture was taken
when I was nineteen years old.

Pepi in 1937,
at age twenty-four.

After the Germans took over Austria—the Anschluss of 1938—all Jews were given new identification cards. Men were given the middle name Israel. Women were given the middle name Sara.

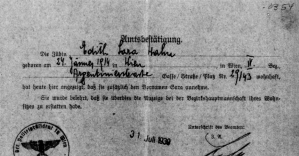

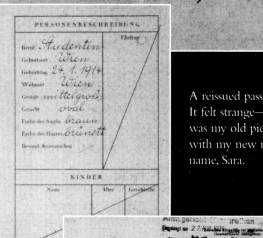

A reissued passport. It felt strange—it was my old picture with my new middle name, Sara.

The eviction notice that banished Mama and me from our home. After this, we lived in the Vienna ghetto.

The asparagus plantation at Osterburg. These were some of my co-workers, bending over the furrowed fields.

Our overseer's little daughter, Ulrike Fleschner, then about four years old, holding a Nazi flag.

Herr Fleschner, the overseer, is on the left, wearing a white shirt. Next to him are Frau Telscher, one of my roommates at Osterburg, and Pierre, a French prisoner of war whom the Germans called Franz. The baskets are for asparagus.

These are letters Pepi and I exchanged to practice English when I was in the slave labor camp. He corrected me but I never corrected him. I was by choice the pupil and he the teacher.

The Nazis required that all ID pictures show the left ear. I used this one, which Pepi took in 1939, because it was the least recognizable photograph of me. The Gestapo had a copy in its files.

Absender:

Wohnort, auch Zustell- oder Leitpostamt

Straße, Hausnummer, Gebäudeteil, Stockwerk oder Postschließfachnummer

Postkarte

Altkleider-
und
Spinnstoffsammlung 1942
1.–15. Juni

Herrn

Dr Josef Rosenfeld

Wien X

The last notes Mama
wrote to Pepi before
she was deported.
"They won't let me
stay behind," she
wrote. "I have to
go.... Please tell
Edith.... God will
stand by her and me."

Lieber Pepi!

Lieber Pepi!

In this letter, I wrote to
Pepi that my friend Mina
Katz and I had enjoyed the
sweets he'd sent me and
that my quota had been
raised to 35,000 boxes
per day.

28.II-

Liebe Edith!

        Ich komme eben aus der Prinz-Eugenstrasse, habe keinen Auf-
schub mehr bekommen und muss noch heute in die Schule. Es ist
blödsinnig, jetzt habe ich Herzweh, weil ich doch damit gerechnet
habe, dass ich noch ein paar Tage draussen bleiben kann. Nun, kann
man nichts machen. Die Schule und Schnee schaufeln ist ja nicht das
Ärgste, wenn nur der Transport nicht ginge. Ich glaube aber schon,
dass er gehen wird, schon weil ich Unglücksrabe dabei bin, ist ja
nichts anderes möglich. Schreibe weiter an Tante, ich werde sicher
mit ihr irgendwie in Verbindung bleiben. Sei aber vorsichtig, nachdem
Du ja jetzt im Heim bist und die Briefe nicht desinfisziert werden.
Jemand anderer soll das Kuvert schreiben und sie wird die Briefe
vorsichtig öffnen.
        Bei Deiner 1. Mama war ich zweimal umsonst, gestern traf
ich sie zufällig in der Stadtbahn und sie sagte mir, ich soll be-
vor ich einrücke zu ihr kommen, weil sie mir was mitgeben will.
Ich nehme dankend an und gehe jetzt gleich zu ihr, denn in der
Schule kann man alles brauchen. Sie sei recht brav. Auch Lieserls
Vater besuche ich über seinen Wunsch noch heute, mit einem Wort,
ich lebe von schnorren.
        Sei nicht traurig, mein liebes Mädel, es besteht ja noch
immer die Möglichkeit, dass noch alles gut wird, also wollen wir
die Hoffnung nicht aufgeben. Du musst recht rasch ganz gesund
werden, Aschersleben nicht zu schwer nehmen und vor allem, mich
recht lieb behalten. Ja, willst Du. Natürlich schreibe ich wenn
ich kann, wenn Du aber keine Post von mir hast, sei versichert,
ich denke an Dich.
        Ich küsse Dich recht herzlich,
                                        Deine
                                               Mina

The last letter I received from Mina before she was deported. She wrote in
code. "Prinz-Eugenstrasse" refers to the headquarters of the Gestapo in
Vienna. "Tante" ("Aunt") refers to Frau Doktor Maria Niederall, who helped
me so much.

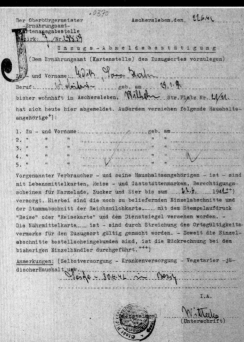

My Jewish ration card.
I was supposed to use it
when I returned to Vienna
from Aschersleben, but
I never did.

I borrowed my friend Christl Denner's lilac blouse for this picture, which I gave as a gift to Pepi in 1940 just before I was taken to the *Arbeitslager,* the labor camp. When Pepi died in 1977, it was still sitting on his desk at home.

Christl Denner Beran, my dear friend, who died in 1992. She gave me her identity papers and saved my life. Christl is wearing a dress my mother made for her.

Maria Niederall gave me this picture of herself. I kept it with me in Brandenburg.

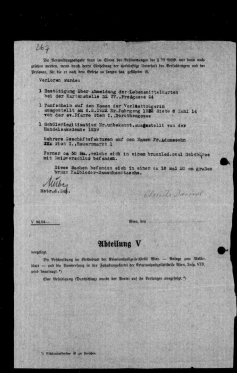

Christl made this application for new papers to replace those she told the police she had accidentally dropped into the Danube.

The marriage certificate of Werner Vetter and "Margarethe Denner." You can see the "proof" that we were both "German-blooded" *("deutschblütig"),* as well as additional notes about the birth of our daughter and the revision, in July 1945, when my real name was noted.

Werner Vetter
before the war . . .

. . . and after he was
drafted into the
Wehrmacht in
September 1944.

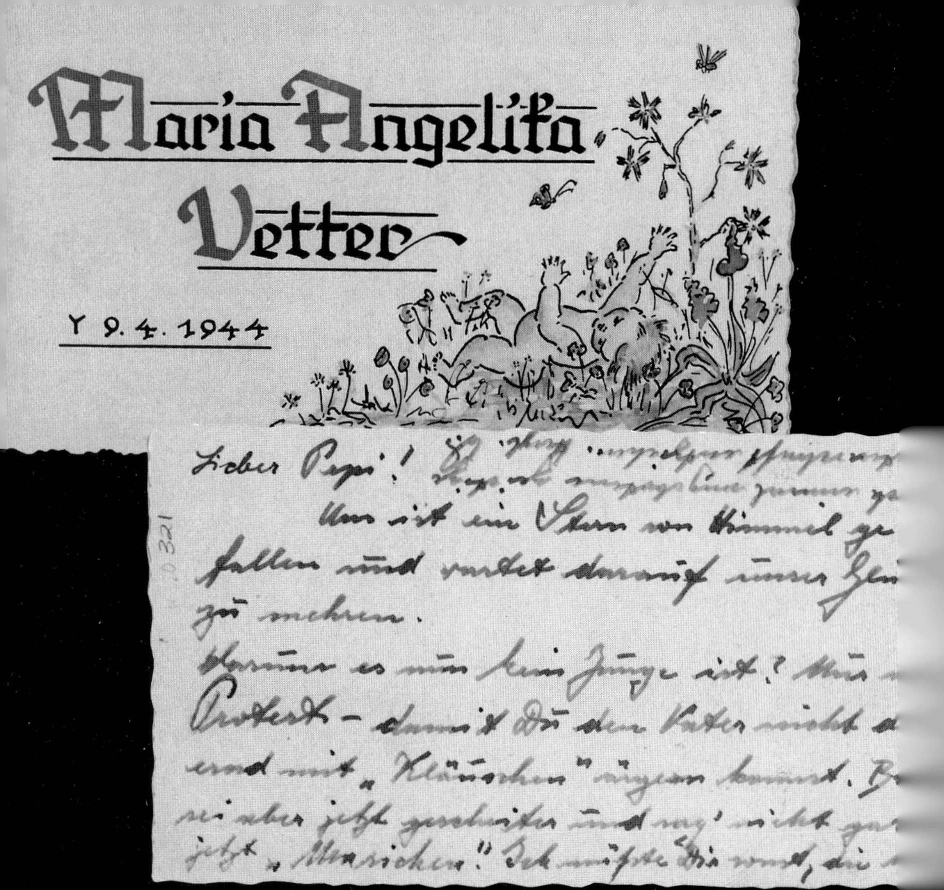

Maria Angelika
Vetter
9. 4. 1944
Lieber Pepi!
Uns ist ein Stern vom Himmel ge-
fallen und wartet darauf unser
zu suchen.

Werner designed and hand-painted this birth announcement after our daughter, Angela ("Angelika"), was born in April 1944. This one was sent to Pepi with a nc on the back: "A star has fallen from the heavens. . . ."

In the summer of 1944, Werner took this picture of me pushing Angela's pram and walking with Bärbl, Werner's four-year-old daughter from his first marriage.

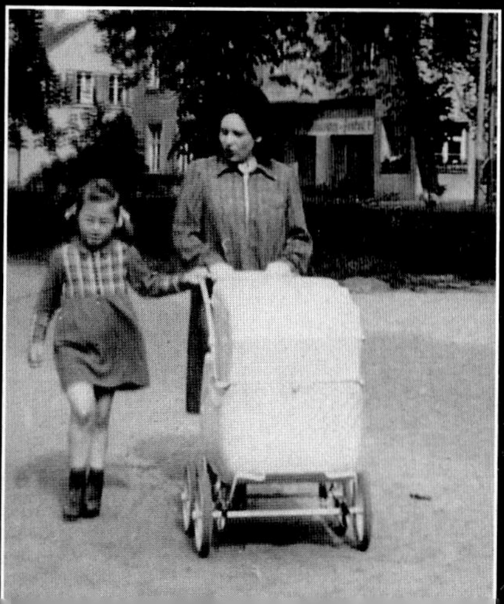

Werner smuggled out this letter to me from a Siberian prison camp. It was packed into the lining of an eyeglasses case and delivered by a man who tossed it through my door and left instantly.

Angela was three years old in 1947 when this photo was taken by Werner, after his return.

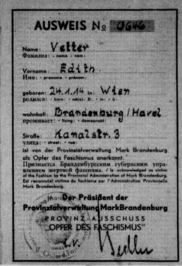

My identification when I was a judge in Brandenburg. "OPFER DES FASCHISMUS" means "A Victim of Facism."

I acquired this ID in 1948. It gave the false address I needed for my flight to England. Although I paid the rent for months, I stayed there only a few weeks before my departure.

This picture of Christl Denner Beran and me was taken in 1985 at the Israeli Embassy in Vienna, where Christl received a medal for her heroism and permission to plant a tree in the Garden of the Righteous Gentiles at Yad v'Shem in Jerusalem.

David Harrison

Edith Hahn Beer and her daughter, Angela Schlüter, in 1998.

NINE

■

A Quiet Life on Immelmannstrasse

$\mathcal{I}$ BEGAN TO live a lie as an everyday ordinary *Hausfrau*. It was as good a lie as any that a woman could live in Nazi Germany, because the regime celebrated female domesticity and made itself extremely generous to housewives.

My manner was quiet. My habit was to listen. I behaved in a friendly way toward everyone; I became close to no one. With all my strength, I tried to convince myself that I was really and truly Grete Denner. I forced myself to forget everything dear to me, all my experience of life, my education; to become a bland, prosaic, polite person who never ever said or did anything to arouse attention. The result was that on the outside I seemed like a calm, silent sea and inside I was stormy—tense, turbulent, stressed, sleepless, worrying constantly because I must always appear to be worried about nothing.

Werner lived in company housing, in one of more than three thousand apartments built for employees of the Arado Aircraft Company in an embankment of identical straight-faced buildings on the east end of town. Our flat was on Immelmannstrasse, which is now called Gartz Street. They took the rent right out of Werner's salary before he brought it home.

Arado Aircraft made war planes, among them the world's first jet bomber. During the war, it was the biggest armaments industry in Brandenburg district, which included not only the city of Brandenburg but Potsdam and Berlin. The company's directors, Felix Wagonfür and Walter Blume, were rich and famous. Blume became the head of military economy for the Reich, and Albert Speer made him a professor.

By 1940, Arado had 8,000 workers; by 1944 it had 9,500. Almost thirty-five percent were foreign-born. You may ask why the Nazis would allow so many foreigners to work in a high-security company. I tell you, I really believe it was because Hitler insisted that Aryan women must be protected breeding machines whose major task was to stay home and have babies.

We heard that the Americans and the British encouraged mothers to work in the war industries, that they provided child care and paid high wages to a highly motivated, patriotic workforce. But the Führer rejected this idea. German women received extra rations, even medals of honor, for breeding profusely. So places like Arado depended mainly on boys who were too young, men who were too old, girls who knew they would be better off pregnant, and workers from conquered countries, a group not especially motivated to break production records for the Luftwaffe.

Arado's foreign workers lived at eight labor camps. The Dutch, especially the aircraft designers, lived quite decently. So did the French, whom the Germans had come to admire for their skill and diligence. And so did the Italians, who were supposed to be our allies. Some alliance! The Germans generally thought the Italians were cowardly and ill-mannered, and the Italians thought the Germans were bombastic and uncultured. Also, the Italians hated German food. A neighbor of mine once told me, with horror, that she had seen an Italian worker at a restaurant spit out his sausage with a disgusted "Yuch!" ("Right onto the floor!" she exclaimed) and then storm out, shouting that only the barbarian Huns could possibly consume such offal.

All the "Eastern" foreign workers—Poles, Serbs, Russians, and others—lived in squalor, under guard, in fear.

Thankfully, it was mostly the French and Dutch who worked under Werner's supervision in the Arado paint department. He made sure that there was enough paint and that the insignia on the aircraft were applied correctly, and he earned quite a good salary. His apartment was by far the nicest in our building.

Each of the workers' buildings had four stories, with three apartments on each floor. Our flat was on the first floor, facing the street. The big vacant lot across the way, scheduled to become a park, as yet contained nothing but a row of trash bins. We had a bedroom, a big combination kitchen and living room, a smaller room, and a bathroom—with a bath! Actually, it was a gas heating unit with a large kettle on top. You could heat water in the kettle and then empty it into the tub for a bath. We alone, among the tenants, possessed this luxury.

Our stove came already prepared for war. It was electric; but if the electricity were to be cut off, coal bricks could fuel it.

Werner took great care not to tempt the neighbors to gossip. He did not bring me to live in his flat until his divorce was final, in January 1943. Before that time, I stayed with his friend's wife, Hilde Schlegel, a warmhearted girl with bouncing curls, who lived a few houses away. Hilde's husband, Heinz, also a painter, had been sent to the Eastern front. She longed for a child and had recently undergone an operation to help her conceive. Since the Nazis were generous to the wives of soldiers, she had plenty to live on and did not have to work.

"When Heinz went to the army, they gave me enough money to go see him," Hilde said. "He had been wounded, but only slightly, and he was in a military hospital in Metz. Ach, what a wonderful time that was, Grete—a real honeymoon, my first vacation ever. Because, as you must know, it wasn't always like this. Let me tell you, we had some hard times back when I was a kid. For twelve years Papa had no steady job. We lived on charity mostly. Then, when our dear Führer came to power, things got much better. Just about all the young people we knew joined the Hitler Youth. When I was fifteen I went to a Nazi Party banquet, and they served rolls with butter. It was the first time I ever tasted butter." Is that the reason? I wondered. Is that why they averted their eyes, made themselves blind? For the butter? "I feel that everything we have we owe to our dear Führer, may he live forever."

She clinked her teacup against mine.

Hilde became my closest "friend" in Brandenburg, if you can say that about a woman who has no real idea who you are. She walked me down Wilhelmstrasse toward the town, to show me the stores where I could do my marketing. And she told me all about Werner's first wife, Elisabeth.

"Huge! Taller than Werner! Gorgeous. But temperamental! Ach, what shouting, what fighting! Ask Frau Ziegler in the flat across the hall from Werner if I'm not telling the truth. They had terrible battles. He hit her! And she hit him back! No wonder he finally went and found himself a proper sweet little girl like you."

Elisabeth had taken most of the furniture when she moved out, but we were left with quite enough to get along. Werner lugged all his tools and paints and brushes into the "little room," transforming it into his workshop. We kept a single bed in there, in case anyone came to visit. Against the interior wall, he put together a work table; and then, on little hooks, he hung all of his tools, neatly organized by size and function. To make me feel welcome, he decided to decorate the colorless apartment by painting all around the living room a mural on the wooden section of the wall.

Every night, he would come home from work, change his clothes, and eat the evening meal, which I prepared; then, he would go to work on that mural. He used a technique called *Schleiflack*. I seem to remember that it required several steps of sanding, varnishing, painting, and finishing—a messy, dusty, slow job. He stole paint from the Arado warehouse, bright colors which usually sparkled on the wings of the planes bombing England. Night after night, Werner scraped and sanded, sketched an outline, put down a base coat, let it dry, sanded again, painted again. I sat in a chair near the doorway and watched him, remembering the craftsmen I had seen in Vienna, climbing like acrobats an their scaffolding, painting the facades of the boutiques and the hotels. I was so impressed with him, so filled with admiration, that I needed no other entertainment than to watch him at work. His face was smudged and shining with sweat and the intensity of his pleasure in the project. The gold hair on his strong forearms bristled with plaster dust.

Soon a frieze of fruit and flowers appeared, encircling the kitchen, a network of twining vines, curling leaves, apples, carrots, radishes, onions, and cherries—a garland representing all the bounties of peacetime inside which we two would live, as in a charmed circle.

When he had finished his mural, Werner crouched in the middle of the floor and swiveled slowly on his paint-spattered shoes. His bright blue eyes glittered with critical intensity as he looked for places where finishing touches were needed.

"What do you think?" he asked.

"I think it is beautiful," I said. "And you are a great artist."

I sank down on the floor beside him and held him tight. I did not mind that some paint ended up on my clothes.

In January, after the divorce came through, I moved into that flat, and when Werner closed the door behind us, I became a privileged middle-class German woman. I had a home, a safe place, a protector. I remembered the blessing of the rabbi who had sat by my bed and patted my hand and prayed in Hebrew for me in Badgastein. I felt very lucky.

WE ENJOYED A very quiet, peaceful relationship, Werner and I. But you must understand that I was not a normal companion, like Elisabeth or Frau Doktor, full of demands and opinions. I was concerned only that everything should be as Werner liked it. I never deliberately reminded him that I was Jewish. I only wanted him to forget that, to put that fact away in the back of his mind, as I had put away Edith Hahn, and just let it gather dust there, barely remembered. I put all my energy and imagination into learning how to do the one thing I had lied about being able to do—cook. Frau Doktor sent me packages of lentils and a book of recipes: "Cook with love," it said, and you can be sure that I did.

Every morning I would get up at five, make us breakfast, and make Werner's lunch, and he would go to work on his bike. I ate a potato in the morning so he would have enough bread for his lunchtime sandwich. I could see clearly that before my arrival he hadn't been eating enough, that he could not really feed himself adequately. Early on he had awful headaches in the evening, hunger headaches; I had made their acquaintance myself, so I knew how he suffered, and I tried very hard to feed him well. Just in case I was held up at night at the Städtische Krankenhaus, the hospital where the Red Cross had placed me, I taught him to make *Kartoffel-puffer*, pancakes made of fried potatoes and anything else one could find. Werner Vetter gained two kilos after I moved in.

Tante Paula Simon-Colani, a tiny, powerful woman whom I immediately adored, came often to visit from Berlin, to give herself some relief from the constant bombing there. She told me that Werner's family had an inherited obsession with cleanliness.

"Dust, my dear," said Tante Paula. "Dust as though your life depended upon it."

Good advice, as it turned out. One day, Werner came home before I did and, just to satisfy the family passion, reached up and ran his forefinger along the top edge of the door to see if there was any dust up there. He was tall enough to do that. To clean off the top edge of the door, I had had to climb on a chair. But I had done it, thank God, because Tante Paula had warned me. So there was no dust.

"I am extremely pleased with the way you are keeping the house," he said that evening. "Even the upper edges of the doors are dusted. This is good, very good."

"Ah, well, but I have an advantage—Tante Paula warned me that you would be checking." I laughed, sitting on his lap, wiggling my fingers through the buttons on his shirt and tickling his belly. I think he might have been just a little embarrassed. He never bothered me about cleaning again.

Werner had a problem with authority, which was a very serious problem indeed when you consider that he was living in the most authoritarian society in the world at that time.

I believe he handled his problem by lying. He was an inspired liar. My lies were small, believable. His were huge, colorful. If he didn't want to get up for work one morning, he would say his brother's house in Berlin had been blown up by the RAF, the children were in the street homeless, and he simply had to go and help them. And Arado would believe him.

He loved lying to his superiors at Arado. His lies made him feel free—in fact, superior to his superiors—because he knew something they didn't know, and he was taking the day off while they were working.

Years later, I became friendly with one of his other wives. She said Werner told her that my father had committed suicide by jumping from a window with a typewriter tied around his neck. Why would Werner tell such a story? Perhaps just to entertain her, perhaps just to entertain himself, to make life a bit more thrilling. I sometimes think that was what sparked his interest in me too: the thrill of a lie. After all, an obedient, docile, willing, loving, cooking, cleaning, mending Jewish mistress was not something every German had around the house in the winter of 1942–43.

Werner and I never talked about the Jews or what might be happening to my mother in the east. To speak of it could only have been dangerous for me, because either he might have felt guilty, as a German; or he might have felt frightened, as someone who was running a risk by harboring a fugitive.

He knew that I was a well-educated woman, but that certainly was not something I reminded him about. He didn't like people who had any claim to superiority over him. So I carefully limited my opinions to practical matters. For example, when Werner was divorcing Elisabeth, I told him that in the custody battle for little Bärbl, he should ask for six weeks' visitation.

"If she comes to us for just a short time, you won't be able to have any influence on her," I said. "But if she comes for six weeks, then it will be a real vacation with Father and she will get to know you and love you."

Werner requested this from the court. When his divorce was granted—in January 1943—and he received six weeks' visitation rights, he was so happy that he waltzed me around the apartment, singing (very quietly), "Isn't it just dandy to have a lawyer in the house?"

Every month, he sent out money to buy the car that had been invented especially for the Nazis, to be the dream vehicle of the common man—the Volkswagen. I had no faith in it. I figured it was just something else that the government was doing to get money from the people.

"You will never get that car," I said, as I pressed his shirts.

"I've already paid for several months."

"I promise you, dearest, you will never get it."

He looked at me thoughtfully for a moment. Some instinct must have told him that what I said was true, because he soon stopped paying and thereby became one of the few Germans not to be robbed in this unique manner.

Sexually, Werner was a powerful man. He insisted that we prepare for bed together. He never stayed up after me. I never stayed up after him. Another woman whom stress and tension had rendered sleepless the night before, who had worked all day as a nurse's aide in a municipal hospital, who had cleaned the house and made the dinner, might have said, "No, not tonight. I'm tired." But not I. I knew I was living with a tiger. I wanted the tiger to be sated and happy, with a full belly, ironed shirts, no arguments.

Does that seem like an impossibility? Can a woman be satisfying in bed when she is pretending to be somebody else, when everything she loved has disappeared and she is living in perpetual terror of discovery and death? The answer is, quite truthfully, yes. Sex is one of the few things you can do in life that make you forget all the things you cannot do.

And besides—you must understand this—I cared for Werner, more and more each day,

His first wife, Elisabeth, haunted me. She didn't even live in Brandenburg anymore; she had moved with Bärbl to Bitterfeld northwest of Halle in central Germany—but sometimes I felt that she was sitting at our table, sleeping on our pillow.

"She came by when you were at work," Frau Ziegler told me. "She was asking about you. Who is this Viennese girl, what's her story? I told her, Elisabeth, Grete is a very nice person; you ought to be happy that Bärbl is going to have such a nice stepmother."

I could see from the malicious twinkle in her eye how much Elisabeth's old neighbor had enjoyed increasing her discomfort about me. If she had only had any idea how much she was increasing my discomfort about Elisabeth!

Elisabeth asked another neighbor if there was any chance that Werner still loved her and might want her again. What was I going to do about this? I wanted to stay with Werner, but I dreaded the idea of marriage—the background checks, the papers, and the questions. On the other hand, I lived in fear that if I didn't marry Werner soon, his former wife might take him away.

If it seems that I was haunted by Elisabeth, then you should have seen Werner. There we were in the kitchen one night, the picture of domestic peace. I was darning the holes in Werner's socks. He was reading a novel he had borrowed from the Arado library. Suddenly his book fell to the floor. He stood up straight. He began to speak.

"You are responsible for all of our problems with money," he said angrily. "You have no sense about how to spend or how to save. You buy clothes, you wear them once, and then you throw them away. It's because you are lazy, too lazy to do the laundry, to iron, to behave like a real woman should."

I didn't know what to think. Was he speaking to me? I was the only person in the room, but the person he was speaking to was nothing like the person I was.

"Werner, what's the matter?" I asked in my small voice. He did not even hear me. He began to stride up and down the kitchen, rubbing his chest as though trying not to have a heart attack, dragging his fingers through his neat hair.

"I work like a horse. I lie and invent stories at Arado so that you will have all the things you want. I buy you presents, I buy presents for little Bärbl, and still you are not satisfied, still you say this friend of yours has this, and that friend of yours has that! You want more and more and more!"

I realized that he was talking to Elisabeth, that somehow or other his mind had taken him into the middle of a conversation he had once had with her, probably right here in this room.

"Werner, please, you were divorced from Elisabeth. You are a wonderful provider. Look at me; I am Grete. We are living together here in peace and happiness. I am mending your socks. Please. Stop yelling."

He smashed his fist down on the kitchen table. The forks and knives flew up. The dishes rattled.

"I will not take this anymore," he yelled. "I am the master in my house, and I expect to be obeyed! Nothing new will be bought here until The Victory! You will have to live with the clothing you have! And anything that is bought for Bärbl I will buy myself!"

He fell back into his chair, panting and exhausted. I waited for him to return to himself. It took some time. I thought: Edith, you are living with a lunatic. But then again, who else but a lunatic would live with you?

WERNER'S PRIZED POSSESSION was his radio, a fine piece of equipment. On the dial, he had inserted a little piece of brown paper. As long as that little piece of brown paper stayed in place, you could hear nothing but the German news.

The radio was our chief source of entertainment, our terror, and our solace. The "Army Report" was available to everybody. This was what Werner and I had heard when we were dating in Munich. The radio brought us our favorite music request show, romantic songs from Zarah Leander, short concerts by the Berlin Philharmonic on Sunday nights, and Goebbels declaiming his weekly editorial from *Das Reich*, the Nazi "newsmagazine" (if one can imagine such a thing). If you dared listen to the foreign news, and you were caught, you could be sent to a concentration camp—and thousands were.

During the first days of February 1943, the radio told us about the defeat of the German Army at Stalingrad. Even this terrible news was presented in a theatrical, almost beautiful way by order of the brilliant Goebbels.

We heard muffled drums—the second movement of Beethoven's Fifth Symphony.

"The Battle of Stalingrad has ended," said the announcer. "True to its oath to fight to the last breath, the Sixth Army under the exemplary leadership of Field Marshall Paulus has been overcome by the superiority of the enemy and by the unfavorable circumstances confronting our forces."

Hitler declared that there would be four days of national mourning during which all places of entertainment would be closed.

So closely controlled and manipulated was the news that even this disaster could somehow be made to stimulate renewal of the Germans' fighting resolve. On February 18, the radio brought us Goebbels's "total war" speech at the Sportspalast, in which he called on Germans to make greater and greater sacrifices, to believe with greater and greater fervor in ultimate victory, to give themselves body and soul to the Führer, to adopt the motto "Now, people, rise, and storm and break loose!" Meanwhile the thousands in the stadium were screaming wildly: *Führer befiehl, wir folgen!* "Führer, command us and we shall follow!" With such hysteria, with such total control of the news, it was entirely possible not to feel how severe the defeat at Stalingrad had been, not to put it together with the news of Rommel's defeat at El Alamein and the Allied landings in North Africa, not to understand that the war had turned against Germany and that this was the beginning of the end, but to still believe that Hitler would soon conquer England and the world.

To live in ignorance, all you had to do was listen only to the Nazi news.

It was evening. Werner was working late, and I was alone. I sat looking at that piece of brown paper holding the radio dial firmly and permanently at the politically correct place.

"What if I were to move?" suggested the little piece of paper.

"You can't move," I answered.

"I could slip from my spot."

"Not all alone without help."

"You could help me move . . ."

"No! Impossible! Anybody who does that will go to Dachau or Buchenwald or Orianenburg or God only knows where. A Red Cross nurse who helped you move from your spot on the dial could end up in Ravensbrück."

"So, if you're so afraid," said the little piece of brown paper, "leave me where I am and continue to live in darkness."

I turned my back on the radio, thinking to myself that I was going mad like my husband, arguing with chimeras. I got down on my hands and knees and scrubbed the kitchen floor. But the little piece of paper called to me.

"Hello, there! *Hausfrau!* You know what's on the other end of this dial? The BBC."

"Shh!"

"And Radio Moscow."

"Quiet."

"And the Voice of America."

"Shut up!"

"All in German, of course."

The man upstairs had started hammering on a bookcase he was building, as he did most nights after work. His wife—I think her name may have been Karla—was singing as she ironed their clothes.

"Have you ever considered these lines by Goethe?" said the little piece of paper.

Cowardly thoughts, anxious hesitation,
Womanish timidity, timorous complaints
Won't keep misery away from you
And will not set you free.

So, challenged by my own motto, I at last snatched the brown piece of paper off the radio dial and threw it away. Under cover of the racket upstairs, for the very first time, I tuned in the BBC.

Werner came home from work, tired and hungry. I gave him his dinner. I held him tightly in my arms. And right before we went to sleep, I said to him, "Listen . . ." Very, very quietly, using pillows and eiderdowns to muffle the sound, I turned on the BBC news. We were told that of 285,000 German soldiers at the battle of Stalingrad, only 49,000 had been evacuated. More than 140,000 had been slaughtered, and 91,000 had been taken prisoner. The prisoners were starving, freezing, frostbitten, being marched away in the subzero cold. Although we could not know it then, only about 6,000 of these men would ever return to Germany.

Tears rolled down Werner's face.

From that time on, I listened to the foreign radio three or four times a day, and Werner listened too. Radio Moscow we did not believe. (Its broadcasts always began with "*Tod der Deutschen Okkupanten!*"—"Death to the German invaders!") The BBC we thought sometimes exaggerated. The Voice of America did not come in very clearly. Beromünster of Switzerland we tended to find most objective.

We shared our new discovery with Tante Paula during one of her visits. She wrote and thanked us for showing her the "beautiful pictures."

One day when I went across the hall to bring some flour to Frau Ziegler, I heard a familiar sound from Karla's flat. It was just one tone, but I recognized it as one of the call notes of the BBC. Instantly I understood that our noisy upstairs neighbors had fooled us and everybody else with their hammering and singing. They were listening to the forbidden radio stations, just as we were.

Outside of our house, Werner appeared to be a party stalwart, unshakable in his faith in Hitler. I know this because I met people he worked with at Arado, who spoke to me as though they expected me to share the opinions they thought Werner held.

"I agree with Werner, Fräulein Denner," said one of our neighbors. "Churchill is a drunkard and an upper-class English snob, and he has no rapport with his people. They don't adore him the way we love our Führer. They will abandon him sooner or later and England will be ours."

"As Werner always says, the Führer knows best," said another— this about a man who was living with a Jewish fugitive and listening every night to the foreign news.

WORKING AT THE Städtische Krankenhaus solved one problem for me: I no longer had to go every month to have my ration card booklet stamped.

You see, ordinary Reich citizens like Werner received their ration cards from a delivery man. Not me. I had to go to the food ration office in person—a terrifying trip, because I had no legal registration card, no identification that said who I was and where I lived. That card, which enabled a person to acquire all the other cards needed for food and clothing, was sitting in a file in Vienna and belonged to Christl Denner.

When you changed your address, your card went into a sort of transit file. When you arrived at your new address, your card followed you. My last registration had taken place at Aschersleben. When I returned to Vienna, I should have registered there, but of course I had not. So now I lived in fear of conducting some transaction that would force the Germans to look for my card and say,

"Well, but Fräulein, where is your card? And who is this other Fräulein Christina Maria Margarethe Denner in Vienna?"

I had to avoid such an encounter at all costs—it would have meant disaster for me and for Christl. So I continued to eat from cards issued against Christl's registration for a six-month holiday. Her ration card book was almost completely filled, and I was very afraid they would tell me that I could no longer use it, that I must actually live in the place where the holiday was being spent. I was terribly afraid of that. For days before I had to go to the food office, I would lie sleepless with anxiety. I rehearsed my lies over and over. At the desk in the office, waiting for the bureaucrat's stamp, I would tremble and pray, "One more time, dear God. Please let them overlook the overfilled ration card booklet one more time." I never shared my fears with Werner because then he might be afraid as well.

Imagine, then, what a relief it was, as of February 1943, to be registered in the Red Cross *Gemeinschafts-verpflegung*, the group catering service at the hospital. I no longer had to make the terrible trip to the food ration office, because I didn't have to get that card stamped.

I worked a twelve-hour shift and received 30 reichsmarks per month. This was more pocket money than pay, but of course it was monumental compared with the starvation wages at the *Arbeitslager*. All the nurses ate the midday meal at a long table. The head nurse sat at the top; the others, arranged by rank, sat along the sides. I was at the very bottom of the table. At first, the head nurse would say a prayer before we ate, but by the spring of 1943 the prayer was outlawed.

On my uniform I had a Red Cross brooch, and in the center of the cross was a swastika. I was supposed to wear it over my heart but I couldn't bear to, so I didn't. Every once in a while one of the senior nurses would notice and reprimand me.

I would make my face humble, stupid. I mumbled that I had forgotten, hoping that after a while they would assume I was a fool and had just lost the pin. This was my response to many "Aryan" matters—appear slightly foolish and they will leave you alone.

For example, when I was working with foreign patients, I always tried to speak French to the French.

"Tell them," said one of my colleagues with a laugh, "all French are pigs."

"Oh, I am so very sorry," I said, "but I don't know the word for pigs."

And then there was the issue of party membership.

"Fräulein Denner, you have been told more than once that we expect all our aides to belong to the Frauenschaften, the women's auxiliary of the party. Is that clear?"

"Yes, ma'am."

"Go tomorrow afternoon and join."

"Yes, ma'am."

"That will be all."

I saluted. We were always supposed to salute a superior, coming and going, as though the German Red Cross were the German Army.

"Uh, where is it I am supposed to go, ma'am?"

My superior would sigh with great patience and tell me, yet again, where I should go. And yet again, I would "forget" to go.

One day as I stood at the window of the ward, facing the gardens, two grizzled men in rags suddenly dashed out of the bushes and scurried toward the back door. They disappeared for a moment, then reappeared, trying to hide chunks of bread and cheese beneath their shirts. My superior—the nurse from Hamburg who had saved an onion for a dying Russian patient—came into the ward to change some bandages. I said nothing. She said nothing. I knew she was feeding these men. She knew I knew. Not a word was spoken about it. When her parents' home was bombed in air attacks on Hamburg in July 1943, she had to leave. I was sorry to see her go, and with reason, because another nurse took her place as my superior, and almost immediately denounced me as a young silly girl who was much too nice to the foreigners and demanded my transfer to another service.

That was how I eventually came to work in the maternity ward—a wonderful spot for me, as distant as possible from the war and its losses.

At that time it was customary for a woman to stay in the hospital for nine days after giving birth. The babies were kept in a special room and brought to the mothers for feeding. Usually maternity patients were farmers' wives with big families. Their older children would come to visit, bringing dolls and little wooden horses as though the infant were already a toddler and their playmate. How bizarre it was to see these plain, hardy folk wrapping their newborns in the finest pure silk baby clothes sent home by the occupiers of Paris!

We had no incubator, so when infants were born prematurely we fed them with an eye dropper. I cuddled the babies, changed them, and helped them to the mother's breast. If the mother had no milk, I prepared tiny little bottles. A few times, people asked me to come to church and stand as godmother. I always said yes, but then I would make some last-minute excuse and not go. If I went to church, it would be obvious to everyone that I had never been at a Christian service in my life.

I loved this work. I felt that my mother walked with me through the maternity ward, steadying my hand. I spoke softly to the children, with her soft voice. At a time when every footstep in the hall, every knock on the door, created panic, it brought me some peace of mind.

There were moments of crisis, of course. One woman developed a thrombosis after giving birth, and her leg had to be amputated. Another woman arrived at the hospital beaten and lacerated. Her child did not live ten minutes. She already had three other young children, barely two years apart. They waited for her outside, dumped there by the father. When she was recovering, she spoke to me of his brutality, his rages. When he came to get her, she didn't want to leave with him. Her bruised eyes were glazed with terror. But we had no way to keep her.

What most impressed me was the fact that when women were given anesthesia for the pain of childbirth, they would babble, saying all kinds of things that could have gotten them into serious trouble.

One girl virtually admitted that her baby was not her husband's but the child of a Polish slave laborer. She kept calling, "Jan! Jan, my darling!"

I put my hand over her mouth, leaned close to her ear, and whispered, "Shhh."

A farm woman who had just given birth to twins admitted that she and her husband had been hoarding cheese and illegally slaughtering pigs. Another woman blurted out deliriously that she had heard her oldest son's voice on Moscow Radio, which had begun broadcasting personal messages from captured German soldiers. This was by far the most serious political offense anyone spoke about. I could imagine her joy at knowing that her son had survived the Russian slaughter. How fortunate for her that I was the only one who heard her admit to it.

■ ■ ■

IN MAY 1943 one of the doctors in the hospital noticed that I seemed thin and exhausted and called me in for an examination. He diagnosed malnutrition and recommended a few days in bed and some concentrated eating.

Werner and I used the unexpected vacation time to take a trip to Vienna, for I had told him about Frau Doktor, Jultschi, Christl, and Pepi, and he was very keen to get to know them. I introduced him with a combination of pride—*Look, I have found a friend, a protector; he says he loves me*—and trepidation—*but he is quite eccentric; he has a dangerous temper; on the other hand, maybe he can help in some way.*

Werner stayed in the Hotel Wandl on Petersplatz. I did not dare register at any hotel, so I stayed with my cousin. I took Werner to the Wienerwald to enjoy the panorama of the Danube. I took him climbing in the hills above the city.

This is where I came as a girl, I did not say. *On these trails I sang "La Bandiera Rossa," in the days when a citizen could sing a socialist song like that aloud, in freedom.*

A sudden storm cracked in the sky overhead—lightning and thunder. I was scared, but not Werner; he enjoyed a good storm. We found shelter in a lean-to by the trail and he held me in his arms and comforted me while the wind howled outside. When we returned to Vienna the next day, Christl was ready to leave town, Jultschi was frantic, and Frau Doktor was pacing in her office like a lioness, grim with worry. They all thought we had been caught, you see. They thought we were in the hands of the Gestapo.

Before we left, Christl showed us a large bolt of silk she had bought. It was hard for her to acquire stock for her shop, and she was thinking she might cut the silk into squares for souvenir scarves. But how should she decorate them?

Werner smiled. He had an idea. "I will imprint each scarf with a scene of Vienna," he said. "Saint Stephen's on the corner of this one. The Opera on the corner of that one. This one in blue, that one in gold."

"But where will you get the colors?" Christl asked.

"Leave it to me," he answered.

I understood that a few more jars of paint would soon disappear from the shelves of the Arado warehouse.

I hated to leave my friends again, but I knew that now I had crossed some line; I had become Werner's woman in their eyes as well as my own. They evaluated his strength and said to themselves, "Edith will be safe with this man"—just as I said to myself, "Hansi is safe with the British." I was no longer a desperate victim in their eyes, starving, homeless. Now, by virtue of my protector, with his imaginative gifts, his skill as a craftsman, and his access to materials, I was actually in a position to help them.

I HAD REACHED a new plateau of well-being. But not for one moment could I let down my guard. The price I was paying for my ascent was simultaneously to sink so deep into my disguise that I ran the risk of losing myself completely. With Vienna loosening its hold on me, I felt more and more unconnected to anything I had once called "real." I began to fear that soon I might look in the mirror and see someone I myself could not recognize. "Who knows who I am anymore?" I asked myself. "Who knows me?"

There I was in the maternity ward, with all the tiny babies, bathing and feeding them, cuddling them, soothing them when they cried. I watched the delight of their mothers when we brought them to be fed.

I thought: "I am almost thirty years old. Not so young. I know firsthand the hideous feeling of losing my menstrual period and living without hope of having a child. Now I am fertile again, but maybe I won't be for long. Maybe they'll catch me and starve me again. Who knows? Who knows how long this war will last and what the future will bring? Maybe now is my only chance. I have a strong and virile lover, who has the wit and the will to tell fantastic lies, who is not afraid. Maybe he can give me a baby. If I have a baby, I will not be alone. Someone will be mine."

I began to talk to Werner about having a child. He did not want one, not with me. You see, he had absorbed much of the Nazi race propaganda, and he believed that Jewish blood would some- how dominate in any child of ours. He didn't want that. I had to find a way to overcome his reluctance.

I waited for Werner to come home at night. I stood at the stove and listened for his footsteps on the short flight of stairs outside. I knew he often peeked through the keyhole, just because it pleased him so much to see me standing at the stove cooking his dinner. Frau Doktor's words came back to me. "They all want a woman waiting in a comfortable room, with a good meal ready, and a warm bed." I could feel him watching me. My scalp tingled. He came in the door. I pretended to be so engrossed in cooking that I did not notice him entering, and he came up behind me and lifted me away from the stove, with my stirring spoon still in my hand.

After dinner, I suggested that we play chess. I played badly and he always won. And because it was chess, he always knew ahead of time that he was going to win, understanding, as I pretended not to, when I had made a wrong move. I loved watching Wer- ner's body relax and his face light up when he realized that he would win. The transparency of his happiness I found adorable. Chess always did the trick—it was the perfect mating game.

I pondered each move. I dangled the rook between my forefinger and my thumb. I rolled the king thoughtfully between my palms. I put it down in the wrong place. Werner captured it easily. My queen was completely exposed.

I looked at him and smiled and shrugged helplessly. "Well, it looks as though you have triumphed again," I said. "Congratulations." I leaned across the table and kissed him.

Werner caught me in his arms and picked me up and carried me to bed. Rushing, he reached into the drawer where he kept the condoms.

"No," I whispered. "Not tonight."

"I don't want you getting pregnant," he said.

"I don't care if I get pregnant," I whispered. "I want to get pregnant."

"No," he said.

"Please," I said.

"No," he said.

"Dearest . . ."

"Stop, Grete . . ."

"Shhh."

It was the first time I had ever dared argue with Werner Vetter. But it was worth it. By September 1943, I knew I was going to have a baby.

T E N

■

A Respectable Aryan Household

$\mathfrak{A}$LTHOUGH I WANTED to have a baby, that didn't mean I wanted to get married. The idea of another stern Nazi bureaucrat scrutinizing my fake papers in order to qualify me for a marriage license made me sick with fear. And what could the notion of illegitimacy mean to me in my situation? I thought that by the time the ninth month passed, the Nazis would have lost the war and I would take my illegitimate baby and maybe marry its father or, if we didn't want that, maybe marry somebody else.

But Werner Vetter was a *real* citizen of the Reich. He had a reputation to uphold, and he absolutely refused to father an illegitimate child. "Besides, Tante Paula insists that if I am not good to you, she will never speak to me again," he said lightly. "So I must make an honest woman of you."

There was no fighting him. We had to get married.

I walked down the main street in Brandenburg, nodding hello to acquaintances, oblivious of the sparkling weather. At some grim administrative office, I met a man who was to me the keeper of the gates of hell, a humorless, gray-faced registrar. From my papers I gather that his name may have been Heineburg. He hung like a dark spider among his files, lists, and boxes of index cards and potentially deadly records, waiting, I daresay hoping, for some enemy of the state like me to come walking into his lair. Next to him was a stone bust of Hitler. Behind him was the Nazi flag.

"Your father's parents are Aryan, I see. Your mother's father, I see, has a birth certificate, a baptismal certificate. Now. (Looking at the papers.) Now. Now what about your mother's mother?"

"Mother came from White Russia," I offered. "Father brought her back from there after the First World War. He served with the Kaiser's engineers."

"Yes, yes, yes, I see all that. But. (Looking again.) But. But what about your mother's mother? Where are *her* racial papers?"

"We have been unable to receive copies of them because of the battles and the interruption in communication."

"But this means we cannot know who she really was."

"She was my grandmother."

"But she may have been a Jewess. Which means that you yourself may be a Jewess."

I gasped in simulated horror and squinted at him as though I thought he had gone mad. He tapped his teeth with his fingernail and looked at me calmly through thick glasses that were speckled with dust. He had tiny eyes. My heart made a noise like a kettledrum in my chest. I did not breathe.

"Well. (Looking at me.) Well. Well, it is obvious just from looking at you that you could not possibly be anything but a pure-blooded Aryan," he said.

Suddenly, with a loud grunt, he smashed his rubber stamp down on the forms. *"Deutschblütig"*—"German-blooded"—said my papers at last. He gave me the marriage license, and I breathed again.

The same man married me and Werner, at the same desk with the same bust of the Führer and the same flag, on October 16, 1943. Try to imagine what a romantic event it was, with this registrar presiding. I think the ceremony took all of three minutes.

Hilde Schlegel, who was now six months pregnant herself, and her husband, Heinz, home from the front on leave, served as the witnesses. I wore a dress that my mother had made for me, to summon her presence in spirit, as though that might protect me in this potentially fatal charade. But I was a wreck. I was scared to death that I would forget to sign all my names—Christina Maria Margarethe Denner—and that somehow the pen would just write by itself, "Edith Hahn, Edith Hahn, that's who I am, you bastards, I hate you, I pray that an American bomb falls right on this office and turns your statue and your flags and all your evil fascist records into dust."

We were supposed to receive a copy of *Mein Kampf*—Hitler's gift to all newly married couples—but just that week the supply in Brandenburg had run out.

We were entitled to extra ration cards because of our marriage: 150 grams (about 3 ounces) of meat; 50 grams of real butter, 40 grams of oil, 200 grams of bread, 50 grams of cereal, 100 grams of sugar, 25 grams of coffee substitute, and one egg per wedding guest. I had been afraid to go and pick up this treasure. "Here I am pregnant," I complained to Hilde. "Werner demands that the house should be so spotless that you could eat off the bathroom floor. When do I have time to go to the ration office and pick up my extra cards?" Thankfully, Hilda agreed to go and pick up the marriage rations for me.

Heinz Schlegel suggested that we all go out to a restaurant to spend the extra ration cards and have a little celebration. It was especially pleasant because my famous patient, who had recovered enough to return to Berlin, had asked his sons to send me some Moselle wine on the occasion of my marriage, a rare treat for ordinary citizens of the Reich in wartime.

You will ask how I felt about spending so much time with people who supported the Hitler regime. I will tell you that, since I had absolutely no choice in the matter, I no longer dared to think about it. To be in Germany at that time, pretending to be an Aryan, meant that you automatically socialized with Nazis. To me, they were all Nazis, whether they belonged to the party or not. For me to have made distinctions at that time—to say Hilde was a "good" Nazi and the registrar was a "bad" Nazi—would have been silly and dangerous, because the good ones could turn you in as easily and capriciously as the bad ones could save your life.

My new husband was the most complicated of all. An opportunist one moment, a true believer the next. On our wedding night, when I was washing the dishes, Werner walked up behind me and put his hands on my small belly. "This is going to be a boy," he said with absolute confidence. "We will name him Klaus." He wrapped me in his arms. He had often said that he felt that the Jewish race was stronger, that Jewish blood always dominated. He had learned this idea from the Nazis, and he still believed it. He would always say that he felt himself to be only the "trigger element" in my pregnancy, *"das auslösende Element"*— those were his words. But it didn't seem to bother him as long as he could have what he desired most—a son.

Why my new husband didn't believe that German blood was stronger, that the child would always be an Aryan by virtue of his father's participation, I will never understand. When an idea is idiotic to begin with, its applications never make any sense.

THE DOCTOR EXAMINED me and shook his head. He had found something that I myself had completely forgotten. As a child, I had endured a bout of diphtheria, and it had left me with a heart murmur. The Viennese doctor had told me at that time to take great care with pregnancy. But the tumultuous events of the ensuing years had made such considerations insignificant.

"You've taken a big chance here, Grete," said the German doctor. "You have a weak heart. The murmur is very strong. You should never have become pregnant. But now that you are, I am going to write you a prescription for digitalis and recommend that you quit your job and stay home until the baby is born."

Wonderful news? Well, not exactly, because now I had a new crisis with my rations. I had been receiving rations suitable for a Red Cross employee eating with the group at the hospital. Now that I was going to be out of work and at home for six months, how would I eat? I needed a new ration book. But I could not receive one without a national registration card, an index card issued for each Reich citizen by the Office of Economics, the Wirtschaftsamt. And how was I going to get one of those without coming to the attention of the Gestapo?

"Please, dear God," I prayed, "get me through this. I will soon have a child to protect. Help us pass this test."

For the first time, I decided against looking nondescript, made myself as presentable and attractive as possible, and walked to the central registry. This time I encountered a woman, fat, neat, perfumed. She kept a little potted plant on her spotless desk. I gave her the Red Cross document, which showed that I had been let off from work and should now receive ration cards at home because I would no longer be eating at the hospital.

She began looking for mỹ index card. There was no sign of it in the main file. She checked four times. I stared at her fingers picking through the little cards on which all the citizens of the Reich were neatly stored.

She glanced at me.

"It's not here."

I smiled. "Well, it must be somewhere."

She searched for a hint of reproach in my face or my voice, but I made sure she found none. I did not want her to feel guilty. I did not want her to feel defensive. I wanted her to feel safe.

She grinned at me suddenly and tapped her forehead with her palm to show me she had just had a wonderful idea; with renewed enthusiasm, she looked in a series of files for the cards of people who had moved from other cities, which were not yet transferred into the main file. Surely my card must be in there. She looked. She looked again. She looked again.

"It's not here."

A film of sweat glistened near her ears and on her upper lip. She was terrified. I concentrated every ounce of my emotional strength on concealing the fact that I was terrified too.

"Well, perhaps you can find the card of my husband," I said.

She looked and immediately found Werner's card. I could see her mind working. How could a Red Cross nursing assistant, an employee of the Städtische Krankenhaus, the pregnant wife of an Arado supervisor who was also a longtime member of the Nazi Party, not have an index card? Impossible!

"There has to be some mistake . . ." she murmured.

I said nothing.

"I know what I must do," she said.

I waited.

"Since your card has obviously been misplaced somehow, I will make up a new card for you right now," she said, and she did. It went into the file: Christina Maria Margarethe Vetter.

I concentrated every ounce of my emotional strength on not looking happy. But I tell you, if I could have, I would have hugged and kissed that nice fat insecure woman and danced on her spotless desk. Because at last I had a registration card and I could receive my rations in an ordinary, unremarkable way. One of my greatest vulnerabilities, by which the Gestapo could have found me at any moment, had been erased.

I still had the problem of what to wear. Remember that Herr Plattner, the *Sippenforscher* in Vienna, had warned me never to apply for a *Kleiderkarte*, a clothing card. If my shoes needed repairs, Werner fixed them. If I needed a dress, I sewed somebody else's rags together and made one for myself. Now that I was big with child, Frau Doktor sent me some fabric and I made a pinafore that fit loosely over all my other clothes as they grew tight. Finally I gave up and just wore Werner's old shirts. But the child—what would I put on the child? After all, I had no soldier in Paris to provide me with silk baby clothes. Christl sent me a knitted bed jacket, so I could rip the wool and make a little sweater.

Then, out of the blue, Werner received a letter from Tante Paula.

"What kind of a brother are you?" she wrote. "Your poor brother Robert is at the front, his wife and three children have been evacuated to East Prussia, their flat is being bombed, the doors don't work, the windows don't close, every robber and squatter and deserter in the city can just march in there and settle down. Take your tools and your clever hands and go over there right this instant and fix everything!"

Well, of course my big strong husband could not withstand such a directive from his diminutive aunt. He told some lie at Arado and raced to Berlin.

His brother's home was nearly empty. Gertrude had taken almost everything. Only a few items still remained, including a folding crib and *forty* baby jackets and diapers! Werner wrote to Robert to ask if we could use the baby things, and since Robert's children were too big for them, he was happy to give us permission. Werner battened down the windows, fixed the doors, and locked up the flat. In the end, with all the bombing in Berlin, this particular flat was never touched.

IN A MATTER of a little more than a year, I had gone from being the most despised creature in the Third Reich—a hunted Jewish slave girl dodging a transport to Poland—to being one of its most valued citizens, a breeding Aryan housewife. People treated me with concern and respect. If they only knew who I had been! If they only knew whose new life I was breeding!

The insanity of it all made me a little hysterical.

I looked up at the American bombers that passed over every day on their way to nearby Berlin. I saw them as though the sky were a huge movie screen, on which some great fictional epic were being played—planes flying in formation like big ducks across the clouds, black puffs of flak and antiaircraft fire rising up to engulf them. I sent messages of victory skyward to my saviors. When I saw an American airman go down, my heart fell to the ground with him. I prayed for a glimpse of his parachute; the possibility of his death made my bones ache with mourning.

The appearance of the Allies in the sky, the real possibility of a German defeat, the autumn weather, my new sense of safety, all combined to put dangerous thoughts into my head, thoughts that I had long repressed: the Jewish holidays, my father, my sisters, my Mama, my family in Vienna. Where was everybody? Was anybody out there? Did the others long for me as I longed for them?

Alone in the house, cooking, cleaning, I listened to the BBC and suddenly, to my astonishment, I realized that instead of the usual news, I was hearing a message meant precisely and particularly for me. It was part of a sermon that the British Chief Rabbi Hertz was giving with the approach of Rosh Hashanah and Yom Kippur. He spoke in German.

"Our utmost sympathy goes out to the remnant of our brethren in Nazi lands who walk in the valley of the shadow of death," said the rabbi.

He means me, I thought, me and my baby. But why does he say "remnant"? Are we all that is left? Can it possibly be that everyone else is dead?

"Good men and true the world over remember them in their devotions and ardently yearn for the hour when the land of the destroyer will be paralyzed and all his inhuman designs frustrated."

They remember us, I thought. Those of us who are hunted, stalked, hiding in the darkness, are in the prayers of our brothers and sisters. We are not forgotten.

"And I know that my Jewish listeners will, in anticipation of the Day of Atonement, fervently join with me in the ancient prayers. Remember us unto life, O King who delights in life, and inscribe us in the Book of Life, for Thine own sake, O living God!"

Werner came home and asked me why I had been crying. I suppose I said it had something to do with the mood changes of pregnancy—anything not to burden him with my true thoughts on the eve of Rosh Hashanah 1943.

WHEN I WAS about six months pregnant, in the winter of 1944, a great sadness came over me. It disturbed Werner; he liked to see me happy.

"I'm just so homesick," I wept.

Without a second thought, he said, "Pack."

He biked over to Arado, and I imagine that he told them that his mother's house had been bombed and she had been evacuated and now the house had been broken into by a gang of deserters who stole everything and broke all the windows and doors, and so he had to go and fill out a police report, or some such thing, and they believed him—and we went to Vienna.

Everything was the same, but everything was different. The Austrians had begun to suffer now. Their little dictator from Linz had not proved to be the military genius everyone thought he was in 1941. They were losing sons, enduring air raids. They had liked it when they could just loot the lives of a helpless civilian population, but these enemy armies—this Zhukhov, this Eisenhower, this Montgomery—this was not what they had in mind when they voted for Anschluss.

During this second trip Werner and I made to Vienna, I walked slowly on the Ringstrasse, trying to summon memories of my girlhood. The police had the whole place cordoned off because Hitler was coming to stay at the Hotel Imperial and there was to be a gigantic rally.

A policeman approached me. My stomach tightened. My throat

went dry. Frau Westermayer has spotted me, I thought, and fulfilled her threat to call the police.

"Perhaps you would like to walk over there, madam," he said, "because we are expecting masses of people to come here very shortly and a lady in your condition should not be caught in such a great crush."

I walked off several blocks and waited for the masses, but they did not come. I suppose the local Nazis felt frightened that the Führer might be displeased with empty streets and take it out on them, so they finally bused in a lot of schoolchildren who were instructed to scream *"Wir wollen unser Führer sehen!"*—"We want to see our Führer!"—so the madman would be "compelled" to appear on the balcony, like royalty.

The next day Pepi and Werner and I met in a café. These two men of mine had developed a certain rapport, not exactly a friendship but more like an alliance. Everyone in my Vienna group had admired Werner's ability to supply Christl with printed souvenir scarves that her customers bought up eagerly. Now it was Pepi's turn to ask for help.

He looked awful—older, shabby. "Men are deserting," he said softly. "The worse things go at the front, the more hostility the regime turns on its own people. So they send out the police, even the SS, to find the deserters. Any young man who is not in uniform can be picked up at any time."

I had never seen him so grim, so scared.

"What shall I do when they stop me and demand to see my reason for not being in the army? Pull out my blue identification card that disqualifies me from the draft because I am a Jew?"

"You need an excuse," Werner said thoughtfully.

"Yes."

"An official excuse . . ."

"That I can carry in my pocket . . ."

"Attesting that you are doing some important work required for the war effort."

"Yes. That's it. Exactly."

We sat in silence in the café, all of us thinking. Then Werner said: "Go and get some pieces of letterhead stationery from your stepfather's insurance company, and a sample of the chief executive's signature."

"There must be a stamp as well," Pepi added nervously. "From the Labor Ministry or the Interior Ministry or . . ."

"This will not be a problem," Werner said.

Pepi laughed without mirth. "Not a problem? My dear fellow, everything is a problem."

"You can trust Werner," I assured him. "He has golden hands."

When we returned home, Werner went to work. He bought some ready-made office stamps with date, invoice number, "Received with thanks," and such already on them. Then he removed some letters from one stamp and cut out new letters from another stamp; fitted the second into the first; and soon had a brand-new stamp that said what he needed it to say. With his tiny knives and chisels, he carved the right design, then with a tweezer inserted the letters and the date. At Arado, he typed a letter on the stationery Pepi had brought from Herr Hofer's company. It stated that Dr. Josef Rosenfeld was *Unabkömmlich*—busy—needed by the Donau Insurance Company to do vital work on behalf of the Reich. Then he forged the signature of Hofer's boss. Then he added the incredibly believable, official-looking stamp. Then he leaned back and gave his work a narrow-eyed, critical last look.

"Pretty good, huh?" Werner said.

"Absolutely wonderful."

In my eyes, it was perfect, a magic document that would keep

Pepi secure for the duration of the war. I don't know whether he ever used it, but he *had* it, you see. It gave him confidence that he was protected; and that was half the battle for U-boats like us who were hiding among the enemy. If you had confidence, the terror and stress of daily life would not show on your face and give you away.

"I'll bet I could have made a lot of money doing things like this back in the thirties. Papers people needed, documents . . ."

"Yes, I suppose you could have."

"Damn. Just my luck. I'm always too late to cash in."

"But you are my genius," I said, kissing him.

He was something special, Werner Vetter. A truly gifted man. I wonder if anybody again ever appreciated his talents as much as I did.

IT WAS APRIL. Werner had begun to travel a lot to find supplies for Arado because the war had disrupted normal deliveries. He was tired. We played a little chess, listened to a little news, then went to bed, and he fell asleep instantly.

I felt the first pains of labor. But I didn't want to wake him right away. I walked back and forth in the bathroom, then went back to bed, then back to the bathroom. About eleven, I woke him up.

"I think I'm having the baby, Werner."

"Ah. All right. I will read you what happens." He pulled a book from the bookshelf. "First, the pains are widely spaced apart and very gentle. Then as the baby positions itself . . ."

"Fine fine, it sounds great in words and sentences, but now let's go to the hospital."

We walked through the quiet streets of Brandenburg. I held his arm. It took us almost an hour because I moved so slowly. At the hospital, the nurses put me into a large room with other women in labor.

The clocks on every wall ticked loudly. They were mad for clocks, the Germans. I could hear the other women groaning. The doctor came in to take a look at me. He said to the nurse: "Wait a little while. Then we'll give her a sedative."

I was concentrating on managing the pain, and so I did not say anything right away. But then I began to remember all the patients I had seen who had come out of surgery or had been sedated during childbirth, and who said things that could incriminate them and their loved ones. Suddenly I realized the predicament I was in—I could not take anything for the pain, because if I did, I too might become delirious. I might mention names. "Christl," "Frau Doktor." God forbid, I might say "Jew." I lectured myself like a propagandist.

"All the people you adore will be dead because you were a weakling and could not stand the pain of childbirth. For thousands and thousands of years, women have gone through this ordeal without anesthetic. You must be one of them. You must be like your grandmothers and great-grandmothers and have your baby as an act of nature."

When the nurse came with her needle, I croaked: "No. No. I am young and strong, and I do not need anything for the pain."

She did not argue. She packed up her needle and left. As long as I didn't scream and make a commotion, what did she care?

And after that, for the only time during that terrible war, I really wanted to die.

On Easter Sunday morning, April 9, 1944, my child was finally born. The doctor came in during the last few crucial minutes and tugged her into the world. When I saw that she was a beautiful girl, that she had a sweet little face and two good eyes and all the right fingers and toes, I was overjoyed.

"My husband wanted a boy," I said to the doctor. "He may be very unhappy about this."

"So what shall we do, Frau Vetter? Shall we push her back in and hope that she will be reborn a male? Tell your husband that to have a healthy child at such a time is an even bigger miracle than it usually is. Tell him to thank God and be grateful." He started to leave and then turned back to me and said: "And remember, it is the man who determines the sex of the baby. So your husband cannot blame you for this lovely girl. It is all his fault."

They laid her in my arms. I was torn and bleeding, in pain, but I took a deep breath of peace and happiness.

All of a sudden, the sirens screamed—an American air raid. The bombers were in the air above us, and this time it looked as though they were going to bomb not just Berlin and Potsdam, but Brandenburg as well.

Everybody who could walk ran for the shelter. Somebody pushed the gurney on which I lay into a dark, airless place. How lucky that my baby was with me just at that moment, that they had given me a little bottle of water for her, to teach her how to suck. We all listened in the blackness, with the practiced ears of people who had been bombed before, to hear where the bombs were dropping.

I thought: "Stupid girl! What have you done? You have brought a doomed child into the world. If you are not buried by the American bombs, you will be discovered by the Nazis! Your whole family, everything you once knew, could be lost and gone. And when you die, who will sit *shiva*?"

I was so lonely at that moment, so scared. And all I could think of was my mother.

Werner tried to make his way to the hospital, but he was stopped because of the "all points" warning in the streets. It took some time for the all-clear. As it turned out the Americans did not bomb Brandenburg but went to Berlin as usual.

When I saw him wandering through the bunker, calling my name, my heart melted with affection. He looked so sweet. He had not shaved. His face was lined with sleeplessness. His hair, usually perfectly combed, was all messed up.

"Grete!" he called softly. "Grete, where are you?"

I thought that I answered him loudly and strongly. But probably my voice came out in a whisper because he passed me by a couple of times before he saw me.

He leaned over me, smiling, his blue eyes sparkling with pleasure. He picked up the baby, unwrapped the blankets, saw that she was a girl, and turned to stone.

"This was your idea! This whole pregnancy was your idea! And what do I have now? Another daughter! Another daughter!"

Werner was in a fury. It seemed to me that his eyes turned white. The flame of love that I had felt for him moments before went out. A Nazi husband: What could I have expected? Was this not a regime which despised women and prized only their ability to breed? Was this not a country that had made a religion of twisted, primitive virility? He paced back and forth by my gurney, fuming and sputtering with anger. I hated him so much at that moment, I never wanted to see him again. And I said to myself, "This is my child, my child, my child. This child is only mine."

The next day, I received a letter from Werner apologizing for his bad behavior in the bunker.

You know, we have moments of passion when we are in pain. And then of course the moment ends, and with it the passion and the pain, and we forgive and forget. But I think that every time you hurt somebody you care for, a crack appears in your relationship, a little weakening—and it stays there, dangerous, waiting for the next opportunity to open up and destroy everything. Still, I was not in a position to hold a grudge against Werner. He was the father of my baby, my protector, *her* protector. So when he returned again to the hospital and held my hand to his lips, I allowed my heart to soften.

"You will see," I said. "She will bring you joy." He smiled a little and tried to look fondly on the new baby; he really tried. He made a lovely birth announcement and sent it to many friends. But it was like the garland of fruit and flowers in our kitchen, only a decoration to mask more serious matters. The truth was that Werner was deeply disappointed and would be for the rest of his life. He had wanted a son.

As the days went by, he looked more and more disheveled. He was getting thinner. I honestly believe he was completely incapable of feeding himself. He had grown used to having a woman to take care of him, and he couldn't manage on his own. Maybe he thought that if he appeared like a derelict at the hospital, with his shirt dirty and his face gaunt from hunger, I would be sympathetic, stop bleeding, recover quickly from the birth, and come home. If that's what he thought, well, he was absolutely right. Every time I looked at him, my heart turned, and I did not stay in the hospital for nine days as I should have. I went home in a week because my husband was so lost without me.

I named our daughter Maria for Frau Doktor, my savior in Vienna. We further named her Angelika, for the great eighteenth-century painter Angelika Kauffman—friend of Goethe, Herder,

Joshua Reynolds, Thomas Gainsborough—a woman whom Werner admired. Her mythic canvases depicting scenes from the Germanic wars against the Romans were now hanging in the Reich's Chancellery, for she was Hitler's favorite too. (In later years, when we moved to England, our daughter gave up the name Angelika and called herself Angela. I will use it to refer to her from now on in my story, because she much prefers it.)

You may ask why I did not name my baby for my mother. It was because it is a Jewish tradition to name children only for dead people, and in April 1944, I believed that my mother was alive.

I felt her presence in everything that I did with the new baby, felt her hovering over the crib, smelled her perfume in the air. I felt her so vividly, so physically, that I was absolutely certain she must be alive and well.

Little Bärbl, Werner's four-year-old daughter, arrived early on a Tuesday morning shortly after Angela's birth. The minute she walked into the house, clutching her ochre-haired doll, she raised her little arm and shouted: "Heil Hitler!"

Her mother, Elisabeth, smiled approvingly.

I think that I have rarely in my life met anybody who terrified me as much as Elisabeth Vetter. She was very good-looking, very tall, very strong, and, to me, ice-cold. I suppose she could feel as soft and tender as my magic statue. But she struck me as marble through and through. Werner had stayed late in the morning to greet her and Bärbl. The electric hostility and attraction between him and his ex-wife made the air in the apartment close and hot. I could clearly see that he still wanted her. He kissed his little girl and hastily went off to work.

Left alone with Elisabeth, I adopted my most innocuous personality. I practically whispered. I scurried around offering her coffee and cake, a chair, a tour of the flat. Bärbl stood in the corner, a tall blond child, naturally shy with me.

Elisabeth gazed down at Angela in her laundry-basket bed. "They certainly don't look much like sisters," she said.

She looked at the painted garland around the kitchen. "Well, Werner made efforts for you that he did not make for us—right, Bärbl?"

She looked at the neatly aligned tools and paints. "He thinks he's an artist. Too bad he has no talent."

I do not remember whether Elisabeth kissed Bärbl when she left. I waited for her to be outside in the hall. I stood at the window waiting for her to be down in the street. I waited and waited until she had disappeared down the block. Not until she was completely out of sight did I breathe a little easier.

"Where is the picture of Hitler?" Bärbl asked. "We have a picture of Hitler in every room in our flat."

"We are having it repaired," I said. "It fell down and broke, and we have to have the pieces fixed. It will take some time, but eventually we will get it back. Would you like a cookie?"

"Yes," she said.

I gave her Knödl, little sugared potato dumplings, each with a single strawberry on the inside. When she was an adult, far away in another country, married to a Scotsman, the mother of British sons, that was what she remembered—the Viennese Knödl with the strawberry surprise.

Every day we went for a walk: myself, my baby girl in the pram, and the tall four-year-old. Everything that I did with Angela, Bärbl did with her doll. I gave a bath; she gave a bath. I pumped milk from my breast to put into a bottle. She tried to play at pumping and gave her doll a bottle as well. Whenever we met anybody on the road and I would say "Good morning," Bärbl would say "Heil Hitler!"

"Heil Hitler!" to the gardener, to the woman who cleaned the streets, to the man who delivered the rations. People must have thought I was a splendid Nazi mother.

But truthfully, I loved Bärbl. She was a sweet little girl, and after a while she stopped saying "Heil Hitler," because she was under my roof. I was not strict. I was not working. I had nothing but time for the children.

Bärbl's six-week vacation with us went so well that Elisabeth must have felt quite threatened. In keeping with the spirit of the times, she denounced Werner and me to the authorities, giving some reason why we were "unfit" to house her daughter. The court sent a delegation of two women social workers to come and visit our home.

As usual with the bureaucracy, I was in a state of panic. I had been living with Werner for quite some time, more than a year, and we had grown relaxed with each other. Was there some sign of my Jewishness that he didn't even notice anymore but they might see? Was there anything in the house that might say "This woman went to a university, studied law, knew how to dress with style . . . ?"

I asked my upstairs neighbor Karla if I could borrow a picture of the Führer, since mine was being repaired. She found one in a drawer.

The social workers arrived without warning—the usual self-important Nazi women with notepads and hats. I invited them in. My beautiful little angel was sleeping in her laundry basket. I thought: "My God, in that little wicker nest she looks like Moses floating among the bulrushes!" They asked me about the routine of our day, the nature of our meals; they opened the stove to see if it was dirty; they checked for dust in every corner; they noted every title of every book in the bookcase. Then they left.

In several weeks we received a letter saying that we had passed inspection, we had proved ourselves to have a respectable Aryan household, and that Elisabeth's petition to acquire sole custody of Bärbl had been turned down. "It can only be good for this child to spend as much time as possible in the home of Herr and Frau Vetter," they wrote in their report. I always wanted to show those two Nazi women that report. In later years, I would have been thrilled to march into their offices and say, "Look, this is what you wrote to a Jewish woman, you unspeakable hypocrites!"

But fate rarely grants us these satisfactions.

ELEVEN

■

The Fall of Brandenburg

I LIVED IN hope. I did not think of my sisters except, some-times, to comfort myself with the idea that they were safe in Palestine. I did not think of Mina or any of my other friends from the labor camp. I tried desperately not to think of Mama. Because, you see, if I thought about them, I would have lost my mind. I would not have been able to bear my disguise another minute. So I did everything in my power to protect myself from the depressing power of Rabbi Hertz's suggestion that I was only a "remnant" and to delude myself that I was leading a "normal" life.

"Normal." That's what I said to everyone in later years. I lived as a housewife, a mother. We had a "normal" life. My God.

The milkman delivered our ration of milk. The Nazi paper— *Der Völkische Beobachter*—was delivered every day by a boy on a bicycle. I tried to go shopping where one did not have to greet the storekeeper with the Nazi salute. We lived on our rations. Frau Doktor sent us some extra things: nonperishables like rice, noodles, lentils, and peas. Frau Gerl sometimes sent me ration cards for bread. I sent as many of my milk rations as I could to Jultschi for her Otti, and I saved all of my coffee rations for Tante Paula, who loved her cup of coffee more than anything. We had cabbage and potatoes; we had bread, sugar, salt, and occasionally a little meat— and this was enough for me to feed our family.

The farmers outside the city made fortunes from bartering, because people would bring their most valuable furnishings to trade for some carrots, maybe a slab of bacon, or some fresh cheese. People joked that the farmers now owned so many Persian rugs that they put them in the cowsheds. I heard that there were used clothing exchanges, but I feared they would require me to show my nonexistent clothing card, so I never went. I just sewed all the time.

I was friendly enough with Karla, the singing lady upstairs. She and her husband, an older man, had long wanted to adopt a child, but for some reason, even with all the orphans in the country, they couldn't find one. One day, they came home with a brand-new infant. I knew they had received her almost directly from the mother's arms, and I could imagine from what sort of liaison she had originated. But what did it matter? She was a lucky child to have these nice people for parents. I often gave Karla baby clothes that Angela had outgrown. Karla, in turn, saved everything for my neighbor across the hall, Frau Ziegler, who already had a toddler and was now pregnant again since her husband's last leave from the front.

The only person who ever came over to talk was Hilde Schlegel. She would sit in the kitchen and tell me how she longed for Heinz's forthcoming furlough. We talked about the weather, rations, the difficulties of washing, how lucky I was that a friend in Vienna had sent me some washing powder. (Actually, the powder belonged to Anna Hofer; Pepi had stolen it from under her sink.) Hilde often went on and on about her mother-in-law. That gave me an idea.

"Let's invite your mother for a visit," I said to Werner.

"What?"

"She's never seen the baby."

"She won't care about the baby."

"That's impossible. Who could not be charmed by our little sweetheart?"

The elder Frau Vetter stayed with us for a week. She had a flat blank wrinkled face and wore her hair in a gray bun at the back of her head. She hardly ever spoke to me. She wore a starched white apron. She was so neat and tidy that she didn't even want to touch Angela for fear of being soiled by a dirty diaper or a bit of drool. She drank beer all day, quietly, and fell asleep snoring, her apron still unsullied. She reminded me of Aschersleben in the snow—white and clean on the outside, but inside a hopeless corrupt drunk who felt no love even for her own son's child. One day, I came home with Angela and she was gone. She had brought nothing. She took nothing. Werner had been absolutely right about his mother.

I cuddled my pretty baby and whispered: "Don't you worry, little one. It doesn't matter that Grandma didn't say good-bye. Soon the war will be over; we have only to wait and be rescued by the victorious Soviet army. And when the ghettos of Poland are opened, your other Grandma will come out and you will see, she will sing to you and cradle you and kiss your eyes."

■　■　■

As Pepi had said, the Nazis grew more dangerous as the war turned against them. The propaganda machine tried to foster hope in the population with talk of "secret weapons." But these weapons never quite seemed to materialize. The Gestapo didn't trust the people to be loyal to the Führer in times of trouble. They hunted for deserters, who were shot if discovered. They ransacked the huts of foreign workers, looking for signs of sabotage. They despised the lonely married women, many of them widows by now, who took up with foreign workers. By 1944, almost a quarter of the court cases concerned illicit liaisons between German women and foreigners, and every day three or four workers were executed for crimes like pretty thievery and adultery.

Sudden *razzias* would occur, poof, like that, for no reason, putting ordinary citizens on edge and filling my days with tension. Once I remember, I was at a pharmacy with Angela when two SS men walked in and demanded to see the papers of the proprietress. She handed them over without a word. The SS men scrutinized the stamps, the official signatures. I hung back among the medicines, planning my strategy, as I always did: If they ask for my papers. I'll give them. If they think there is something wrong with my papers, I'll act dumb and sweet. If they imprison me, I'll tell them *I stole the papers, all by myself, me alone—no one helped me, my husband had no idea . . .*

Satisfied, the SS men gave the papers back to the proprietess and left the store. One of them stopped to smile and cluck sweetly at my baby in her carriage.

Werner now worked a seven-day week, twelve hours a day. His Dutch employees declared themselves too religious to work on Sundays. Although it seemed odd that foreign laborers should have a shorter work week than Germans, Werner defended them to the company, and they got their way in the end. You see, every able-bodied German was fighting, making the loss of skilled labor so critical that these foreign prisoners had now become too valuable to offend. Werner made a concerted personal effort to treat them decently. An appreciative Frenchman sent us a beautiful box, intricately carved and inlaid with tiny pieces of wood and metal. I understood that he had probably kept his soul alive by concentrating on making this object of beauty. I had been there myself.

The supply lines were being bombed. Production slowed. Werner had to travel to companies like Daimler-Benz, Siemens, Argus, Telefunken, Osram, AEG, and others to acquire materials for Arado. Inside the factory, constant propaganda exhorted the workers to greater and greater efforts. Large photos of Arado employees who had died at the front hung on the walls, a stark reminder that no matter how long and hard you labored at home, it was better than dying in Russia. Incidents of sabotage increased. We later heard that French workers at Arado colluded with German communists to build a secret radio and send messages to the Allies.

In addition to his endless work week, Werner also had to put in time for civil defense because we were now living under almost constant bombardment.

If Werner was home, and the air raid sirens sounded, we would put Angela in the laundry basket and each of us would take a handle and carry her down to the shelter together—just as Mina and I had carried potatoes in Osterburg. But if I was by myself, I tried to take Angela down there as little as possible. There was no air, no light, and all the mothers and children were packed in together—it seemed to me like a recipe for disease because one infected child could sicken the entire group. A little boy in our building (Petra was his name, I think) did contract whooping cough in just that way, and died in his mother's arms.

My greatest fear was of being caught *inside*, crushed inside the house or buried inside the shelter. My plan for a bombing was to run out into the open. Of course this seems idiotic now; but in wartime, people develop superstitious ideas of how they would and would not like to die. So when the bombers roared overhead, I would stay aboveground. I would put Angela in her basket on the floor, making little "walls" around her out of furniture and pillows. I would sit with my back to the window, so that the flying glass would hit me and not enter the flat and hit her. I kept a blanket ready in case I had to grab her and run.

In summer, the bombers came over from eight o'clock in the evening until midnight. The Americans flew in formation, so low that you could see their insignia. I organized my housework with the thought that, since the bombing would begin at eight, I must cook dinner and the next day's breakfast and make sure the laundry was done and nothing was hanging outside after seven o'clock.

Every once in a while, the Americans surprised me. One day I had taken my usual walk with Angela in her pram, down the Wilhelmstrasse, away from the center of town. We had stopped to sit on the grass under a tree so I could give her a bottle. (You must understand that after three months I had no more milk in my breasts, an effect of the hunger I had endured in Osterburg and Aschersleben. Werner brought special milk from the pharmacy.) My baby lay on a blanket, laughing and cooing, wriggling with happiness as I nuzzled her little belly. And meanwhile the bombs smashed into the city over the horizon, the sky flashed with orange and black waves of death, the antiaircraft cannons roared. The earth beneath her shook and trembled—and Angela kicked her legs and laughed.

She kept me sane. She made me smile in the presence of death.

She was my miracle. As long as I had her, I felt that *any* miracle could happen, that all the world could be saved.

I had always been able to catch a glimpse of Edith in the mirror. Now what I had feared when I became a U-boat began to happen. I did not recognize myself. I knew I was a German woman with a baby, but where was this lovely child's grandma? Where were her aunts? Why wasn't a great, warm, loving family swarming around her crib, bringing her presents, commenting on her extraordinary feats? I ached with longing for my mother. She would know who I was. She would recognize Grandmother Hahn's fingers or Aunt Marianne's nose in my baby.

"What's the matter?" Werner asked.

"Longing," I said. "I have this longing. . . ."

"Don't say another word. Put some things in a bag. I'll be back at noon, and we'll be on our way to Vienna."

I did not say: *It isn't Vienna that I miss, it's my mother who is lost out there somewhere in the empire your Führer has torn from the world's heart.*

Werner rode his bike to Arado and told them, again, that his mother's home in the Rhineland had been bombed and he had to go help her, and they believed him again. (With this kind of competence at the top, it is no wonder that the French workers and the German communists had so much success with their secret radio.)

What a strange trip that was! While exhausted Wehrmacht soldiers stood in the crowded train corridor, the nurse attendants fussed over Angela, I was helped to a seat, and I rode with my husband in a compartment like a queen. Having a baby in Germany had become, next to dying at the front, the highest form of service to the state. I think that by then the Nazis no longer wanted babies because they felt it was their racial destiny to repopulate a "new Europe." I think they wanted babies to repopulate Germany itself because the country had lost so many people in the war.

We rang the bell at Jultschi's house. She took one look at me with my Nazi husband and my German baby and she said, "You are insane!"

Maybe I *was* a little insane by then just from being invisible.

Only Frau Doktor gave me the reaction I longed for. "This child is named Maria. For you," I told her. Her strong face melted. She cooed to Angela, cuddled her; she bounced her and changed her and crawled on the floor next to her—everything that I knew my mother would have done.

Frau Doktor went out of town for a few days, and I stayed in her flat on the Partenstrasse. Werner stayed in a hotel.

Pepi took a walk with me down the streets of our youth. The baby was sleeping. Pepi was pale. The dark circles around his eyes told the story of the constant fear under which he lived. His hair had almost completely disappeared. He didn't look twenty years older than I; he looked forty years older.

Remind me of the carefree girl I used to be, I wanted to say. *Tell me that Mama is safe, tell me that this baby of mine will grow up in freedom.*

But it was too late. He was too old, too beaten. I had always been the student, he the teacher. I had always been the starving prisoner, he the comforter. Now it was my turn to try and comfort him.

"Everything will be all right," I said to him. "Just be patient. Be strong. Think of the socialist paradise. . . ."

Pepi answered with his mirthless laugh. He showed very little interest in my baby.

■   ■   ■

WERNER WAS DRAFTED on the first of September 1944, part of a last-ditch conscription of Germans with stomach trouble, asthma, sensory losses, bad feet, and any other ailments now considered too slight to exempt a man from service in a losing cause. Soon the government would be enlisting boys and old men to defend German cities. Werner was part of these cannon-fodder brigades.

He did not report to the army until September third. If he had dared, he would have pretended that he had never received the draft notice and tried to hide somewhere. But even Werner knew better than to attempt to lie his way out of this.

The country was falling apart. Sabotage. Desertions. Thousands made homeless by the bombings. And with the last of its strength, this dictatorship could think of nothing better to do than sacrifice my husband.

He took all our savings—ten thousand marks—out of the bank in case he fell into enemy hands and had to bribe somebody for his freedom. I never dreamed of protesting. I lived handily on his salary from Arado, which was still paid even after he was drafted, and I saved every pfennig I could.

Werner sighed and hung his head. I knew I was about to hear a confession.

"Listen, Grete," he said. "When you go to the pharmacy for the special milk for the baby, don't be surprised if they treat you as a tragic heroine. Because to tell you the truth, I lied to them. I told them you had already buried three children and therefore they simply had to give you the milk so that this fourth child of yours would not also enter eternity."

Even now, I have to smile when I think of this. I tell you, of all the things about Werner Vetter that appealed to me, this most of all warmed my heart: He had no respect for the truth in Nazi Germany.

All the other men stayed in their barracks. My Werner came home every night on his bicycle and spent the evening hours with me until he had to leave and return to the base. What lie he told his superiors to justify this, I do not know, but I can imagine.

He disliked wearing his uniform and always changed out of it right away when he came home. Symbols of authority irritated him—unless the authority was his own.

One night when he left to go back to the barracks, he found that a part of his bicycle had been stolen. This was a potential catastrophe. If he didn't return on time, he would be declared absent without leave, considered a deserter, and shot before he could make an explanation. So what did he do? He found another bicycle belonging to some other citizen, and he stole and installed the part that had been stolen from him. It seemed fair enough.

He made a friend at the base, a young man who badly wanted to leave his wife pregnant when he went forth into the final battle. The young couple had no place to be together. So Werner, without asking me first, invited them to stay in our little room.

I was shocked when he appeared at our door with them. To bring strangers! It was so dangerous! What if they were committed Nazis who snooped and pried?

I sat outside with my baby to give our guests some privacy, and all the while I worried. Would they notice that the radio dial was not set to the government station? Would they notice that we did not have a picture of Hitler on the wall? Did we not hear every day of neighbors denouncing each other for minute infractions in order to win some advantage? How could Werner have toyed with our safety this way, after we had been so careful, so quiet and circumspect, for so long? The answer of course, was that he had never felt as frightened of exposure as I. Why should he? If I was

caught, he would deny having known about my true identity—
and I would support his denial. He would come out all right.
Angela and I would disappear.

The sweet young couple thanked me for my hospitality, wished
me well, and went on their way. I suppose they would have been
horrified to know that I was afraid of them. I sometimes wonder
if they ever had the child they wanted so much.

Around Christmas, most of Werner's unit was shipped west to
confront the Allied invasion. But Werner—who was clearly
brighter than most, had supervisory experience, and was a good
enough shot to win an award for marksmanship even with only
one eye—was sent to Frankfurt an der Oder for further training
before he went to the Eastern front.

They had decided to make him an officer.

"Come and spend New Year's with me," he said. I could hear
the urgency in his voice—one last weekend before he had to face
the Russians. I hastened to make arrangements. Hilde Schlegel said
she would keep my baby.

I waited for Werner at a little inn, really just a private home that
sometimes rented rooms to soldiers and their women.

The innkeeper and his employees behaved deferentially toward
me—oh, yes, they treated me with great respect. Because you see
my disguise had now reached the outer limits of absurdity, its most
fantastic incarnation: I had become the best thing a German
woman could be in that time and place, a Nazi officer's wife.

When I saw Werner in his officer's uniform, I did not know
whether to laugh or faint. That hateful collar! The brass! The eagle!
The insignia of the would-be conquerors of the world! He pulled
me to him. But I twisted away, repelled. I could not bear to have
that uniform touch my skin.

"Oh, take that dreadful thing off!" I cried.

We did not go out that whole weekend. We stayed in our room and told each other jokes. I mean it. We told each other every funny story we could think of. One of them stays in my mind. A German citizen wants to commit suicide. He tries to hang himself, but the rope is of such a poor quality that it breaks. He tries to drown himself, but the percentage of wood in the fabric of his pants is so high that he floats on the surface like a raft. Finally he starves to death from eating official government rations.

The darkest joke of all was that as Werner was marching east with his comrades into the teeth of the advancing Soviet army, he passed thousands of Germans fleeing for their lives in the opposite direction. They knew the war was over and lost.

"Keep your fingers crossed for me," he wrote.

MY UPSTAIRS NEIGHBOR and her husband left right after the New Year, very early in the morning.

I saw them leave only because Angela had awakened me before dawn. They were creeping out, carrying with them all their possessions and their sleeping child. I opened my door.

"Good luck to you," I whispered.

"And to you, Grete," Karla answered. "I hope your husband comes home safely."

We shook hands, and they left. But that night, I heard someone moving in their supposedly empty apartment. Footsteps. Shuffling. The clink of a teakettle. The creak of a bed. I wondered who it was. Then I decided it was not my place to wonder.

The following morning, while I was in the bathroom, boiling diapers, I heard a terrible pounding on my door.

"Frau Vetter!" a man called. "It is the police! Open the door!"

It was the young couple, I thought—they had turned me in because Hitler's picture was not hanging on the wall. It was Frau Zeigler across the hall, I thought—she had turned me in because she heard a tone from the BBC and knew I was listening. It was the registrar, who had always suspected me; or Elisabeth, who had always wanted me out of the picture. It could be anyone. What mattered was that we had almost reached the end of the war, and in the last moments, somebody had denounced me. I had been discovered.

My stomach knotted. My legs turned hot and trembled. My throat felt dry. The story I had rehearsed a thousand times flew through my head.

These papers belong to Christl Denner, Fräulein. She lives in Vienna. Who are you? How did you get these papers?

I stole them. I was walking on the path by the Alte Donau, and Christl was out on the river rowing, and I saw that she dropped her handbag in the river and then she and her companions rowed away, and as soon as they were out of sight, I jumped into the river and swam to the place and dove down again and again until I found the handbag and I retrieved the papers and made them into false papers for myself. This was my crime. My crime alone. No one helped me . . .

I closed my eyes, pictured my mother's face, held it before me like a light, and then I opened the door. A policeman was standing there. He was not such a young man. He looked tired.

"Good morning, Frau Vetter. We have reason to believe there is a deserter hiding out in the vacant apartment of his sister and her husband in this building, right above you. He would have been here last night. Did you hear any noise?"

"No," I said. "Nothing."

"Maybe you slept through it."

"No, I would have heard because I am up so often with my baby in the night."

"Ah, well, if you hear anyone moving about in that apartment, please call this number."

"Yes, of course, officer. I certainly will."

He bowed politely and left.

THE BBC PROGRAMS best suited my work schedule. I tuned in one evening and found myself listening to a broadcast by Thomas Mann, the Nobel laureate, author of masterpieces like *The Magic Mountain* and *Death in Venice*. He had lived out the war in California and had been making anti-Nazi broadcasts to the German people for years. This was the first time I had heard him.

"German listeners!

"If only this war were at an end! If only the horrifying things that Germany has done in the world could be set aside. . . . "

If only, I thought.

"But one thing is necessary for a new beginning. . . . It is the full and absolute realization of the unforgivable crimes, which you indeed know very little of, in part because they locked you out, forcibly consigning you to stupidity, . . . in part because you concealed the knowledge of this horror from your consciousness through your instinct of self-preservation."

I thought, what is he saying? What is he talking about?

"You, who are listening to me now, do you know of Maidanek at Lublin in Poland, Hitler's extermination camp? It was *not* a concentration camp; rather, it was a huge murder complex. A huge building of stone with a factory chimney stands there, the largest crematorium in the world. . . . More than half a million European people—men, women, and children—were poisoned with chlorine and then burned, fourteen hundred daily. The death factory worked day and night; its chimneys were always smoking."

No, I thought, this is impossible. This is someone's propaganda.

"The Swiss rescue mission . . . saw the Auschwitz and Birkenau camps. They saw things that no feeling person is ready to believe who hasn't seen it with his own eyes: the human bones, the barrels of lime, chlorine gas pipes, and the burning facilities. In addition they saw the piles of clothing and shoes, which they took off their sacrifices, many little shoes, shoes of children. . . . In these German facilities alone, one million seven hundred fifteen thousand Jews were murdered from April 15, 1942, up until April 15, 1944."

No. It can't be. No.

Turn it off! I said to myself. Make him stop!

But I could not move. And Mann did not stop.

". . . The remains of the burned were ground up and pulverized, packed up and sent to Germany to fertilize the German earth . . ."

Mama.

"I have given only a few examples of the things that you will discover. The shooting of hostages, the murder of captives, the torture chambers of the Gestapo . . . the bloodbaths which took place in the Russian civilian population . . . the planned, wanted, and accomplished deaths of children in France, Belgium, the Netherlands, Greece, and especially Poland."

Inside myself I felt a terrible silence, as though I had been hollowed out and become a cave.

Angela began to cry. I did not go to her to comfort her. I sank to the floor.

My blouse felt so tight at the throat that I tore the collar, just to breathe. But I could not breathe. I lay on the floor; I could not get up.

Angela was screaming now. And then I was screaming. But I could make no sound. Because the Germans would have heard me.

I lay on the floor, unable to absorb the horror of what I had just been told. Who can imagine a living, breathing, laughing mother as smoke and ashes? No one can imagine that. My mind shut down. I sank like a rock to the bottom of my soul.

The true meaning of the term "U-boat" came clear to me in that moment. I felt myself buried alive, in silence, under an ocean of terror. I was living among accomplices. No matter that they looked like housewives and shopkeepers, I knew that their acquiescence with Hitler's war against the Jewish people had led to the nightmare Thomas Mann had described.

I don't know how long I lay there. I don't know when Angela fell asleep, worn out from screaming.

The next day came and the next day, the weeks went by, and then Mama returned to me in my imagination. She sat on my bed at night and reminded me of poems long forgotten that I had recited for my grandfather. It must have been so, because the following morning, I knew them once again and could say them for Angela. When the baby started crawling, I imagined that Mama clapped her hands with happiness. "You see, Edith, she's a clever girl. Soon she will be running across the bridge at Stockerau. . . ."

AN OFFICER OF the Wehrmacht sat at the kitchen table. He held his hat in his hands. I thought he was going to tell me that Werner was dead. Hot tears rolled down my neck.

"No," said the officer. "Don't cry. Werner is not dead. He is a Russian prisoner of war. His unit was attacked at Küstrin. They pulled back until they could go no farther. They were surrounded, and they surrendered. They were all taken."

"Was he wounded?"

"I don't think so."

"Oh, thank you for telling me this!" I cried.

"He'll go to a prison camp in Siberia. You won't see him for a long time."

"Thank you! Thank you!"

He put his hat on and went to notify the next woman.

As far as I could see, this was the best possible outcome. Not only was Werner safe, he had been captured whole, not wounded, and I had no doubt that he would manage as well as any German soldier in the Russian prison camp. I thought of him as I thought of my sister Hansi—safely stowed in the hands of an ally. His brothers, Gert and Robert, would not be so fortunate. They would die of their wounds in battlefield hospitals.

Hilde Schlegel's husband, Heinz, had been killed in one of the last battles on the Eastern front. She had sent her baby girl Evelyn to stay with her mother, and anticipated with grave fears the occupation of the city.

"Everybody says the Russians are monsters who will rape us all," she said. "I have heard that before they shoot off a cannon, they tie some poor old woman across its mouth so that she is blown to pieces when the cannon goes off."

I no longer responded with disbelief, no longer countered with "Ah, this is someone's propaganda."

"Maybe you should do what Werner did—take out all your money so that you'll have something to bribe somebody with if you need to."

"Ach, that is a terrible idea, Grete. I am keeping all our money locked up in the bank where they can't get at it."

On Easter Saturday in 1945, Brandenburg was bombed. We lost our electricity and our gas. The SS brought in a brigade of Russian soldiers to dig trenches in front of our houses and defend us. I suppose they were prisoners of war. These men were so afraid of the approaching Red Army that within minutes they were inside our flats, cowering behind the people they were supposed to protect. So the SS took them away.

We heard a siren that lasted for an hour, and we knew that Brandenburg had fallen. We all went down into the shelters and stayed there with the children, maybe twenty children. One little girl cried and screamed because she had left her doll upstairs and was afraid it would be lost in the bombing. Her mother could not resist her pleas and went back up to get the doll. The minute she came down again, a bomb hit the roof with such a loud explosion that the mother got scared and dropped the doll, and that was the end of that. The little girl was crying; the mother was crying. Everyone was tense and frightened.

I went to sleep on my mattress, holding my well-behaved Angela in my arms, certain that our saviors would soon arrive. One of the old men working in civil defense came down to tell us that a supply train loaded with food had stopped on the tracks. Many people went out to loot it; they shared the food they brought back.

A German soldier awakened us. "The Russians have broken through," he said. "Time to evacuate the town."

So I did what everybody else did: I put my baby in her carriage and I ran. There were soldiers all over telling us which way to go, and we ran and ran; everybody was running. The city was burning. We could hear the bridges exploding behind us as the Wehrmacht blew them up to slow the Russian advance. By the time it grew dark, I had reached a little town on the outskirts of the city. I ran into a barn and found a corner to hide in. I wrapped Angela in my coat, and we both fell asleep. When I woke up, the sky outside was on fire. So was Angela. She was covered with red spots and running a high fever—measles.

I didn't have anything with which to care for her, no water, nothing. I went from house to house, weeping, begging to be allowed in because my child was so ill. A neighbor from Brandenburg saw my distress and pleaded on my behalf. Everybody said no. Everybody was afraid. Finally, in the last house, the smallest house, a woman and her daughter let me in. They had both had measles. They told me to keep Angela in the shadows and give her water.

The whole city seemed to be fleeing through that little town. On the heels of the civilians came the army that had once seemed invincible, now utterly beaten, desperate not to fall into the hands of the Russians. Some soldiers came to the little house to rest and hide for a bit. One of them had a battery-operated radio. We gathered around it, I and my suffering child, the old woman and her daughter, the haggard soldiers. Admiral Doenitz spoke to us. He told us that Germany could no longer defend itself, the war had been lost, and German citizens should obey the commands of the victors.

Silence. No one wept. No one even sighed.

"So. Is anybody hungry?" I asked.

They gaped at me, astonished.

"Go to the farmers hereabouts and ask them for flour and eggs and milk and jam and bread," I said. "Bring the food back here, leave your weapons outside, and I will make you something good to eat."

And that is exactly what happened. All day long, as the men streamed into the little house, I made hundreds of delicate Viennese crepes for the Wehrmacht, and the woman and her daughter served them. As I stood at the stove, a song from a million years ago came into my head, and I sang:

One day the Temple will be rebuilt,
And the Jews will return to Jerusalem.
So it is written in the Holy Book.
So it is written. Hallelujah.

One of the soldiers whispered in my ear: "Don't act so happy, madam. Hitler may hear you."

"Hitler has killed himself, Sergeant. That's for sure. Hitler and Goebbels did not wait to greet the Russians along with us plain people. That's why it was the admiral we heard on the radio."

"You never know," he said. "Careful."

In the middle of that tremendous defeat, the sky blazing with bombs and roaring with Russian cannon, he was still afraid to say a word. It was the habit of silence, you see. The habit of silence gets into you; it spreads from this one to the next one. If the Germans wanted to be phobic about an infectious disease, they should have picked silence, not measles.

Before this soldier left, he gave me some glucose tablets. We called them sugar pills. What a treasure they turned out to be!

Now, in this little town, every house hung out a white flag of surrender—a rag, a sheet, a towel. My two kind hostesses were not eager to stay there and say hello to the victorious Red Army, so they left. And I was not so keen to receive them on my own, so I decided to go back to Brandenburg. I took as much food as I could and walked back with Angela in her carriage, heading east on the road as the defeated German soldiers headed west.

I came to a bridge that spanned a very deep ditch. The bridge had been smashed in the middle. The two sagging, cracked sides of the bridge were connected by a toilet door, the kind of wooden door they have in the countryside, with a heart carved out of it in the center. This little door was barely wide enough to support the wheels of the pram. I looked down through the open heart and saw boulders and debris and death. I imagined the pram slipping off the thin bridge, the baby hurtling downward.

"This is the end," I thought.

I closed my eyes and raced across the door to the other side. When I opened my eyes, Angela was sitting up, looking at me. Her fever was gone.

The road back into Brandenburg was strewn with German corpses. If they were lucky, somebody had put newspaper over their faces. I tried not to walk on them, but sometimes it was impossible to go around them. There were huge piles of rubble from the bombing. I picked up the pram and climbed over them.

The Russians came down the street on giant horses, towering over the city.

I MET UP with my neighbor, Frau Ziegler. Far gone in her pregnancy, she was pushing her other baby, a little boy, in a baby carriage just like me. We decided to stay together and try to make it back to our building.

We passed the bank. The Russians had broken into the vault and taken out all the reichsmarks, and now they threw the money into the street so that it blew like flying leaves in the hot wind from the fires all around. When the Germans ran after the money, the Russians roared with laughter.

Our house on Immelmannstrasse was burning. The Russian soldiers had run inside, taken out mattresses and quilts and pillows, and tossed them into the vacant lot across the street, and now they were lounging there smoking and laughing, watching the building burn. Much of the facade had fallen away, exposing the cellar where I stored my Viennese suitcase, the one that Mama had left for me with Pepi. I could see the suitcase, shimmering in a haze of heat and smoke.

"I have to get that suitcase!" I screamed, and I ran like a madwoman into the fire. The terrific heat forced me back. Frau Ziegler pleaded with me to forget it; what could be so important that it was worth risking my life for? But I ran back into the blaze once again. The heat overcame me, burning my eyebrows and my hair. "Help me, someone, I have to get that suitcase! Help!"

A Russian soldier who had been watching this scene threw one of our quilts over himself, dashed into the cellar, and brought out my suitcase. I couldn't stop thanking him. I think I may have kissed his hands. He and his comrades watched curiously as I opened the suitcase, imagining, I suppose, that something incredibly valuable was stored there—jewels, silver, paintings. When they saw that what I had been so hysterical to retrieve was a faded blue volume of Goethe, rather clumsily bound, they thought I had lost my mind.

Now that our home was destroyed, we had to find a place to stay for the night. In the street we met our doctor, the old man who took care of our children. He directed us to a Protestant girls' school nearby. The teachers there showed us to a tiny room, a sort of dressing room, at the back of the stage in the assembly hall. Two medical stretchers, a broom, a sink. We were exhausted, and so were our children. So we lay down on the stretchers and we went to sleep. We did not think of locking the door.

During the night, I woke up. There was a wailing sound all around me, not like a siren but rather a soft, sustained screaming. It seemed to come from the sky and the earth. Outside the little room where we cowered, drunken Russian soldiers passed back and forth. They didn't come in, because we had not locked the door and when they pushed it open they saw nothing but darkness, and they must have thought it was a closet. Frau Ziegler and I lay there holding hands the whole night. We scarcely dared breathe, and we prayed that the children would stay quiet.

In the morning we went back into the streets and searched until we found an abandoned apartment. The doors didn't close, the windows didn't close, but nobody bothered anymore about such minor matters. We had nothing to eat except some cold pancakes. In the street, though, there was a hydrant which we could open to get some water. I dissolved the glucose tablets in water and that was how I fed my baby.

The systematic rape of the women in the city went on for a few days and then abruptly stopped. Most women had some relatives they could contact. Frau Ziegler left to go and stay with her mother. But I was alone, so I stayed there in that apartment near the water hydrant.

I went out to find people I knew. One of my friends lived in a building that had not been destroyed. She was sitting on a chair, staring out the window at the blasted city: the smoldering shells of buildings, the Russians sauntering and smoking. Her eyes were ringed with purplish bruises. Her nose was caked with dried blood. Her dress was torn.

"I offered him my husband's watch," she said, "but he already had an armful of watches." She didn't weep. I think she was finished weeping. "Thank heaven the baby was with my mother."

"Our old pediatrician is about," I offered. "Maybe he could help you . . ."

"No, it's all right. I have water. I have food." She looked

around, knowing that her old life was over, missing it already, missing her dead Führer, her dead husband, and the regime that had promised her world conquest. "This was the nicest apartment I ever had," she said.

EVENTUALLY THE OLD PEOPLE who owned the apartment I was staying in came back. They were delighted that I had not stolen anything, and they let me stay on. I do not know what my baby ate at that time, how we ate, what we ate; I do not know that anymore. Every day was an adventure in hunger. We stood on long lines waiting for some authority to give us a little food— some pasta, some dried peas, some black bread. For breakfast we had a watery flour soup mixed with a little salt. Angela ate it with bit of sugar. I was so thin and weak that sometimes I could not even lift her.

Soon not one dog or cat remained alive in the city.

For months and months, there was upheaval: no order, no transportation or electricity, no water in the tap. Everybody was stealing and everybody was starving.

Every lightbulb in every fixture in every corridor in every building was stolen. If somebody offered you a meal, you had to bring your own utensils. The mail came by horse and wagon. Pepi sent me a Christmas card in 1945. I received it in July 1946.

Cigarettes became currency. The Americans joked that you could get any woman in Germany for cigarettes. The Germans brought their china and their laces and antique clocks to certain places at certain hours; and since the Russians were not allowed to socialize with the Germans, they would sell these things to the British and American soldiers in exchange for the ordinary necessities of life.

Immediately after the Russians came, everybody put on a white armband, a sign of surrender. Not I. After all, I felt myself to be one of the victors. The foreign workers found ways to put the colors of their flag on their sleeves, so the Russians would know who they were and give them food for the long trek home. I saw an Austrian wearing red, white, and red—the colors of the Austrian flag—so I did the same, and the Russians gave me some food.

They opened the jails and released all the prisoners, murderers, thieves, and political prisoners all together. One such man noticed my makeshift armband as I stood in a food line and told me, rather merrily, that he too came from Austria and that he had been in jail "for subverting the German army." He asked for my address. I gave it to him. He disappeared. I forgot him. More than a week later, a truck pulled up to our building and unloaded what was for us a vast quantity of potatoes and vegetables, even fruit.

"It was the Austrian," I said to my thrilled neighbors. "I don't even know his name."

"He was an angel sent by God," said the old people.

It took almost six months before we had ration cards again, and then we received a quarter of a liter of skim milk per day for a child. We had been living on the money I had rescued from our bank. I carried this cash on me or in the pram under the baby. Now it was all gone. I needed a job. But to find one, I had to have a real identity card. And that posed a grave problem because I was still afraid to tell anybody that I was a Jew.

All through the war, nobody had talked about the Jews. Not one word. It was as though no one even recalled that until recently, Jewish people had been living in this country. But now, the Germans talked constantly about the possibility that the Jews would come back and take revenge. Every time a group of strangers entered the town, my neighbors would turn tense and appre-hensive. "Is it the Jews?" they would ask, fearing, I suppose, an attack by well-armed, hate-filled people seeking "an eye for an eye." What a joke! No one could imagine yet how utterly the Jewish people had been destroyed, how starved and diseased and exhausted and powerless the surviving remnant would be.

In such an atmosphere, I was afraid to reveal that I was Jewish. I was afraid that the people who had taken me in—who may well have been living in a Jewish house and wearing a dead Jew's clothes—might think I would want to take something away from them and would throw me and Angela into the street.

Only in July, two months after the Russian victory, did I slice open the cover of the book that Pepi had made for me and retrieve my real papers.

I went to a lawyer, Dr. Schütze. He applied for a court order to have my name changed from Grete Vetter née Denner to Edith Vetter née Hahn.

Then I went to the radio station and arranged to have my mother's name announced every day on the program that listed missing people: "Does anyone know the whereabouts of Klothilde Hahn of Vienna, a skilled seamstress, deported to Poland in June 1942? Has anyone seen her or heard anything at all about her? If so, contact her daughter. . . ."

The communists who returned from the camps corroborated the story told by Thomas Mann. One of them told me that he had had the job of going through the clothing of Jewish people after they were stripped and sent to the gas chambers. His job was to find jewelry or money sewn into the lining. I remembered my mother's brown coat, her fine silk blouses. I imagined this man going through them, slitting the seams.

No, I thought. No. Impossible.

You see I could not accept that Mama had met such a hideous fate. I just couldn't. This was not complete folly on my part. Every day people who had been given up for dead walked out of the dust and rubble into the arms of their loved ones. So I kept Mama's name on the radio. I expected her to return.

I WENT TO the Central Registry and to my horror found myself looking at the same man who had officiated at our wedding ceremony.

"Ah, Frau Vetter! I remember you."

"And I remember you too."

"It still says here that we have no background papers for your mother's mother. Perhaps now that our Russian friends have come, they can supply them."

"I think not. Those were false papers."

"What?"

"Here, these are my real identity papers. And this is a court order commanding you to register me as the person I really am."

He stared at my Jewish identity papers, shocked.

"You lied to me!" he exclaimed.

"Yes, I certainly did."

"You falsified your racial records!"

"Right."

"This is a high crime against the state, what you did!"

I leaned toward him. Close. Close. I wanted him to feel my breath.

"Well, I don't think you will find any attorney in Brandenburg to indict me for it now," I said.

I was now the real me, for the first time in years. How did that feel, you will ask? I will tell you. It felt like nothing. Because, you see, I could not immediately find the old Edith. She was still a U-boat, deep in hiding. Just like the rest of the Jews, she did not bounce back quickly. It took time, a long time.

Forever.

I took my new identity and went to see the mayor of the town, a communist who had spent many years in a concentration camp.

"From which camp did you come?" he asked.

I said, "I managed without a camp."

He looked at my school records, which Pepi had preserved. He saw immediately that I had the qualifications of a junior barrister— a *Referendrar*. So he sent me to the Brandenburg courthouse, where I got a job right away and suddenly, incredibly, a new life.

TWELVE

■

Surfacing

THE HIGH-RANKING NAZIS had long ago taken off with their loot. What we had left in Brandenburg were a lot of little Nazis who tried to lie about their background. However, the courthouse with all its files had not been bombed, so the Russians possessed fairly accurate records of who was and who was not a friend of the Nazi regime. You could see correspondence from individuals you knew, who closed with "Heil Hitler!" The really enthusiastic ones would add *"Gott Strafe England!"*—"May God destroy England!" Few, then, could lie and get away with it. Since the Russians, unlike the Americans and the British, would not knowingly employ Nazis, those of us who could prove that we were not Nazis and who had some actual legal training were rare and suddenly valuable in the new labor crisis.

On September 1, 1945, I went to work on the second floor of

the district court. The director of the court—Herr Ulrich—gave me old cases to study, so that I could bring myself up to the present on the legal system. A distinguished jurist, fired because he wouldn't join the Nazi Party, he now loved to ask people, "Tell me, sir, were *you* a member of the party?" And then he would sit back and watch them squirm and sweat and lie.

My first job was as a *Rechtspfleger*, an attorney who helps those needing guidance in court. After some time I was appointed as *Vorsitzende im Schöffengericht*, a judge on a panel of three which also included two lay assessors. (To find a jury of twelve non-Nazis would have been impossible.) The court administration, dominated by the Russians, wanted me to work in a special court dealing with political matters. I refused and finally became a judge in the family court.

My greatest ambition, stimulated by the Halsmann case, fired by my relationship with Pepi, long ago totally abandoned, now became a reality. I was a judge.

I was given an office. I wore a robe. Before I entered the court, the foreman shouted out, *"Das Gericht!"* People stood up and remained standing until I was seated.

It was the most wonderful time in my life, the one and only time when I was able to work to the maximum of my intellectual ability—a pleasure beyond description—and the one and only time I had even the slightest power to alleviate any of the suffering in this world.

RIGHT AFTER I secured my first court job, I became ill. I had skin eruptions due to nutritional deficiencies. My feet were permanently twisted from wearing ill-fitting shoes. I was exhausted. I wound up in the hospital. My landlady kept Angela.

When I recovered, I applied to the housing office for a new place to live. It took two months, but finally I was assigned a very nice flat on Kanalstrasse, in the best district. It had belonged to a Nazi lawyer who had fled. It had a balcony.

A man who had taken over a Nazi furniture factory, which the Nazis had stolen from the Jews, arranged for me to acquire furniture at good terms. I remember one beautiful desk, very ornate, with brass decorations and feet like the claws of a lion. It looked as if it had come from a palace—a real SS desk.

To add to my good fortune, the boss of the electric service, a communist who had returned from the camps, lived in my building and arranged to put us on the Russian grid. So, unlike most Germans in Brandenburg, we had light.

You will ask how we ate in those days, what we ate. I will tell you that it was like the English song: one got by with a little help from one's friends.

I joined an organization, Victims of Fascism, full of people just like me, who had somehow survived. These were not just communists but other Jews who had existed as U-boats with falsified papers, or by hiding in the countryside, or escaping from the death marches or the camps. It meant everything to me to discover that I had not been the only one. We looked into each other's faces and without a word we understood each other's stories. The thing I had sought and found less and less in my successive trips to Vienna—surcease from lying and hiding and fear, *someone who would understand*—I now found among the Victims of Fascism.

My new friends gave me a bottle of wine. I traded it to a Russian soldier for a bottle of cooking oil, a deal that delighted both parties.

On a bread line, I befriended a woman of my age, named Agnes. When I was in the hospital, trying to recover on meager rations, she brought me something extra to eat every day. Her brother had been in the SS. Her husband—perhaps his name was Heinrich—was a communist who had spent ten years in the Orianenburg concentration camp. Toward the end of the war, he had escaped and found shelter with fellow communists who were distributing flyers to encourage foreign workers to commit acts of sabotage. Now he had become an official of the Brandenburg municipality, so highly placed in the Communist Party that he had a car.

Then there was Klessen the fisherman. During the war, he let the communists use his fishing boat as a floating headquarters where they printed anti-Nazi leaflets. Klessen had lost his youngest son at Stalingrad. One day a Nazi officer who chartered his boat was talking about the loss of lives at the front in such an uncaring manner that Klessen became enraged and shot him. Of course, he had to flee. He hid in the woods. The war ended. He came home.

The Russians trusted him. He and his wife became friends of mine. They gave me fish, vegetables, and potatoes—so much, in fact, that I had some left over to send to Tante Paula and my sister-in-law Gertrude in Berlin. Once Klessen came to my office with a bag of eels that he had caught in a secret trap. I put them into my desk drawer. I was conducting an interview with someone, and suddenly the desk began to shudder and shake, because even though they were dead, the eels were still jumping.

From the moment I joined the court, I made petitions to the Russian administration, called the Kommandatura, to get Werner out of Siberia.

"My husband is a German officer," I said. "But he was captured only at the end of the war and saw almost no active duty. He is disabled, half-blind. He doesn't deserve to be in a prison camp. He's a good man who hid me and helped me. Please . . . let him out."

Now, when you asked these Russians for something, they did

not say yes or no; they said nothing, and you did not know what the outcome would be until it happened. So I kept asking and they kept saying nothing and I kept asking.

As the mail began to arrive again and as an occasional telephone began to work, I heard news of my friends and family. My little sister Hansi had arrived in Vienna with the British Army and knocked on Jultschi's door. The happiness of their reunion spilled over into my pulverized little German city like a joyous flood. I heard that my cousin Elli was safe in London; that Mimi and Milo were safe in Palestine; that my cousin Max Sternbach, the artist, had survived by pretending to be a French prisoner; that Wolfgang and Ilse Roemer had been saved by the Quakers; that my cousins Vera and Alex Robichek had survived their Italian exile; that Uncle Richard and Aunt Roszi were safe in Sacramento.

Could I imagine that almost all the rest were murdered? My friends from Vienna, the girls from the *Arbeitslager,* dozens of relatives, all gone . . . could I even imagine that?

My work as a judge centered on children. Destitute German children were everywhere in those days, begging in train stations, sleeping on piles of rags on the pavement. Of course, they turned to lives of crime. They sold precious food on the black market. They sold their sisters and themselves. They stole whatever they could find to steal. These youngsters were brought before me at the family court. Remembering Osterburg, the best of my prisons, I never sent them to languish among hardened criminals, but I sentenced them instead to outside work—clearing the rubble, paving the streets.

The Russians searched the country for the children of Germans and slave laborers; took them from their mothers, natural or adoptive; and transported them to the Soviet Union. This was retaliation for the heartless kidnapping of thousands of Russian children by the Nazi forces, for slave labor or "Aryanized" lives in Germany.

However, a matter of policy for nations can be a matter of personal tragedy for individuals. This is what happened to Karla, my former upstairs neighbor, who came to see me at the court.

"Is it true you are a Jew, Grete?" she asked.

"Yes. My name is not Grete. It's Edith."

"So maybe I can tell you what my trouble is and you will understand. You know, my husband and I had no kids, but we could never get a baby because we were not members of the Nazi Party and the adoption agencies, which had so many babies, would never give one to us."

"Ah, so that was why . . ."

"We found a child, the daughter of a French prisoner and a farm girl from East Prussia. We paid her family everything we could gather. And you know how much I love my little Elsie; she's my whole life. But the Russians are taking away all these children now, Grete . . . I mean, Edith . . . and that was why we ran away so quickly before dawn like that . . ." (She lowered her eyes.) "Also to make room for my brother . . ."

"Yes, I understand."

"I have broken so many laws, signed all kinds of false papers, to protect her identity and make people think she is my baby out of my body. But now all these children are being taken. And I am so afraid—not to go to jail; I would gladly go to jail—but to lose my child. Grete . . . I mean Edith . . . I will do anything not to lose my child. Can you help me?"

"Yes," I said.

And I did. Finally it was my turn to save someone's life.

One custody battle emerged over and over again. A German officer is in a prison camp. He has been divorced and his second wife is taking care of his children. The mother of the children says the father was a Nazi and not able to educate the children "in a democratic way," and seeks sole custody.

I thought of my Werner in the Russian snows. I thought of Elisabeth trying to use this Russian occupation as an excuse to take little Bärbl away from him, and I never acquiesced in such an application. Never.

A very old judge, brought back from retirement, told me that during the war he had tried the case of a man who was half a Jew himself and married to an Aryan. When the Nazis forced this man to clean the streets, he shouted out horrible curses against Goebbels, the propaganda minister. The police were ready to drag him off to a concentration camp. But the old judge had only fined him for libel and told him, please, in the future, for the sake of his family, to keep his mouth shut.

In 1946, the daughter of this same Goebbels-curser came into my office and asked for help to emigrate to Palestine. A near-impossible request. There were almost a hundred thousand leftover Jews in Europe, wild to escape the continent where six million of their people had been incinerated. Britain would not let *them* into Palestine, much less a German Christian.

The girl went everywhere I could think to send her—to the American Joint Distribution Committee, to the Hebrew Immigrant Aid Society, to the British Consulate—and finally she got out to Israel. She married there. Her parents joined her and made their lives in this country.

MANY PEOPLE COMMITTED suicide at the end of the war, not just Goebbels and Hitler but my teacher from Vienna and her husband the Nazi judge and my Latin teacher from the south Tirol.

So when they brought me a woman who had tried to kill herself, I assumed she was a Nazi with a fear of the Gulag. She was babbling madly that I, only I, must be her lawyer.

The minute she walked into my office, I understood.

She was a woman whom I had met on the maternity service at the Städtische Krankenhaus—the one whose husband had raped and beaten her, the one who was afraid to go home. She was at the end of her rope—she had thrown her three children into the river and then jumped in after them. A Russian soldier had pulled her out. She was about to go on trial for murder.

The lawyer who had been assigned to her case withdrew, and I represented her. It was the only time I ever argued in court on behalf of any defendant.

"This is insanity," I said. "Caused by sadistic cruelty beyond imagination. Who would not be insane after suffering this way? Who would not want to see her children dead rather than to continue a life of torture and agony? If my mother had known what would happen to me in my life, she would have murdered me the moment I was born."

The woman was acquitted.

WANTING ANGELA TO have a playmate during my long work-day, I went to the orphanage and arranged to take in a little girl named Gretl. She called me "Auntie" and became like an older sister to Angela. Every night I made the girls supper, read them a story, and tucked them in.

"When will Mommy come back, Auntie?"

"I'm not sure, Gretl."

"And Papa, when will he come back?" Angela asked.

"They will both come back soon, children."

"What is Papa like?"

I had told them a hundred times, but they always wanted to hear again. "Well, Papa is big. And strong. And very handsome. He can paint beautiful pictures. And he can eat more than all of us put together!"

They giggled. I kissed them good night. These are the perfect moments that live in my memory—the times when I saw those children fall asleep in peace and comfort, their eyelashes lying down on their faces.

For the first time in ten years, I had begun to feel real. I had a decent home for myself and my child. I had friends who understood me, with whom I could be myself, to whom I could say the truth of my heart. I had a wonderful job, which challenged me and enabled me to heal the world a little. My reality—the true Edith Hahn—was returning. I laughed again, argued again, dreamed of the future.

In my dream, Mama would come back. Of course, I said to myself, she would look older and would probably be exhausted from her long ordeal in the Polish ghetto. But soon, with rest and food and the love and care Angela and I would shower on her, she would be my witty, energetic mother again, and I would keep her with me always. We would never be separated.

In my dream, Werner would return. He would feel comfortable in our new home. He would find work as a painter and we would be a family again, maybe even have another child. I closed my eyes and imagined the little ones sitting down for lunch with big white napkins tucked under their chins.

Hilde Benjamin, a minister in the new government, called a meeting of the women judges every month in Berlin. During one of these trips, I contacted the American Joint Distribution Committee (the "Joint"), a group of American Jews trying to help the remnant of our people in Europe. The Joint began sending me monthly parcels: cigarettes that I could trade to a shoemaker for shoes for Angela, sanitary napkins, socks.

One time in Berlin, I saw an English soldier climbing a telephone pole, setting up phone lines between the Russian and British zones.

"I have a sister in the British Army," I told him, "and my cousin in Vienna has given me her *Feldposte* number, her military address. But I cannot write to her because I am a civilian. Could you get a letter to her from me?"

He lowered himself down to the street, a polite British boy with freckles and protruding teeth. "Why certainly, madam, it will be my pleasure."

I sat down on a ruined remnant of a staircase, wrote the letter, and gave it to him.

"Tell her if you see her that I am a judge in Brandenburg. Tell her that I am all right and that I love her . . . She is my baby sister . . . Tell her how my heart reaches out for her every day . . ."

In only a few weeks, my British soldier friend walked right into the courtroom and delivered a letter from Hansi. Thereafter, he became our go-between. She sent me elastic for my underwear and sewing needles and cod liver oil for all that ailed my adored little girl. She said she had been with the British Army in Egypt, assigned to interrogating captured German soldiers.

"You speak good German for a Brit," one of them said. "Where'd you learn such good German?"

"I am asking the questions now," answered Hansi.

Sweet victory.

■   ■   ■

IN THE AUTUMN of 1946, one of my colleagues told me about a transit camp in the French zone where Jewish survivors were gathering. Although I still kept Mama's name on the radio every day, and no news of her had materialized, I thought I might find someone who knew of her in the camp. Besides, it was around Rosh Hashanah, and I longed to be with Jews. So I asked my superiors for a few days off, and the old communists let me go.

It was hell to travel at that time. The trains ran when it pleased Providence. Warnings painted in poison green told of the dread diseases you would catch if you dared use public transportation.

In the stations, serpentlike men offered stockings, coffee, chocolate, and cigarettes at black market prices. To walk in the streets you had to scale or somehow circumnavigate mountains of debris. Pipes rigged for heating protruded from holes in the buildings where windows had once been, emitting the terrifying smell of gas. Most of the time, on that arduous journey to the transit camp, I carried Angela and pushed the pram instead of pushing her in it.

I believe the camp may have been in a school. There were large rooms, full of beds, set up like a shelter after a hurricane or a flood. On one side, they housed the very old people and the little children. But perhaps the old people were not as old as they looked, because you see, they all looked as though they had been dug up from the grave—colorless, emaciated, toothless, shaking, staring. I carried Angela among them. They reached for her, just to touch her, a healthy child. My mother was not there.

I left Angela with one of the attendants and walked to the other side of the transit camp, where the younger people were. Grizzled men with stony eyes came up behind me and stroked my arms.

"Come here to my bed, sweetheart, I haven't seen a woman like you since the beginning of time."

"Get away from me! I am looking for my mother!"

"Are you a Jew? Where are you from?"

"I am a Jew. From Vienna. I am looking for Klothilde Hahn!"

They surrounded me. I was terrified. I could not see anybody to help me.

"Leave me alone!" I cried. "I am married. My husband is a prisoner of war. He is in Siberia. My child is here with me. I came only for Rosh Hashanah, to be with some Jews. How can you be Jews? This is not possible! I do not recognize you!"

One of them pulled my hair, yanked my head backward. He was tall, gaunt. He had a shaven head and black eyes set in watery reddish shells.

"So you married a German soldier, huh, bitch? This is why you look so good, so healthy and pink and clean." He turned to his fellows. "How do you like this, comrades? She sleeps with the goyim. And now she's too good to sleep with us."

He spat at me. He had only one or two teeth in his mouth and they were like fangs.

It seemed to me that to get out of that place, I had to run a gauntlet of a thousand grabbing hands. How could these brutalized rapacious men be Jews? It was impossible! Where were the sober, mannerly yeshiva scholars from Poland that I remembered from Badgastein? Where were the refined young men with brilliant minds who went with me to the university? What had the monsters done to my people?

For the first time I experienced the awful, irrational guilt that besets all survivors. For the first time it occurred to me that maybe my life as a U-boat did not weigh heavily on the scales of suffering, that the hideous experiences which had transformed the men in the transit camp might make it impossible for them ever to accept me as one of their own.

I could not stop trembling; I could not stop weeping.

I went back to the other side of the camp, to be with the old people, to help with the children, the orphans of this storm. I held them close to me; I let them play with Angela; I taught them little games to make them smile. With them I had some peace.

But for the journey home, my strength failed me. To drag and push Angela to the station again now seemed an impossible task. I left her with an attendant in the transit camp and said I would come back for her with a car.

At the station one of the black marketeers told me, "There is a train that passes through Brandenburg, but it's a Russian train. Maybe a woman like you shouldn't travel that way."

I felt that I had no choice.

The train came. It was empty. "This is my train," said the officer in charge. He had straight blond hair and Asian features. "If you want to travel with me, you have to go into a compartment."

So I did. I was too nervous to sit down. I stood looking out the window. The Russian came and stood next to me and slipped his arm around my waist.

"I am not German," I said. "I am Jewish."

He took his arm away.

"There is a Jewish officer on board. He's the boss of all the trains. Come on. I will take you to him."

The Jewish officer had dark hair and eyes like my father's and spoke to me in Yiddish.

"I don't know Yiddish," I said.

"Then you are not Jewish."

"I came from Vienna. We never learned."

"All the Jews from Vienna are dead. Gone. Murdered. You are a liar."

"*Shema Yisrael,*" I said. "*Adonai eloheynu. Adonai echod.*"

I had not said it since my father's funeral—ten years, time for a world to disappear. I bit my lip and choked on my tears. I leaned on his desk to keep from falling.

Finally he said, "This train comes empty to this cursed country every week, to pick up Russian prisoners and bring them home. Here is the schedule. You may take this train at any time when it suits you, and I will guarantee your safety."

He held my hand until I regained my composure. But in fact, sometimes I think I have never regained my composure since that visit to the transit camp in the French zone.

What you see is a mask of calm and civility. Inside, always, forever, I am still weeping.

The next day my friend Agnes's husband, the communist, drove me back to the camp and I collected Angela. The attendants were surprised; I suppose they expected never to see me again. But I did not have that baby in the middle of a war in order to abandon her.

ONE NIGHT, SOMETIME in late 1946, I was sitting in my apartment, working on a brief, when a man knocked on my door. He thrust into my hand a case containing eyeglasses. Then disappeared. I locked my door, threw the glasses onto the floor, dug and dug into the lining of the case, and finally found a letter—written in almost infinitesimal handwriting—from Werner.

He was all right. I had been writing to him for more than a year, but he had not received any mail from me until my letter of October thirty-first. In fact, the mail that he *had* received came from his sister-in-law Gertrude; it was intended for his brother Robert, who was lying wounded in a military hospital.

For a moment, I just looked at Werner's letter and enjoyed a flood of relief. Then I read . . .

"I send you and our Angela best greetings and wishes. I hope that fate will keep you from poverty and give my dearest Grete a strong heart . . . to endure this time of separation . . ."

On March 10, 1945, he had been wounded by shrapnel in the right arm. On March 12, he was taken prisoner. After a hellish ride on a military transport, he ended up at a hospital in Poland, where he tried to heal despite near-starvation rations. In May he was brought to a prison camp in Siberia, a miserable, frozen, ugly place, every bit as harsh as I had imagined.

But Werner was a talented man. His virtuosity made him useful, and he found inside work. He did carpentry, repaired locks, wired lamps, decorated the grim Russian offices, painted portraits that the Russians sent home. Just like the French prisoner who made me the beautiful inlaid box, Werner knew that the way to soften a superior's heart was with a charming gift for his wife.

His letters ached with the fears that came with isolation. How well I recalled them! Was I trying to get him out? Could I pull any strings? Did anyone in Germany remember the prisoners of war? Would they just be a burden to the Fatherland?

He begged me to tell the Russians the circumstances of our marriage, "which clearly depict my anti-Fascist behavior long before the fall of Hitler's system."

He asked me to watch over Bärbl.

Now that I was a judge, would I still need a husband to take care of me? Would there be anything for him to do when he got home?

"What an indescribable torment it is," he said, "to not know whether loving hands are waiting to comfort you after the torture of imprisonment."

I knew exactly how he felt. I remembered writing to Pepi in Vienna. *Are you there? Do you remember me? Do you still love me?*

I imagined the screaming Arctic winds, the white wasteland, the endlessly lit sky and then the months of darkness.

"Please," I said to the court director, Herr Ulrich, "use your influence. Bring my Werner home."

I imagined the prison rations, the hard bread. I saw Werner shivering under thin blankets, wearing all his clothes to bed as I had done, his capable hands wrapped in rags of gloves.

"Please," I said to the lawyer, Schütze, "you know some of the Russians. Tell them what a good man he was, how kind to the Dutchmen and Frenchmen at Arado, how they loved him and sent him gifts."

I imagined the snow. Deep. Up to his knees. I imagined him working next to SS men, butchers from the death camps. "Get him out," I begged the Russian commandants. "He's not like the others. He deserves to come home to his wife and his child. Please."

The Russians looked at me without expression, denying me nothing, promising me nothing. I did not stop asking. I sent letters to Berlin, petitions to every office I could think of. "Please," I begged.

Even as I begged for Werner's release, I feared his homecoming. No matter how deftly I limited my social life to the Victims of Fascism and other anti-Nazi survivors, I knew I was still living among the most virulent anti-Semites the world had ever known, and one of them—albeit the least virulent—was Angela's father. I had often heard Werner's views about the "power" of "Jewish blood." What if he refused to accept our beautiful, lively three-year-old because of this? I felt that I must do something to neutralize the effects of the Nazi propaganda, to make sure my Angela had a loving father. So I arranged for a Lutheran minister to come to my home, and I had Angela baptized as a Christian.

You will ask why I did not go to church for this ceremony. I will tell you. I felt compelled to do it, but I was miserable about doing it, and I didn't want anyone to see.

It was an evening in the summer of 1947, about seven-thirty. The streets outside were quiet. The boats on the canal made soft scraping noises at the dock. The trees, which were beginning to grow again, filled the night with a perfume that can be enjoyed only in peacetime. I happened to be alone in the apartment. Gretl was with her little brother at the orphanage. Angela had been taken ill with diphtheria and needed penicillin, which was available only in the west, so she was staying at a children's hospital in West Berlin.

I heard a gentle knock at the door. I had the chain on, and I opened the door a crack. "Who's there?" It was dark in the corridor—hard to see. "Who's there?" A tall, haggard, thin man. Grayish stubble on his face. Too exhausted even to smile.

"It's me," he said.

I gathered him into my arms, then washed him with warm water and laid him down to sleep.

"We have made it through the nightmare," I thought. "Now at last everything will be all right."

I really thought that.

For the next few days, we were happy. But then, as Werner recovered his strength and got his bearings and understood our position, his anger found its voice.

Nothing about the new situation pleased him. Well, yes, he did like the apartment; he said it looked like something out of a movie. But when he would wake up and find that I had gone to work and my helper was there to make him breakfast, he did not respond well. He wanted me home as before, serving, cooking, waiting.

"But I must work," I said. "I'm a judge; I have cases . . ."

Angela returned from the hospital. I had dressed her like a lovely doll, in a pretty dress, with bows in her dark hair. She hung back in the doorway, gazing at Werner with his own large, round light eyes. "Go to your papa," I said, crouching next to her. "Go and give your papa a big kiss."

She cuddled close to Werner, seeking to adore him and be adored by him. He patted her absently. To my huge disappointment, it made absolutely no difference to him that she had been baptized. He still said it was "Jewish blood" that counted. I felt lost, brokenhearted, ashamed. I had betrayed myself and contravened the will of my father for nothing.

Werner didn't like the fact that I had an office with a secretary and a receptionist out front, that he couldn't just walk into my office but had to be announced. He hated it if somebody was in my chambers with me and he had to wait outside. He had thought he would be treated as a hero, but he was disappointed. Nobody regarded him as a hero. Anyway, there were too many other returning "heroes" to deal with. Of course, I understood his frustration. How could I not understand? Imagine how hard it was for him, to come home in defeat, to a country which had no economy, no opportunities to offer him, and which was being run according to a new system by people who had been despised and imprisoned when he left.

The labor office was ready to put him to work clearing streets and redigging sewers. He thought that I could use my connections to get him a supervisory job, like the one he had had at Arado. But there were no such jobs for noncommunists. People like Tante Paula advised him to be grateful that he had a working wife who could house him and feed him decently. He did not seem to understand (nor did I understand fully) that getting him out, when others would not come home for two more years or four more or eight more years, was enough to indebt me to the Kommadatura in ways as yet unimaginable.

He expected me to clean and take care of the house and the baby as I had done before, but I had no time for that. I could not do his laundry—he was furious about that. The happy little girls, racing about, shouting and laughing, irritated him no end. He wanted me to send Gretl back to the orphanage for good.

"She's not mine!" he yelled. "It's not bad enough that I have two daughters to take care of! Now you foist a third on me, and she isn't even mine!"

I asked him to go to Herr Klessen, the generous fisherman, and pick up some fish for our dinner. He refused. "This is your job!" he snapped. "I don't go and collect the food in this house. My job is to sit down at night at my table and eat it!"

"But I have no time to go. There are all these cases . . ."

"The hell with your damn cases!"

"Please, Werner . . ."

"I am not going to beg some socialist fisherman for our dinner! This is a woman's job!"

He was full of energy, and he had nothing to do. He was restless, angry, but there was no one to rage at. His old friends at Arado could not help him. The plant itself was an empty ruin. It had been bombed repeatedly, and the Russians had dragged off any equipment left standing. In later years, Angela went back there and asked where the Arado plant was, and the citizens of Brandenburg had no recollection that any such place had ever existed.

One night I came home late from work, tired, my mind crowded with the sad stories of German women and their children. Werner had been working himself into a fury all day because he had found a hole in his sock, and his pent-up rage burst over me like an American bomb.

"Did you forget how to sew?"

"No, I . . . I still sew . . . It's just that . . ."

"It's just that you are a big judge under the Russian regime and you have no time for your husband."

"Stop it! Don't you understand that the reason you were able to return home so soon is that I have begged and pleaded and worked for the Russians? Don't bother me about a hole in your sock! You are home! You are safe! Try to count your blessings!"

"What blessings? An overeducated wife who is nothing like the woman I used to know?"

"I am the same woman . . . Oh, God, please darling, try to understand . . ."

"No, you are not! My wife, Grete, was obedient! She cooked! She cleaned! She ironed! She sewed! She treated me like a king! And I want her back!"

Everything I had so long repressed, my true instincts, my real personality, all my grief and my bottomless rage, roared to the surface.

"Well, you can't have her!" I shouted. "Grete is dead! She was a Nazi invention—a lie, just like the propaganda on the radio! And now that the Nazis are gone, she is gone too! I am Edith! I am Edith! I am who I am! You cannot have a meek, scared, obedient little slave laborer like H. C. Bestehorn anymore! Now you have a real wife!"

He hit me. I went flying across the room. I literally saw stars. My brain rattled.

Werner walked out. I felt as though my heart would break.

He came back several days later, looking content and smug. I knew he had been with a woman. He took some money and went to his first wife, Elisabeth. And a few days after that, he came back again.

"Little Bärbl is coming here to live for a while."

"What?"

"Send Gretl back to the orphanage. I want Bärbl here. Elisabeth needs a break."

"No. I will not throw Gretl out. Bärbl has a mother. Gretl has no one."

"I am your husband. You will do what I say."

"I will not take over the upkeep of Bärbl so that you can renew your romance with Elisabeth in a child-free house, no, I will not. I love Bärbl; I would love to see her again. But this is not fair. This is wrong."

"I don't like this person you are now," he said. "I liked you the old way. I want you to write to your rich relatives in London and get them to send me some paints . . ."

"My rich relatives? Are you crazy? My family was robbed of everything! My sisters have nothing! You have ten thousand reichsmarks!"

"Oh, that. I threw it away because this Russian was taking me prisoner and I didn't want him to think I was a capitalist . . ."

I didn't know what to say to that. Probably I should have laughed, but I was too unhappy. He told me he wanted a divorce—the faster, the better.

"Are you going back to Elisabeth?"

"Of course. I have to save my little Bärbl."

I cried and cried when I finally realized I could not keep him. It seemed to me that now I would be alone forever.

Then one day something happened to bring me to my senses. Angela had been naughty—she had thrown a toy, raised her voice—and I scolded her, "Stop that right this minute or I will punish you."

"If you punish me," she said, "I will tell Papa and he will hit you and make you cry."

Right then and there, I made up my mind to agree to the divorce Werner wanted.

A colleague of mine did the work on the divorce. Werner asked me to speed up the process. He had already emigrated to the west with Elisabeth. He wanted me to lie and say they had divorced the first time only "to save me," that he had never courted me in Munich, or loved me for one minute, that our marriage was all just an anti-Nazi charade.

I told my colleague to say whatever was necessary to make the divorce go like lightning.

In fact, that was how Werner's second marriage to Elisabeth went, as well. Like lightning. Poof. A flame. Poof. Gone.

Werner.

THIRTEEN

■

I Heard the Fiend
Goebbels, Laughing

$\mathcal{A}$T THAT TIME, the Nuremberg trials were just ending, and the trials of the smaller Nazis were beginning. Judges were needed. The Russians chose me, but I didn't want to be involved.

"Who will regard a sentence of mine as fair?" I said to them. "Everybody will say: This is a Jewish woman; she is seeking revenge. And I certainly wouldn't want to bend over backward the other way. I am *befangen*, not impartial; I am not qualified to do this."

It meant everything to me not to have my integrity called into question, because, you see, for two years, not one of my decisions had been appealed. I did not want to lose the trust and respect I enjoyed.

The commandants did not agree.

I went to Potsdam and appealed to the superior counselor in

the Department of Justice, Dr. Hoenigger. He agreed with my point of view and said he would talk to the Russians for me. But the order to do the work came anyway. I went back to Hoenniger. This time he threw me out of his office.

I went to the Minister of the Interior and waited for hours before he finally saw me. He had no idea why I should be so reluctant. "But since you want so much to be disqualified," he said, "I will help you."

I was notified that I would not have to judge the Nazis.

But then I was further notified that I could no longer work as a judge at all. In the future, I would serve only as a public prosecutor.

My sense of safety began to fray and tear. I felt the presence of someone in the shadows of the hall. When I opened my door at night, I was not absolutely sure that I would find everything in order at home. It seemed to me that the letters I received from Hansi and Jultschi had been opened and then resealed.

The Russians called me in for a meeting.

They asked me questions about my life, my relatives, and my friends. They made me write down the names and addresses of everyone with whom I corresponded. They sent me home. Then they called me in again and asked me more questions, to which I understood they already knew the answers. Something about their tone reminded me of the registrar: *"But your mother's mother, Fräulein. What about her?"*

My blood ran cold. My stomach knotted—an old feeling, all too familiar.

"We helped you," said the commandant. "Now you must help us."

"But how?"

"We understand that you are a very good listener, and people trust you and tell you the truth about their lives. All we want is for you to tell us what they tell you."

They wanted me to spy on my colleagues, on Agnes and her husband, on the caretaker and the secretary and Klessen, on the lawyers and the litigants, on everybody I knew. They gave me a telephone number where I could always reach them. "We expect to hear from you in short order," said the commandant.

The old terror returned. My knees trembled. I heard my voice growing smaller. I mumbled. My eyes grew vacant, and I pretended to understand nothing of what was going on. I didn't say yes. I didn't say no. I stalled, hoping they would forget me. But this was the NKVD, the secret police. They forgot no one. They had ways. People disappeared. There were rumors of beatings, of torture. They could make your job disappear, your apartment. Your children.

They interviewed me again.

I couldn't sleep. I jumped at every sound in the hallway. I began to suspect my friends. After all, if I had been asked to watch them, maybe they had been asked to watch me.

Ulrich said I shouldn't worry so much.

"So you tell them things. It's up to you what you tell them."

"But it's up to them how they use what I tell them."

He shrugged. I suppose he thought this wasn't such a big problem. But for me, you see, for me, it was *the same problem*, all over again.

"We haven't heard from you yet, Frau Vetter," said the commandant.

"Oh yes . . . yes . . . I was supposed to call you, that number . . ." I fumbled in my bag. "I wonder if I still have it . . ." Did I really imagine that I could convince him I had misplaced his number the way I had "lost" my Nazi Red Cross pin?

"The number is on your desk," he said with a smile.

"Ah. Yes. In my office."

"No. Not that desk. The antique desk with the brass fittings and feet like the claws of a lion, the desk you have in your apartment."

In my mind's ear, I heard the fiend Goebbels laughing.

A young girl whom I knew missed the last train home and came back unexpectedly to stay the night with me. When she knocked on the door, a cold sweat popped up on my skin. By the time I opened that door, I was weak with fear. Every terrible memory—the preparation for arrest, for interrogation, for death—had come back.

"You are a messenger from heaven," I said to the girl, welcoming her in. She did not understand what I meant. I meant that I knew beyond any doubt, from my reaction to her knock on my door, that I could never again live as part of a system of denunciation and intimidation and tyranny, where you always feared the unexpected guest. I knew I had to get out.

I told people who I knew would tell the commandant that I wanted to visit my sister in England for two weeks. Then I went to Berlin and inquired at York House about the best way to get a visa. An Englishman—a complete stranger, with a large mustache and a fat briefcase—told me that I should rent a room in West Berlin and ask there for a passport.

I went to the headquarters of the Jewish community. There I met a man who said he could rent me a room. I told him that I did not actually wish to live there, that I would pay the rent but that really all I needed was the address so I could qualify for an *Ausweis*, a residential identity card. I went to the police station and waited for a long time. Finally an officer came. I told him that I did not want any food, just a *Personalausweis* so that I could visit my sister in England.

You must understand, at that time there was a blockade of Berlin. It was impossible to secure permission to travel. But this policeman gave it to me. He just gave it to me and wished me a pleasant journey to England.

It took months to assemble the rest of the papers I needed—the passport, the visas, the clearances. Meanwhile, I was working at the court as though I planned to be there forever. Every ten days or so, I would travel to the British zone to collect the papers that had come in and pay my rent to the Jewish couple.

I knew I would eventually have to end our relationship with Gretl, but I didn't want to do it at the last moment, for fear that it might signal my imminent departure. So one day without any particular warning, I gathered my courage and strength and took her back to the orphanage. I started to tell her some lie about how we'd see her again very soon.

She covered her ears. "No," she said.

Children always understood everything.

I kissed her. That was a mistake. I should never have done that. She began to cry. And I began to cry.

When I left the orphanage, she was screaming "Auntie! Auntie!" The woman there could hardly hold her. I ran from that place.

This was part of the price I had to pay for leaving Germany: to turn my back on that shrieking child. Baron de Rothschild, signing over his steel mills and his palaces, did not pay a higher price.

DURING THE LONG, clandestine arrangements before my departure, I often had to stand in line for hours with Angela. Although she was the most mature of little girls, a typical war baby, never demanding or complaining, she would sometimes grow restive and irritable on the long lines. She would whine or make a fuss. And pushing her pram through the ruined streets exhausted me beyond endurance.

One time when I was trying to make my way through the rubble, a Russian soldier fell into step with me and helped me keep the pram upright and Angela inside it.

"Your daughter reminds me of my niece," he said.

"Oh, then your niece must be adorable."

"My niece is dead," he said. "The SS came into our town in Russia and went on a hunt for all the Jews and when they found my sister and my brother-in-law, they just killed them where they stood and threw their little girl out the window."

It was getting to be the end of the day. The sun was somehow setting again. A man could stand in the street and tell a perfect stranger a story of such incomprehensible evil that it really seemed as if the sun should stop shining altogether. But there was no alteration in Heaven, no sign that the cries of children had been heard.

"You speak excellent German," I said. "I would never have been able to tell you were Jewish."

He laughed. "And I knew you were Jewish the minute I saw you."

An astonishing statement, don't you agree? For years the Germans had not been able to tell I was Jewish by looking at me. The registrar had stared into my eyes and into my past—and he couldn't tell. Now here was a complete stranger, a foreigner . . . and he had known in an instant.

"I have been thinking about trying to get over to the western side of the city, so I can see my relatives who are still alive. But I have had no luck in getting to the visa office, because I must bring my little girl with me, and it's impossible to spend all the time necessary to stand in line and wait with this child."

"Leave her with me," he said. "Tell me when you want to come back here from Brandenburg, tell me where you wish to meet me, and I will be there and I will keep her with me for as long as you need to get your visa."

A fantastic offer—and equally fantastic that I accepted it. I returned to Berlin the following week and met the Russian soldier. I left my precious child with him the whole day, and never for a minute thought that he might abuse her or steal her or sell her or hurt her in any way.

Why did I have such trust? Because he was a Jew. And I could not believe that any Jew would want to hurt my baby.

Something always happened, you see. A Yiddish song on Hanukkah, a British rabbi's prayer on the radio, some kindness on a train or in the street that reminded me, no matter how far I retreated, no matter how deep into self-denial my fear drove me, that the Jews would always be my people and I would always belong to them.

YOU WILL ASK me why it took so long for me to think of leaving Brandenburg, why I had even dreamed of being able to lead a normal life in Germany. I will tell you. It was because I could not imagine a normal life anywhere else.

I couldn't get a visa for Palestine, even if Mimi wanted me there, which she didn't. I couldn't go back to Vienna. To live again in the city that had buried my whole family? Never! In Brandenburg I knew the language and I could get work and support my daughter. Under the communist regime, I had a place, a good job, and a nice flat and friends who had shared my fate. Do you think after all the terror and hiding and hunger and running, I wanted to start again wandering the strange and evil world alone with a child? Lost again, with no place, no home, no husband, no family, *no place*?

When I left Brandenburg and closed that apartment door behind me, I cried bitter tears of mourning for my moment of peace, creativity, and security, so briefly enjoyed.

I left on a Sunday in November 1948. I told no one my intentions so as not to make anyone an accomplice, and left enough money in my bank account to pay the outstanding bills. On the kitchen counter in my flat, I left a loaf of bread so the Russians would think I was coming back.

Angela and I went to the train station and then I lost my courage and went home.

On Monday morning I rang Agnes's husband and asked him to take us to Potsdam, where one could use the underground, avoiding the train and any potential *razzia* by the Russians.

For two weeks I stayed with the Jewish family at 33 Wielandstrasse in Berlin's Charlottenburg district, waiting for a British airline strike to be over so I could use the ticket that Hansi and her English husband, John, had sent me and fly away. A friend back in Brandenburg told me my apartment had been sealed by the police. I guess they understood that I would not be coming back.

Finally the strike ended. Finally everything ended.

I flew to Northholt Airport with Angela.

When I saw my sister Hansi, when I heard her joyous cry of greeting and felt her tears mingle with my tears, when I held her in my arms—my little soldier sister—I knew that Edith Hahn had finally returned to herself. The ocean of terror was lifted from me. I breathed the air of freedom. My disguise became history.

In my sister's eyes I saw a reflection of my own grief, which I had fended off for years with hopeful fantasies, and I confronted the agonizing truth. Our mother, Klothilde Hahn, had been murdered after being deported to the Minsk ghetto in the summer of 1942. She had appeared to me in mirrors, smiling with encouragement; sat on my bed and comforted me with happy memories in my most frightening hours; hovered like a light before me as I opened the door to what I thought must be certain death. Was it not Mama who spoke to me through that cold marble statue and directed me to safety? My angel, my beacon, she was gone forever.

And my little daughter and I, because of random good luck and the interventions of a few decent people, had been saved.

FOURTEEN

■

Pepi's Last Package

$\mathcal{I}$N BRANDENBURG, I had been a respected official of the court, a middle-class woman with an adequate salary and a decent home.

In England, I arrived as a destitute refugee with a sixty-day visa and no permission to work, knowing very little English, carrying no luggage except a briefcase containing a change of underwear. In the years that followed, I worked as a maid, a cook, and a seamstress for the National Health. I never worked in the legal profession again.

I turned my back on the charade of assimilation, sent my daughter to a Jewish school, and raised her as a Jew.

In 1957, I married Fred Beer, another Viennese Jew, whose mother had been murdered in the Holocaust. We told each other our stories once, only once, and did not mention these dreadful events again for thirty years. We let the past lie and drift, like wreckage on the sea, in the hope that eventually it would sink and be forgotten. In this, I am told, we were not unlike other survivors of terrible catastrophes.

Fred died in 1984, and I moved to Israel in 1987, to live at last among Jewish people in their own country. And though I am surrounded by citizens from cultures very different from mine, I feel a kinship with them all. I am comfortable here. This is my place.

I tried to stay in touch with the people who had been so close to me during my ordeal as a U-boat. When Frau Doktor Maria Niederall was ejected from her stolen shop and fell ill, I saved two weeks' salary to send her a pretty bed jacket. At least it made her happy. She always loved luxurious feminine things. But it did not make her well. She died too young. So had many of the people who might have mourned for her.

I read a novel by the famous Nazi hunter Simon Wiesenthal. One of the characters in it said, "We must never forget those who have helped us . . ." and so I wrote to the author and told him about Christl Denner Beran, my beloved friend who is now gone. She was given a medal for her heroism and her extraordinary courage. A tree was planted in her name at Yad v'Shem, the Holocaust memorial here in Israel—the highest honor our country gives to a righteous gentile.

When Angela was growing up in England, I sent her birthday cards from relatives who had become smoke, to make her feel she had a large and loving family. She always received a card from Grandmother Klothilde.

I stayed in touch with Bärbl and her family. And I tried to keep the extraordinary personality of Werner Vetter somewhere remembered in our lives.

"Your father could have painted that wall," I would say. "Your father would have been able to make the teacher believe that excuse. . . . Your father could have fixed the bike. . . ."

I told Angela that Werner and I had loved each other truly and were separated only because he could not get work in England. I did not tell her until she was almost a teenager that we were divorced. In fact, I arranged several visits with him, so she would know this man whom I had tried so hard to love and would always, despite everything, honor.

Why did I surround my daughter with these pleasant, soothing lies? Because I wanted her not to feel alone. Just as Mama had always sent me the things she did not have—the cake when she was hungry, the gloves when she was cold—I tried to give Angela the things that I had lost: a family, a secure place in the world, a normal life.

So I think I could easily have let this story go untold forever.

Except that Pepi Rosenfeld, with a mad courage quite out of character for him, did *not* burn the letters and pictures I had sent him, as I had instructed him to do, but kept them, every single one.

They could have killed us all, those letters.

"What do you think, my dear Edith?" he suggested with his sly smile when we met in later years in Vienna and introduced each other to the people we had married. "Shall I donate these letters to the Austrian National Archives?" I think I must have cried out in horror. "Yes, I thought you might react that way." He laughed. Decades had passed. And I still fell for that man's little jokes.

In 1977, shortly before his death, Pepi sent me his last package. It contained all the letters I had written to him from the slave labor camps and from Brandenburg when I was living as a U-boat in the Nazi empire.

And my daughter, Angela, wanting more than anything to know the whole truth at last, read them.

A B O U T   T H E   T Y P E

■

This book is set in Bembo, which is considered one of the first old-style typefaces, along with the highly popular Garamond.

Bembo is based on the roman types cut by Francesco Griffo and used by Aldus Manutius in Venice in 1495 to print Cardinal Bembo's tract *De Aetna*. There were no italics at that time. *Bembo Italic* is based on an original print from the writing master Giovanni Tagliente, Venice, 1524. The modern version of Bembo was designed in 1929 by the Monotype Type Drawing Office, supervised by Stanley Morison.

Bembo has been widely used in books, advertising, and display work over the last sixty years. One reason for its popularity is its functional serifs, which help provide readability and guarantee an easy reading experience. Books and other texts set in Bembo can encompass a wide variety of subjects and formats because of its quiet, classical beauty.